SCHOOLS AND MEANING

Essays on the Moral
Nature of Schooling

Edited by

David E. Purpel
H. Svi Shapiro

UNIVERSITY
PRESS OF
AMERICA

LANHAM • NEW YORK • LONDON

LA
217
.S295
1985

All University Press of America books are produced on acid-free
paper which exceeds the minimum standards set by the National
Historical Publications and Records Commission.

Dedicated to
James Bradley Macdonald

ACKNOWLEDGEMENTS

We wish to express our appreciation for the special and sensitive contributions of those who participated in the planning for the conference: William Bennett, Joseph Brooks, John Sullivan, Oakley Winters, and the late James Macdonald. Two other people, Al Rubio and Richard Pipan not only made helpful suggestions in the planning but also provided heroic and vital service to the demands of details, crises, and logistics.

Financial and moral support was provided by many people and institutions including the School of Education of the Univeristy of North Carolina - Greensboro, Greensboro Day School, New Garden Friends School, Oak Ridge Military Academy, Saint Pius X School, and the High Point Public Schools. A very special note of thanks is in order for the generous and active support of the North Carolina Humanities Committee.

We are very much indebted to Leslie Frontz and Dottye R. Ricks for the quality of their work, their patience, and the interest in the preparation of this manuscript. We also acknowledge gratefully the contributions of Sherwood Jones, Robert O'Kane, Martha Hudson, Richard Weller, and Rachel Purpel.

CONTENTS

Appendices

INTRODUCTION

David E. Purpel

The essays in this book had their origin in a
conference sponsored by the Center for Educational
Reform at the University of North Carolina at
Greensboro. The story of how this conference was
planned and what happened at the conference is in
itself of significance and will be noted in the second
half of this introduction. First, let us speak to the
professional and theoretical concerns that provided
the impetus for the conference and also constitute
major themes of this book.

The people who planned the project came from
several different but related fields - curriculum
theory, moral education, the humanities, philosophy,
and social foundations. They have spent most if not
all of their professional lives as educators concerned
less with the technology of education but rather more
with the complex and close relationships between
culture and education. All had been active in one way
or another in cultural and educational movements and
stirrings of the 1960s and early 1970s, particularly
in the efforts to signficantly alter the elementary
and secondary school curriculum. All of us had also
experienced the collapse of these efforts and the
ensuing public backlash of anger and disillusionment
with these efforts which eventually settled into an
inertia and indiffference, the end of which is only
now beginning to appear possible. The mid and late
1970s became for many educators, including the
planners of this conference, a time of re-examination
and reflection on the meaning of these events, a time
of lessons to be learned and consolidated.

One of the helpful insights that emerged from
this re-examination, ironically enough, was the
realization of the failure of the various curriculum
reform projects to have a significant impact on
American education. Basically and broadly these
projects (most, although surely not all, were in the
fields of science and mathematics) operated on the
very reasonable assumptions that curriculum material
planned and developed with imagination, rigor,

thought, and thoroughness were both needed and wanted.
However, in spite of a considerable investment of
money, energy, and talent the net effect of these
efforts was very disappointing. Many explanations
have been offered: insufficient funds for follow-
through and teacher training; resistance by schools
and teachers, and insensitivity to teacher's concerns.
It was not simply, however, that these curriculum
ideas were totally rejected since in fact many schools
adopted in some degree or other such programs as PSSC,
SMSG, "Open Education," MACOS, and the like. What was
significant was not only that some of these programs
were rejected but even where they were, the overall
effect on the quality of the educational process
seemed negligible. In spite of all the energy and
excitement, basically the schools seem to have hardly
changed at all, indeed, in more recent times even the
modest and uneven changes in tone and substance that
did occur seems to have been eroded as a result of the
society's shift to the right. This realization has
led many educators to re-discover with a new and fresh
intensity the truism that schools are more than
syllabi, course requirements, and instructional
materials. A persistent but then quiet voice had long
spoken to how connections between the cluster of
values, attitudes, beliefs, policies, and priorities
that form the social and cultural structure influences
what happens in schools. It is, therefore, no
surprise that the concept of the "hidden curriculum"
came to be a popular one soon after the collapse of
the curriculum reform movement. It is not only a
concept that has the heuristic quality of promoting
fresh conceptual analysis but it also provides a
counterpoint to the growing notion that schools have
only a marginal impact on students and the culture.
Much of the cultural backlash of the 1970s tended to
discount the significance of schools particularly as
it related to social and economic advancement as a
great deal of persuasive evidence was presented to
undermine the prevailing wisdom that "doing well" in
school translated into "doing well" in the culture.

What has changed for many educational theorists
is the notion of what is meant by "doing well'--a
change marked by a shift in emphasis from a focus of
curriculum as the acquisition of skills and
intellectual mastery to a conception of curriculum as
the process by which students assume and learn roles,
attitudes, and postures that are valued by the
culture. As a group curriculum theorists tended to

move away from the relatively technical issues related
to developing materials and procedures for appropriate
and measurable goals toward seeing the educational
program in social and cultural terms. The school came
once again to be seen as an important context for the
transmission and reflection of its political,
economic, and cultural milieu and how schools mediated
that milieu came to be considered of greater import
than the specific content of the program of study.
The theoretical action then shifted from what should
we teach to what is really being taught; from what
program or text is being used or might be used to
what is/might be the prevailing ideology of the
school; from seeing school as an academic work place,
to viewing school as a metaphor of the culture.

This perspective enabled many educational
theorists to widen the scope of their concerns to
include cultural and social contexts and has led to an
increasingly sophisticated body of educational
literature that delves more deeply into the sub-texts
of school life in order to illumine the complexities
and subtleties of meaning reflected in day to day
school practice. Much of this practice has been
hitherto free of such deep analysis, another aspect of
the highly technological and pragmatic quality of post
World War II educational research. It is certainly
not "news" that schools are situated and entangled in
cultural, social, political, economic mileus and
indeed it seems that much of the 19th and early 20th
century dialogue on public education was
philosophical, and theoretical in nature. This shift
in emphasis (and this is by no means no more than a
modest albeit growing movement within the field of
education) can be seen as a fading of the romance with
logical positivism and applied social science and the
renewal of a once intimate relationship with cultural
and social theory. Indeed, this shift in emphasis
within the field of education itself was but one of
the many indications that the culture has as a whole
been rethinking and reexaminining its basic ways of
knowing and seeking truth.

The emergence of the hidden curriculum roughly
coincided with the surge of interest in value
issues and it is hardly an accident that the re-
emergence of the term and field of moral education
came during the era of the Civil Rights movement, the
Viet-Nam crisis; when there was serious concern over
pollution, nuclear war, political corruption, and all

the other issues that make up the agenda of lively and
intense public activism that peaked in the late
sixties but by no means are forgotten. In cultural
terms we as a people continue to face in an ever
intensifying way the deepening sense of alienation and
with it the increasing thirst for ultimate meaning.
We feel the emptiness of materialism and consumerism
and the madness of nuclear confrontation. The
interaction of recent technical triumphs and cultural
catastrophes with heightened consciousness has led to a
deepened sense of the moral and spiritual dimensions
of life. We seem to agree that violence, greed,
perversion, cynicism, rapaciousness, and
destructiveness are on the rise but we do so with deep
loathing and dread, enough to generate the kind of
hope and energy to impel us to understand and
transform these dark forces. This moral concern came
also to be expressed in education generally as well as
more particularly in the curriculum reform movement as
exemplified most powerfully by the Values
Clarification project and the work of Lawrence
Kohlberg and his associates.

This is not the place to either describe or
analyze these two movements nor the other serious
efforts at responding to the issues of moral
education. Suffice it to say that there is general
agreement that such efforts have been enormously bene-
ficial in stimulating research and dialogue and that
they have supplied us with intriguing, ingenious, and
thoughtful educational programs. They have helped to
restore the moral dimension as a significant aspect of
educational theory and practice, an emphasis which in
spite of contrary predictions still persists. However,
there is also a sense in which the specific moral education programs have experienced results parallel to
other curriculum reforms, i.e., a history of initial
enormous interest of a fad-like quality followed by
either rejection or absorption of specific programs
into mainstream school life. Although, there are a
few isolated instances of schools being significantly
altered through such programs there are many more instances where such programs are either now a part of
oblivion or inanity. While the relative failure of
these programs per se to make for significant change
is clear, the net effect of such efforts has been to
keep the moral issue on the agenda, at least for a
large number of educational theorists.

This failure itself took on a significance since

the field had to examine not only the underlying assumptions of the programs but also the nature and quality of resistance to them. Why the virulence? Why the suspicion? Why the anger? Why the fear? These programs had indeed touched highly sensitive and neglected nerves. What was so awful about helping people to clarify their values? What harm could come from trying to promote moral growth? The resistance and critique helped us greatly to focus and sort out major educational questions. It was said that values clarification was not enough, that it promoted moral relativity and that it succeeded only in raising highly sensitive and potent issues without providing sufficient resources to deal with them. It was said that programs for promoting moral growth were too hierarchical and too isolated from the culture. It was said that it was silly to have special courses in moral education since all existing courses inherently had moral dimensions. Indeed it was said that the school itself was primarily a moral institution and perhaps it is the re-emergence of this insight that constitutes the single most important contribution of the moral education movement.

We came to see that the inadvertent, unconscious, or unaware moral messages were probably just as, if not more, significant than the deliberate and calculated ones. This has served to intensify the dialogue on not only what should the school as an institution represent morally but also on which moral principles actually inform existing school practices and policies. Many of us therefore shifted our concern for finding an appropriate moral education curriculum to a concern for those moral values of the culture and society which permeate the schools and to an analysis of how these values get expressed in day to day practice. The intensity of the reaction to moral education proposals revealed both the depth of confusion and interest in the issues and the technical failure of the packages confirmed the notion that moral education action was not to be found in syllabi but in structures. The struggles also helped to remind us of the complexities and subtleties of these issues, of the perplexity and enormity of the dilemmas inherent in providing an education with moral rigor to the American experience so deeply rooted in democracy, pluralism, and individualism.

We have come to see that the dilemmas, paradoxes, and controversies related to issues of moral education have still deeper roots. As we proceed with our onion peeling we find ourselves confronting ever more basic human issues - issues of human nature, of human potential, matters of ultimate meaning, of the relationship between the human experience and nature, between humans and humans, humans and the cosmos. We also come to confront the reality of the dialectic between these issues and our day to day lives, the realization that human nature is not just of hypothetical concern and that theories, values and life orientations are manifested in concrete and specific ways. More particularly, we came again to see enormous issues are manifested in contexts and sites, and that they are situated in particular settings - one of which of course is the school. Thus, we choose the school (perhaps at least as important for some as other contexts) as a place to examine the nature and substance of the major issues of human existence. It is a place to examine how we actually come to resolve or at least deal with these major issues of meaning and purpose. Schools then can be seen as one of the stages where the extraordinary drama of life is scripted, directed, and brought to life, and hence open to critical analysis.

This in research terms means a different kind of analysis than is involved in the use of the concepts and techniques of the applied social and psychological sciences. It means studying education not as a technology but as human phenomena and studying these phenomena not in isolation but in relationship to other human endeavors and struggles. The issues of education speak to the state of the human condition and require the same kind of rigorous, serious, and thorough inquiry that is applied to politics, culture, the arts, the economy, and the sciences.

The separation of the traditional academic discipline from education has been a mixed blessing. It surely has provided for more focused and specialized research but it has also allowed those in the traditional academic disciplines to be less concerned and sensitive if not more cavalier about education. The separation has helped the development of new approaches and methodologies but it has also tended to aggravate the drift toward the reification and reductionism of educational issues. It has had the unintended effect of contributing to the trivialization of educational issues into those of causal relationships between teaching techniques and student learning or more tersely, into input-output terms.

It is indeed encouraging to note the recent strengthening of disciplined examination of educational research and particularly the increased interest in the relationship between the humanities and education. There is a growing and lively literature that seeks to link the perspectives of aesthetics, drama, dance, art, literature, and poetry with educational reasearch that augments the traditional philosophical research. Even the field of Educational Research long dominated by logical positivism and quantitative analysis has been forced to acknowledge the movement as seen in the rapid acceptance of the concept of "qualitative evaluation." This balance in part represents an effort to further the examination of educational issues from the perspective of the humanities. To speak of the humanities is to evoke a variety of meanings and orientations. Here we speak in part to the integration of educational issues with traditional disciplines such as literature and philosophy involving not only the focus of these studies but with its concerns for rigor, analysis, and theory. We, of course, also speak to the fundamental concern for the nature and state of the human condition based on a faith that through reflection and commitment to certain ideals human fulfillment is possible. We, therefore, see the school as a locus for both humanistic study and the practice of human aspirations.

In ways parallel to what we have said about curriculum reform in general and the moral education movement in particular we need to make a brief allusion to a rather diffuse and vague phenomenon often called "humanistic education." Although there is no clear or coherent humanistic education movement or definition, many individual programs and orientations have either used that term or have had that term applied to them. Such programs in a very broad sense also put human concerns as a focus of the curriculum and tend to stress such personal values as autonomy, dignity, free expression, and creativity. Many of these programs have since faded as the general curriculum reform movement faded but these particular programs were especially criticized for excessive reliance on psychological well being at the expense of intellectual rigor. We very much support the goals and aspirations of the programs of both moral and humanistic education but have come to see the efforts at the development of a focused, coherent curriculum (in the narrow sense) as windmill fighting. Clearly those efforts sharpened and reminded us of the school's neglect and/or disregard of these enormously important issues and the, at best, very modest success of the programs highlight for us the extraordinary complexity of our educational institutions. Our focus for this conference came then not to be the development of "new" or "better" materials and techniques for teaching students about morality, values, and the human condition. Rather, our focus came to be on consciousness - on sensitivity to how the schools represent and respond to the profound issues of human existence. We sought a deeper analysis of the school's meaning in relationship to history and culture than can be derived from the limited albeit valuable perspective of curriculum development, intervention, and application.

Our concerns were not just theoretical for we also had a political agenda. First, there is our assumption that issues of power and policy are inextricably bound to culture analysis in general and of course are of enormous significance in educational institutions. Secondly, we wanted to encourage these in the humanities not only to direct attention to educational issues but to do so with the care, rigor, and sensitivity inherent in the traditions of those disciplines. We also wanted to encourage those involved in educational inquiry to consider the possibilities of integrating their work with the disciplined quest for human meaning. We wanted to promote the ideas that schools are not shops that require clever and ingenious bits of engineering to increase productivity and morale but major social institutions where wisdom and courage are required to infuse practice with our highest hopes. We also worked under the assumption that increasing consciousness of these issues would lead to change. Even though many educators are not fully aware of the significance of what they do and what their practice means our faith is that most educators really want to make their practice match our most glorious ideals.

II - The Conference

The actual planning of the conference was done

with great care and lasted for almost two years. We ourselves wanted to attempt the integration discussed above to be expressed in as many aspects of the conference as possible - format, setting, topics, the quality and tone of the proceedings, et. al. We need not here burden the reader with the details of the problems and issues that the planning group faced except to note that the planning process itself was highly stimulating and enlightening for those involved.

Eventually, we agreed on a format - residential, 4 two-day sessions spread over a year, primarily directed at junior high school teachers, administrators, and parents, a focus on four broad values issues, and major reliance on distinguished speakers from the humanties and education. Serious efforts were made to provide for dialogue among all participants and to avoid an experience of the great coming to bestow their gift to the humble. The speakers were chosen in part on the basis of their genuine interest in real dialogue and in mutual learning and teaching.

The conferences turned out to be very powerful experiences for the participants such that we were determined to include in this book a description and sense of those rich experiences. We wanted to convey the feelings of compassion, warmth, empathy, trust and the authenticity, commitment, and hope that was generated. Alas, as the glow of the experiences faded we realized the difficulty if not futility of preserving those moments of powerful existential significance. We realized that to do so required not only a great amount of work but a highly sensitive artistic methodology and so abandoned for the most part this aspect of the project. However, John Sullivan's two essays in this volume make substantial reference to some of the events of the conference. A very vivid account of the conference is contained in a letter we received after the conference. This letter came from a parent with deep interest in education and in it she says:

It is hard to put down in absolute terms why an experience becomes extra-ordinary - a sense while having it that the impacts felt are only tremors of the magnitude of the experience; it is particularly hard to say to what extent such an experience can alter one's being. Yet I had, and still have, that mystical indescribable feeling about my experiences at Quails Roost.

I feel that both for my own benefit, as well as for your committee's, I should make an attempt to crystallize some of my feelings. The first thing that strikes me is that while it was multi-level, and afforded most of us glimpses of genius – the minds and passions of truly extraordinary beings - it was just as strongly multipersonal - that is, demanding the personalized expertise of every participant, be they a "lofty" or a "mere parent."

Perhaps it was because the speakers stayed, because we ate and drank with them, because we heard their fears and passions and saw their humanness, because they joined our discussions. Maybe it was the magic of the idyllic setting - a homey feeling where cows and peacocks were neighbors, where folksy Mr. Phillips demanded that one throw away pretenses; surely the same mystique would not have been possible at the Holiday Inn on the High Point Road. No one closed themselves off in rooms - it was an atmosphere which aided conversation, comfort, and relaxed sharing of concerns. The experience showed an enormous amount of forethought and careful planning; the group leaders were obviously chosen with great care.

My second strong reaction is relief – not in the idea that anyone came away with answers - that we did not. It was relief to find that people were asking questions - questions to stirrings which have plagued me for so long, without knowing how to give those stirrings words. It was a relief to find the words there - to know that the same concerns and doubts and questionings were rumbling in so many other souls - what was what gave me hope and a sense of relief. It was the consciousness raising - the willingness to say "what in the hell

are we doing, and why?" - the realization
that it is in the asking of the questions
that we all share responsibility, not in
providing package deal answers. It was
that my concerns are Maxine Greene's too -
she just says it better, that my wish to
love a subject to the depths of my being -
for my children to know this feeling and
the total joy in truly excelling, in
surpassing oneself - I can see this
embodied in a William Arrowsmith, and yet
know that he, too, despairs and wrings his
hands. I can talk to Oak Ridge people, and
the Friends School staff, and see that the
extremes that I thought would be there,
were nonexistent when it came to concerns.
All of use were painfully, genuinely
involved in sharing our doubts about the
validity of what we do to our kids - and to
ourselves. What methods do inspire
learning, what are motivators, what affords
a concern for others; no answers, but so
many questions that showed so much
humanness - because everyone knew that
there exists no one way - no right way.

I feel most privileged to have been a
participant; that each person's presence
was equally valued and of value; I think
that was a shared feeling - and in a way,
that must have been a large part of the
magical success.

I thank you all for allowing all of us
the opportunity to better understand our
doubts, and to begin asking our questions
together. And in my thanking, I want to
make a request of you, the professional
educators. Schools of Education must make
commitments - moral humane commitments - to
take stands and to buck systems; as
educators, you must shape new attitudes and
teach your students to raise questions.
The formidable public - we - have all been
shaped by our educational experiences - we
do not know how to evalue without
judgement, how to encourage exploration
without offering our critique - we all need
to be taught how to examine our effects on
others. If testing is required, we say

yea!, and that then becomes one's value;
help us to change that, and together, we
can help change each other to be liberators
and humane individuals, with a sense of our
mutual dignity and worth.

III The Papers

This book basically is built around the formal
papers given at the conference, which had been
organized around four general themes or value issues.
These four themes were chosen not only as vitally
important human issues but as ones that strongly
impinge on school practice. The issues we chose for
examination were Equality/Excellence; Schools as
Community/Schools as Institution; Freedom/Responsibi-
lity; and Evaluation/Dignity. We chose to group
the themes in pairs not as polarities or dichotomies
but to indicate some of the complexity and subtlety
involved in the analysis of values. We also were very
much aware that it was indeed very difficult to
examine any one or two major such concerns without
dealing with several other related concerns. The
particular pair ups were made only to clearly indicate
that the two concerns in each pairing had a particular
intimate relationship with each other and hence that
relationship needed to be seriously considered.

This book is also organized around these same
four themes and in each of the four sections there is
a brief introduction followed by two different essays
on each theme. The second part of the book contains a
number of essays written in response to the issues
presented in the papers and proceedings of the
conference.

There is enormous diversity represented in the
essays. First of all the writers come from many
disciplines and professional orientations, e.g.
philosophy, sociology, theology, literature, and
drama. In addition, several orientations and
perspectives are reflected in the papers from
critical theory to analytical philosophy and involving
such traditions as Jungian psychology, existential
philosophy, and Eastern mysticism. As a whole, the
essays reflect a deep sensitivity to the complexities,
ambiguities, and perplexities of the issues
particularly in the way in which centuries-old moral
and philsophical issues relate to school practice.

xxi

The essays provide on the one hand sufficient insight, clarification and direction to justify the project and on the other hand reflect sufficient uncertainty and ambiguity of the issues to demonstrate the necessity for a great deal of further work. What was clear was that not nearly enough has been previously done in the way of examining the school as an arena of the struggle to make meaning and wisdom.

In this regard, the papers all speak to the awesome importance of educational institutions and especially the difficulty and significance of the individual teacher's responsibilities. It is the teacher who actually has the task of deciding on a moment to moment basis how to act and how to concretely inter-relate theory and practice; to make real the questions of the relationship of individuals, groups, and institutions, with moral and philosophical traditions. The papers speak to values not only as rational processes but as they are lived with particular reference here of course to what it means to be human for teachers, students, parents, and administrators. The essays thereby reflect the paradox of the enormous expectations made for schooling - that somehow schools should provide for the development of basic skills, prepare young people for jobs, the culture, and the society, should help students deal with their nutrition, sexuality, health and somehow to do all in a rational, sane, caring, wise and efficient manner. The paradox lies not in the fact that the culture gives this mission to the school but in how the culture comes to trivialize, discount, and deny that mission as shown in the contempt and ignorance of the schools by the culture. On the one hand we say schools are of profound importance and on the other hand we choose to be superficial and patronizing in our understanding of educational processes and miserly in the allocation of human and economic resources to these endeavors.

There is indeed a sharp contrast between the tone and quality of the essays in this book - probing, thorough, daring, a sense of awe for the significance of the issues and of humility in the quest for wisdom, analysis of rich subtlety and of extraordinary diversity - with the quality of the contemporary public dialogue on public education. In the wake of the renewed public interest in public education we see politicians and ambitious educators scrambling to exploit and contain this interest with the familiar cries of "crisis" and lists of scapegoats - television, low salaries, lazy students and/or teachers, schools of education, certification requirements, and the like. We once again hear the simplifications and reductionisms - the equation of academic rigor with requirements, of knowledge with the recall of information, of learning with test scores, the seductive links between "economic growth", national defense and education. It is equally painful to hear the familarly superficial and/or cynical remedies - more homework, less electives, longer school days and years, higher salaries, etc. Schools are seen as agencies of public policy, as generators of jobs and profits, and as adjuncts of our international prestige and power. Among other things, this current scramble itself reveals our anti-intellectual traditions in two ways - the low quality of the intellectual validity of the criticism and the continuing fear of allowing schools to be institutions focused on ideas, on critical reflections, and the stimulation of the imagination. The obsession with test scores, with more compulsion, with stricter controls reflect our historical doubts and fears of the capacity of humans to freely and openly strive to find meaning. This is in sharp contrast to the vision of hope, faith and meaning that is reflected in the essays of this book.

Let me conclude this introduction with an event of the conference which to me crystallizes what this whole endeavor is about and what to me made it so worthwhile. At the conclusion of the conference, one of the participants, an experienced teacher and school administrator stood up and asked to make a few comments before adjournment. This man had been teaching elementary and junior high school students for several years following a disillusioning experience as a university instructor. In a voice full of emotion and in a pace made irregular by his efforts to hold back his tears, he said, "I want to express for myself and I believe the other teachers a deep appreciation for this conference because we have been given in the events of the past few days a chance to remember and rediscover the nobility of our profession."

It is to that passion, that anguish, that commitment, and that idealism of that teacher and his colleagues that this book seeks to speak.

EQUALITY/EXCELLENCE

There can be little doubt that of all the issues concerned with education in America, questions of Equality and Excellence have engendered the greatest degree of contention and passion. In the last two decades, especially, pressures from the bottom of our society have forced the issue of equality onto our political agenda again and again. Characteristic of the debate has been the tendency to present the goals of social equality and educational excellence in a polarity. The pursuit of a more just social order, it has been frequently suggested, is responsible for the corruption of educational values. Presented in this way society is confronted by a terrible and irreconcilable dilemma. It leads us to question whether a serious commitment to equality must lead inevitably to mediocrity and levelling. Or whether we can assume that a commitment to excellence will not end the concern for human equality.

Maxine Greene, in her paper, has sought to root the inequities that disfigure American society in our historically established attitudes towards human nature and human capabilities. From Jefferson to the present time education has been at the center of the process that has sought to select and differentiate individuals from the meritocratic claims of a 'natural aristocracy' of talent. Hierarchical notions, she asserts, infuse teachers attitudes so that they continue to 'freeze' students into superior and inferior categories. Greene also notes that the replacement of notions of excellence that have to do with the 'enlargement of mind' and the capacity for critical reflection have given way to technically constricted notions of competence. Granting that relatively little can be done in schools to counteract the stratification that exists throughout society she calls for a recognition of a 'multiplicty of excellences' that would allow us to combine our concerns for human dignity and worth with the need for an education that encourages students to 'reach out towards possibilities'.

Svi Shapiro, in his paper*, looks at the way schools produce and reproduce inequalities. Working within broadly Marxian categories he considers the way schools in our society help to assign individuals into the class structure, imbuing each with a belief about his or her respective abilities, potentialities and capabilities. In place of the usual definitions of 'excellence' which Shapiro locates in the context of elitist and hierarchical forms of education, he asserts the need for a notion of 'moral excellence' concerned with educating for a more just, non-exploitative, more fully human society.

Finally is William A. Arrowsmith's* poetic vision of the teacher who attains excellence. Deprecating the real status of

1

teachers in most American universities ('a second class citizen')
true teaching, he says, is inseparable from liberation and
transcending ourselves; it is inseparable from 'metaphysical'
concerns - the nature of man and human destiny. It is a process
founded in an Eros-like quest for completion or fulfillment, in
which the educator is a visible embodiment of the realization of
humanity's aspirations, skills, and scholarship. It is, says
Arrowsmith, precisely because the teacher exemplifies this
passion for fulfillment that he or she can influence others to
surpass themselves, to manifest 'a radiant hunger for becoming'.

*Svi Shapiro's paper is an expanded version of his position
paper presented at the conference. William A. Arrowsmith's paper,
while different in some respects from the talk given at the
conference, deals with most of the themes contained in the
original presentation.

EQUALITY/EXCELLENCE

Maxine Greene

At a time of national preoccupation with "excellence," largely defined as a set of technical competencies conceived essential for a "nation at risk,"[1] the commitments to equality have been suppressed. A presumed consensus is used to justify this: Americans, it is suggested, are committed to laissez faire and meritocracy; misfortune is an individual's responsibility; it is a time for the manly virtues, for patriotism, for prayer. Social deficiencies that have long haunted our imagination are set aside as insignificant or repaired. Yet the tension between the values of equality and excellence that has marked our educational history cannot totally be overcome. In many ways, it has made our history distinctive; to attend to it is one way of keeping the faith.

The Declaration of Independence did state (as many people seem to have forgotten) that "We hold these truths to be self evident: that all men are created equal, that they are endowned by their Creator with certain unalienable Rights, that among these are Life, Liberty, and the pursuit of Happiness." It is the case that the Declaration said nothing about women; it is very likely that those who signed the document did not consider slaves as "men." Also, no mention was made of a right to equality of fulfillment, or to equal treatment, or to equal regard. It is not surprising, then, that Thomas Jefferson, the author of the Declaration, later distinguished between the "laboring and the learned" when he devised his plan for education in Virginia.[2]

National Commission on Excellence in Education. A Nation at Risk: The Imperative for Educational Reform. (Washington, D.C.: U. S. Government Printing Office, 1983).

Thomas Jefferson, "Notes on the State of Virginia," Query XIV, in Crusade Against Ignorance: Thomas Jefferson on Education, ed. Gordon C. Lee (New York: Teachers College Press, 1973), pp. 92-97.

Nor is it surprising that, when he developed his concept of a "natural aristocracy," he proposed a different kind of education for those "of the best and most promising genius and disposition" than for the less talented, less likely to achieve excellence. He wrote to John Adams in 1813 about the "virtue and talents" that were the ground of the "natural aristocracy" [3] and made the point that this differed fundamentally from the so-called "artificial aristocracy," based as it was in birth and wealth. That type of aristocracy, he said, "is a mischievous ingredient in government and provision should be made to prevent its ascendancy." And then:

> The natural aristocracy I consider as the most precious gift of nature, for the instruction, the trusts, and government of society. And indeed it would have been inconsistent in creation to have formed man for the social state, and not to have provided virtue and wisdom enough to manage the concerns of society. May we not even say that that form of government is the best which provides the most effectually for pure selection of those natural aristoi into the offices of government? [4]

Concerned as Jefferson was with a society built on a foundation of popular intelligence, he did not have democracy in mind as we understand it, nor did he have in mind actual rule by the people. In the same letter to Adams, he indicated that his hopes for the United States were built upon the continued existence of the freeholder or the small property-owner, interested in "law and order." Such an individual, he said, could be trusted to exert control over affairs and to possess a degree of freedom, which "in the hands of the canaille of the cities of Europe, would be instantly perverted to the demolition and the destruction of everything public and private." [5] He

---

[3] Jefferson, "A Letter to John Adams from Monticello," October 28, 1813, in Adams-Jefferson Letters, ed. Lester J. Cappon (Chapel Hill, N.C.: University of North Carolina Press, 1959), Vol. II, p. 388.

[4] Ibid.

[5] Jefferson, op. cit., p. 392.

did not have what would have been a tragic vision of the future: that, before long, there would be vast numbers of people in this country equally "debased by ignorance, poverty and vice," and that they would be the ones (whose voices had scarcely been attended to before) crying out for democracy and equality.

Jefferson and Adams were dead for only two years when, in 1828, Andrew Jackson was elected president, and the rule of "King Numbers" began. Industrialization and urbanization had commenced to overwhelm the free agrarian society that was the stuff of Jefferson's dream; and Jefferson's arguments for education were taken over by people conscious of very different urgencies. When he was arguing for support of common schools in Massachusetts ten years after Jackson's election, Horace Mann did not talk about a selective education, as Jefferson had done. He understood the sense in which freedom was a function of universal literacy; but he also knew that men with muddy feet, not a "natural aristoi," were now in line to "manage the concerns of society." There could be no guarantee that the most virtuous and the most talented would be "selected" out of the mass; therefore, it was necessary to try to shape all the people, when they were young and malleable, into beings capable of self-control, productiveness, and (if possible) benevolence.

Fearful of disruption and disorder if nothing was done, Mann and other school reformers put their primary emphasis on "voluntary compliance" with the laws of righteousness, on "self-government," on control. They argued for support of education, they described it as the "great equalizer of the conditions of men--the balance-wheel of the social machinery." [6] That meant that a common school training ought to give each individual the independence he would need to resist the selfishness of those around, even as it equipped him with the skills required for making a living and escaping poverty. There was no intention of redistributing wealth or guaranteeing economic equality. It seemed enough to provide equality of opportunity: the opportunity to pursue success,

---

[6]Horace Mann, "Twelfth Annual Report," in The Republic and the School: Horace Mann on the Education of Free Men, ed. Lawrence A. Cremin (New York: Teachers College Press, 1979), p. 87.

create new wealth, and enter the mainstream of
society. From another vantage point, it might be said
that people were assured an equal chance to set foot
on the ladder, soon to be thought of as the
meritocratic ladder. They could expect to go as high
as their skills and intelligence permitted; and that
meant climbing as high as they deserved. It must be
kept in mind that disadvantages, or deficits due to
poverty or sickness or difficulty of adaptation, were
not taken into account. It occurred to few people
(apart from socialists like Robert Dale Owen and
Frances Wright [7]) that, lacking special help or
informed support, the disadvantaged person simply did
not start in the same place where opportunity was
concerned. And only a relatively few, those concerned
about the rights of women and the emancipation of the
slaves, remarked the exclusiveness of a "ladder"
thousands of human beings were not permitted to
approach, much less climb.

Excellence was seldom mentioned as an educational
value; but Horace Mann made two points with respect to
it that affected discourse for years to come.
Challenging those parents who wished to set up private
schools for their children, he said that their removal
of the best students would deprive "the lower classes
in a school" of an "abstract standard of excellence."[8]
As he saw it all children rise easily "to the common
level"; but then they stop. If the school were to
"raise the standard," . . . by a spontaneous movement,
the mass will rise again and reach it." At another
juncture, Mann informed his audiences that self-
government and compliance were, in any case, "the
highest point of excellence attainable by a human
being. No one, however, can consciously obey the laws
of right and duty until he understands them. Hence
the preliminary necessity of their being clearly
explained, of their being made to stand out, broad,
lofty, and as conspicuous as a mountain against a
clear sky." [9] This is very different from the

[7]Arthur M. Schlesinger, Jr., The Age of Jackson
(New York: Mentor Books, 1952), pp. 77-78.

[8]Mann, "First Annual Report," in Cremin, op.
cit., pp. 31-32.

[9]Mann, "Ninth Annual Report," in Cremin, op.cit,
p. 57.

Jeffersonian linking of excellence to mastery of ancient languages, classical philosophy, and natural science (for the talented ones, always the selected few).

The purposes of the common school, of course, had little to do with intellectual pursuits. They were largely utilitarian and moralistic, because of the ways in which the children of the poor and the immigrants were conceived. The overriding idea, after all, was to socialize them into a common belief system and, by so doing, to bring into being a common culture; and then it was to prepare the kinds of citizens who would be virtuous, hard-working, and loyal to the core values of that culture. ("Little children," said a widely used reader, "you must seek rather to be good than wise.") There were strangers' children to Americanize, farmers' sons to urbanize, young girls to save from the "corruptions" of the streets or of the arts. Most importantly, there was the need to guarantee public order and equilibrium. Whatever was considered to be excellent, in consequence, was related to what was called "counterpoise." Excessiveness, even excessiveness in talent or originality, was frowned upon; as in the proliferating factories, standardization was preferred. The anti-intellectualism associated with such an approach was, in part, a response to a felt need for containment; the young were clearly equal in requiring molding and control.

Until the years after the Civil War, most children concluded their education at the end of primary school. Only the few, usually the children of privileged parents, went on to secondary schools. These were ordinarily private academies, sometimes boarding schools resembling the selective grammar schools and gymnasia in European countries. Students could choose between an "English" (or practical) curriculum and a "Latin" (or traditional) one. The first prepared them for commerce, business, or professional training. The other was "liberal," highly intellectual, and prepared for the university. To proponents of mass democratic education, this system often appeared un-American; and, before long, free public high schools began appearing across the country. For a time, they were largely urban institutions; because small communities could neither afford them nor (in many cases) see much justification for them. Not infrequently, a town or village was

7

accustomed to giving financial support or scholarship aid to a private academy in the vicinity. Too much was taken for granted about "natural inequalities" and the need for a specially educated leadership class (for all the arguments regarding common schools) for people to notice that obvious inequity.

Enrollment in the free high schools did not begin outstripping enrollemnt in the academies until the 1880s. Attendance was voluntary in the early years; and, although most students did not plan to go on to college, they were provided an education not unlike that offered by the academies. David Tyack has written about the elaborate Gothic structures built in the cities, clearly to attract families used to the idea of academies. [10] And, indeed, according to Michael Katz[11] and Selwyn Troen, [12] the high school population tended to be upper middle class, with a sprinkling of white collar workers' children and children of professionals. Even though the people at large supported those schools with their taxes (often grudgingly, it is true), a very small percentage of factory workers or unskilled workers of any sort even thought of sending their boys and girls to high school. Some of this can be attributed to family traditions and to a degree of felt security where certain work patterns were concerned. Some of it can be attrributed to a kind of enclave mentality or to a taken-for-grantedness where class membership and mobility were concerned.

As part of the campaign to end child labor, however, efforts were undertaken to make secondary education compulsory; and, between 1890 and 1910, the high school was transformed into a mass institution. the school people did not at first have at hand the categories needed to conceptualize a phenomenon of

[10]David B. Tyack, The One Best System (Cambridge, Mass.: Harvard University Press, 1974), pp. 56-59.

[11]Michael B. Katz, The Irony of Early School Reform: Educational Innovation in Mid-Nineteenth Century Massachusetts (Cambridge: Harvard University Press, 1968), pp. 80-83.

[12]Selwyn Troen, "Popular Education in Nineteenth Century St. Louis," History of Education Quarterly 13 (Spring, 1973), pp. 23-40.

such novelty; and the orientation of the new schools remained predominantly academic in the traditional sense. According to the NEA Committee of Ten, the high school's obligation was "to prepare for the duties of life that small proportion of all the children . . . who show themselves able to profit by an education prolonged to the eighteenth year, and whose parents are able to support them while they remain so long at school." [13] It is evident that a selective principle was still at work: parents "able to support" were clearly upper middle class, affluent parents; those who could "profit" were the privileged. Even so, the Committee asserted that the curriculum was adapted to "the general needs, both intellectual and industrial" of the students. They meant that, in high school at least, training of the mind was of the first importance; but "that small proportion of all the children" was still the fundamental concern.

The NEA's report was issued in 1893; but, as more and more children crowded into the schools, its influence soon began to wane. Educators were forced to come to terms with altogether novel problems; and, as in the common schools, the educational task was now identified as laying the "foundations of good citizenship" and "helping the young make a wise choice of vocation." [14] It seemed obvious that education for the many ought to be more vocational than "bookish"; arrangements could always be made for the well-endowed few. Nonetheless, tracks or no tracks, great numbers of students dropped out or were "selected out" of the high schools. At the end of the second World War, there was such prevalent disinterest that educators felt provoked to develop programs "more in harmony with the life-adjustment needs of all youth," programs suited for the sixty percent of students ostensibly served poorly by both acadmic and vocational curricula. [15] There were the poor, the apparently neglected, the excluded children who had scarcely been noticed before.

_____

[13]Report of the Committee on Secondary School Studies Appointed at the Meeting of the NEA, July 9, 1892 (Washington, 1893).

[14]Ibid.

[15]Lawrence A. Cremin, The Transformation of the School (New York: Alfred A. Knopf, 1961), pp. 335-336.

In times past, young people of this sort would
have found menial jobs and disappeared into the
faceless crowd; but, in an increasingly complex and
technologized society, there were fewer places for
them to go. Their test scores were low; they came
from underprivileged families; they were poorly
motivated. Insisting that they were not in any way
inferior, the manuals on life adjustment emphasized
what they called "life values," those having to do
with morality, citizenship, health, and occupational
adjustment, all of which were piously called more
important than the acquisition of knowledge. Nothing
was said about allaying the crippling effects of
grinding poverty; nothing was said about remediation
or finding ways of enabling different children to
learn to learn. There was a general taken-for
grantedness still about all the factors involved: the
reliability of the tests being administered; the
necessity for measurement; the certainty of the "sixty
per cent" with I.Q.s below 110; the inherent fairness
of focusing on life-adjustment rather than cognitive
growth. Leveling downward as they did, many school
people believed they were realizing the value of
equality.

A variety of attacks on the public schools from
conservative academic, neo-humanist, and religious
points of view marked the decade of the 1950s.
Certain ones focused on the so-called "Deweyan"
influence (either exaggerated or deformed); all
stressed the mediocrity in the schools, the "lollipop"
education, the divorce of the schools from the world
of scholarship, the neglect of tradition, the
subversion of the Good and the True. There was talk
of the need for "basic education," for a return to the
selective principle associated with Jeffersonianism.[16]
John Gardner's <u>Excellence: Can We Be Equal and
Excellent Too?</u> called attention to the multiple modes
of excellence that might be attained if children were
released to develop and to grow.

In 1957, however, all the questions became moot.

---

[16]See Arthur E. Bestor, <u>Educational Wastelands:
The Retreat from Learning in Our Public Schools</u>
(Urbana, Ill.: The University of Illinois Press,
1951) and James B. Conant, <u>Thomas Jefferson and the
Development of American Public Education</u> (Berkeley:
University of California Press, 1962).

With the appearance of the Soviet Sputnik rocket, engineering talent and technical excellence became the primary concern. Even as at present, the paranoid fear of falling behind the Soviet Union in the training of technicians and scientists seemed to cancel out moral commitment and considerations. In the name of national defense, academic rigor and a consequent selection process could be justified. The curriculum reform movement, the inquiries into the "structure of knowledge," [17] the burgeoning interest in Piagetian theory and cognitive development: all these blotted out the memory of "life adjustment." There was some talk of general education for the many, some talk of adjusting the sophistication of what was taught to different ability levels; but the problem of equality was generally set aside, as were the problems of the excluded and the poor.

Then, abruptly, attention was drawn to those who had been "invisible" since the founding the nation; and, at almost the same instant, the civil rights movement began. People who had been inaudible for years, people afflicted by what Reverend Martin Luther King called "nobodiness" took the center of the stage. The War on Poverty, the Elementary and Secondary Acts, compensatory and remedial programs of all sorts made the issue of equality central as it had never been before. The public was being made to understand that the promise of equal opportunity had been an empty one in the face of racial discrimination and the kinds of poverty that caused cognitive and other deficits, deficits that incapacitated children to such a degree that they could not cope with school. There was, in the mid-1960s, a brief moment of optimism with respect to compensatory measures and what they could achieve. Almost immediately, however, such giant studies as James Coleman's on Equality of Educational Opportunity, [18] focusing as they did on achievement scores, convinced numbers of people that the

---

[17]See Jerome S. Bruner, The Process of Education (Cambridge: Harvard University Press, 1960) and G. W. Ford and Lawrence Pugno, ed.s., The Structure of Knowledge and the Curriculum (Chicago: Rand, McNally & Co., 1964).

[18]James S. Coleman, Equality of Educational Opportunity (Washington, D.C.: U.S. Government Printing Office, 1966).

significant variables, after all, were to be found in family background and social class, factors the schools could probably not remedy. This led, in a country preoccupied with protests and with war, to feelings of scepticism and powerlessness with respect to schools.

Various scholars were, despite all this, beginning to make conceptually clear that equality does not mean sameness or equivalence, that treating differently endowed people in identical ways only perpetuated inequalities. It was only those who saw existing inequalities and injustices as somehow "natural" who could continue blandly to believe that the provision of equal opportunity was all that was needed. Myron Lieberman, among others, said that there were at least two definitions of 'equality' that expressed what most people meant when they used the term.[19] One was that two individuals have equality of opportunity when neither has a material advantage over the other in selecting or pursuing his/her educational goals. The other was that two individuals have equality of educational opportunity when the material advantage one may possess over the other cannot be removed without endangering other important values. Values vary from person to person, obviously; the conditions affecting equality of opportunity vary as a result. Equality, at the very least, must be recognized as something other than a given; it is not an aspect of empirical social reality.

The radical historians and the romantic critics who began writing about education in the 1960s were intent on exposing just such "myths" as the idea of an existing equality. As many saw it, the actual purpose of the 19th century reforms had been to impose a system of schooling on the mass of children in response to the needs of the privileged and the owning classes. Michael Katz demonstrated that, in many communities, it was the propertied class and the factory owners who argued most for education, especially high school education, not the working men or the artisans. The reasons had to do with the need to inculcate the kinds of behavior patterns required

---

[19]Myron Lieberman, "Equality of Educational Opportunity," in Language and Concepts in Education, ed.s. B. Othanel Smith and Robert H. Ennis (Chicago: Rand McNally & Company, 1961), pp. 127-143.

in the new factories. Children had to be trained to accommodate to the arbitrary time schemes and regulations that made for industrial efficiency; it was equally necessary to build barriers against what was called the "immoral and degenerate chaos" that seemed incipient in the growing cities and factory towns. The centralization of the school systems and the standardization of curricula were undertaken with such an end in view, the revisionists insisted. As they saw it, the cultural bias of such school reformers as Horace Mann simply prevented them from recognizing that success in school, like success in the larger society, was a function of social-economic class. The interest in control, however, like the preoccupation with moral pieties, represented an acknowledgment that something had to be done to mask the essentially manipulative function of the schools.

The critics believed that there had been and was a deliberate effort to maintain existing inequalities by various tracking devices and, for a long time, by making the academic high school a viable option mainly for those who were "suited" for it. I.Q. tests and aptitude tests, beginning with the end of the First World War, determined who was "suited" and, indeed, who had the "merit" required for advance. Various critics pointed out that the test questions were ordinarily based on "presumed progressive difficulty in performing tasks . . . believed necessary for achievement in ascending the hierarchical occupational structure." In designing the Stanford-Binet I.Q. test, Terman found, according to his test results, that the intelligence of different occupational classes fit a hierarchy he had in mind in the first place. It followed, therefore, that the I.Q. (which Terman thought was inherited) was based on the social class order. [20] But it was pointed out, at the same time, that the rating systems in schools were only partially based on childhood I.Q. Children were ranked and grouped in the light of class-associated information: the way they looked, the way they spoke, the values they brought from their homes. According to the critics, therefore, inequalities have been actually created within the schools, even as the

[20]Leon J. Kamin, "Heredity, Intelligence, Politics, and Psychology," in Shaping the American Educational State, ed. Clarence J. Karier (New York, N.Y.: The Free Press, 1975), pp. 368-369.

knowledge taught has been distributed unequally. The value of excellence, traditionally linked to a high level of cognitive development, becomes irrelevant for those whose achievement is expected to remain--and often does remain--"low."

The radical critique has been frequently countered by those who talk about differentiation among the schools, by those who stress the discrepancies between intent and outcome, by those who object to deterministic analyses, and by those who continue to emphasize the equalizing function of the schools. Diane Ravitch, for example, has talked of the contributions made by the New York City school system in providing "free, unlimited educational opportunities for millions, regardless of language, race, class or religion."[21] She has argued consistently that the public schools have made unprecedented social and economic mobility possible, and that they would not have done so were it now for their commitment to equality of educational opportunity.

Still, such studies as those conducted by Christopher Jencks and his colleagues,[22] have convinced many that the schools are only of "marginal" importance when it comes to the achievement of economic equality; and there has been a growing doubt (nurtured by changing federal policies) that compensatory measures contribute in any significant way to the removal of the worst inequities. The recognition that inequality may be a structural issue, an inevitable aspect of a capitalist and post-capitalist system, has made the contributions of the schools seem increasingly problematic. The Jensen research on the heritability of the I.Q. and the cognitive inferiority of certain racial groups helped to prepare the ground first for a "benign indifference" with respect to the underprivileged and, in time, for the erosion of support systems for the poor and of general social concern. "White flight," conflicts between special interest groups, a swelling

---

[21]Diane Ravitch, The Great School Wars: New York City, 1805-1973 (New York: Basic Books, 1974), p. 403.

[22]Christopher Jencks, et al., Inequality (New York: Basic Books, 1972).

privatism: all have turned attention away from the
great problematic of American inequality.   As cost-
benefit language takes over in the public space, as
the language of value is usurped by television
evangelists and the "moral majority," the "sense of
injustice" [23] itself becomes weakened. People become
increasingly unable even to notice the excluded, the
homeless, the defeated, the unemployed.   They are
preoccupied with their own survival in the face of
economic stringency. They cannot "afford" to pay heed
to others' claims of inequality.

Teachers at the present moment, pressed as they
are by demands for more rigor and higher scores,
realize that the traditional claims and assurances no
longer hold, certainly where the attainment of
equality is concerned. Most recognize full well that
the differences between, say, the performance of the
students in Scarsdale, New York, and the performance
of those in New York City are largely due to economic
differences, not likely to be removed by appeals to
equity or the value of equality. The original ideal,
after all, was articulated with a society of
freeholders in mind, of human beings conceived to be
equal as persons because they shared a common essence
or substance. They were potentially rational beings;
they were perfectible; they shared--in their
communities, in their homogeneous towns--a visible
public space. The "natural aristocrats" among them
were simply those who could be relied upon to guard
their fellow-citizens' liberties and to articulate
their interests or their needs.

The kind of excellence Jefferson had in mind was
the sort that accompanies an enlargement of mind,
scientific understanding, and the "habits of
reflection and correct action" that would render those
appointed to lead "examples of virtue to others, and
of happiness within themselves." [24] This is evocative
of classical norms; and it differs dramatically from
the kind of competence we are told is required by the
technologized mass society that would supplant what

23Edmond N. Cahn, The Sense of Injustice (New
York University Press, 1949).

24Jefferson, "A Bill for the More General
Diffusion of Knowledge," in Crusade Against Ignorance,
op. cit., p. 86 ff.

15

Jefferson thought of as a polis. Nathaniel
Hawthorne's story, "Ethan Brand," may be taken as one
of many metaphors for what happened. The tale is, in
part, a rendering of the contrast between the "simple
and loving man" who once embarked upon a search for
knowledge and the blasted creature who at length
returned with his heart hardened, His "hold of the
magnetic chain of humanity" quite lost. His original
impulse had been to seek the truth out of sympathy for
mankind and reverence for the flawed human heart. But
he was Faustian, on overreacher; and, instead of
remaining a "brother-man," he became a "cold observer,
looking on mankind as the subject of his experiment,
and, at length, converting man and woman to be his
puppets . . . Thus Ethan Brand became a fiend. He
began to be so from the moment his moral nature had
ceased to keep the pace of improvement with his
intellect." [25] Pondering such a story, a reader
cannot but suspect that the increasingly exploitative
society was such as to release many human
perversities, especially those associated with
distancing, manipulations, and controls. And what was
once intended as a sympathetic quest in the interests
of others was transmuted into a drive for technical
know-how, a cold empiricism appropriate to a society
bent on expansion and mastery. A similar theme is
enacted in Herman Melville's Moby Dick against a
larger canvas; and it is not surprising that, when the
ship in that novel sinks beneath the waves, Captain
Ahab would cry out, "Its wood could only be American!"

The problems of equality and excellence must be
confronted today within the contexts of advanced
technology, contexts characterized by complex and
overlapping systems, each one dependent upon what has
been called "functional rationality." [26] The mode of
dominion is largely bureaucratic, a rule by "Nobody,"[27]
under which no one takes responsibility, people play

---

[25]Nathaniel Hawthorne, "Ethan Brand," in The
Portable Hawthorne, ed. Malcolm Cowley (New York: The
Viking Press, 1955), p. 257.

[26]Daniel Bell, The Coming of Post-Industrial
Society (New York: Basic Books, 1973), pp. 165-266.

[27]Hannah Arendt, "On Violence," in Crises of the
Republic (New York: A Harvest Book, Harcourt, Brace
Jovanovich, 1972), p. 137.

roles, and few are personally engaged. Moreover, it remains a meritocracy. A meritocratic social order, John Rawls has said, "follows the principle of careers open to talents and uses equality of opportunity as a way of releasing men's energies in the pursuit of economic prosperity and political dominion."[28] He went on to mark the disparity between the upper and lower classes "in the means of life and the rights and privileges of organizational authority." And then: "Equality of opportunity means an equal chance to leave the less fortunate behind in the personal quest for influence and social position." Under such circumstances, inequalities cannot but be taken for granted; and excellence has largely to do with success in the quest Rawls has described.

The schools, in the present period, are beginning (in response to official demand) to move away from an orientation to "minimal competencies." Certain of the current concerns are legitimated by apparently declining test scores and by an apparent erosion of what is narrowly defined as "literacy." At once, there remains a new consumerism among educational publics that moves them to demand increasingly a kind of "quality control" in the schools, precise measurements of output, and a public accounting of what has been achieved. Affected by the technological ethos, people find it difficult to think in other than calculative terms. Moreover, troubled as they are by the job situation and the calls to prepare for a computerized and automatized society, they have little patience with open-ended goals. Development as an aim is insufficient in most people's eyes; there seems to be too much "risk," in personal life as well as (according to official claim) in the nation's. Whether members of the public are very poor and worried about their children's survival, or very wealthy and worried about status and prestige, they are asking for the kind of education that will guarantee at least the technical or professional literacy supposedly required for success. They are less interested in moral education and citizenship education than those who came before; but they are concerned about discipline and compliance, at least to the extent required for "making it" in the mainstream in a changing world.

---

[28]John Rawls, A Theory of Justice (Cambridge: Harvard University Press, 1971), p. 106.

Equality and excellence become issues at distinctive moments of educational debate. Now and again, the rights of women and minorities are asserted; school people are reminded that the formerly excluded have unmet claims to access to positions of authority. Differential approaches to literacy are occasionally protested; there are arguments over bilingual teaching, both sides apealing to the value of equality. The official emphasis on "excellence," with the accompanying stress on mathematical and scientific literacy (along with writing ability and computer literacy), not only departs from earlier conceptions; it carries with it a hidden message that equality considerations should be set aside. Meanwhile, new attacks are levied at the "mediocrity" of schools, the insufficiency of teachers, the ineffectiveness of teacher education. In the "national interest," we are told, and without federal funding, the systems must be remade.

How, then, is the contemporary teacher to deal with the matter of equality and excellence? It must be said once more that equality ought to be understood as an ideal, perhaps a protest-ideal; in an empirical sense, it may be nearly meaningless. As has been said, it is not to be understood as sameness or identity. If it were, and if equality were taken up as a significant goal, children would have to be removed from their families in infancy and brought up in common nurseries; there would have to be total control of breeding if anything approximating sameness were to be achieved. Surely, there is no teacher anywhere who hopes to eradicate individual differences and create some "brave new world" in his/her classroom. At once, few people can conceive of situations in which all the members of a given group or community are treated in precisely the same way.

There must be an acknowledgment, then, that human beings differ in countless ways: in capacity, in strength, in energy, in virtue, in taste, in many of their needs. In specific ways, and in the light of such differences, they are unequal to one another. Most people cannot climb mountains as skilled mountain climbers do, or open multiple counselling centers as skilled social workers do, or play the piano as Vladimir Horowitz does, or take action in the public interest as Ralph Nader is able to do, or program computers as advanced programmers can. Howard Gardner has developed a theory of "multiple intelligences," [29] or modes of know-how, ranging from the mathematical-logical to the bodily kinaesthetic, from the literary to the scientific to the personal. Even as we take note of human variation, we are bound to think of variable and multiple excellences.

At once, we know that we are equal in certain relevant respects: in our being human, most people would say, and in the rights and freedoms associated with being human. To speak of an "essence," however, to seek out a common denominator that names our "humanness" may be once again to identify equality with sameness. It may be preferable to think of human identity as always future for any living being--to be chosen, to be pursued. It may be that the relevant respect in which human beings are equal is in their integrity and in their freedom, in their right and their capacity to act upon possibility.

When people say that all men and women are equal, it seems evident that they mean (on some level) that everyone is entitled to equality of consideration. This means that every living individual is entitled to the kind of treament and attention that express regard for his/her integrity and permit him/her (or empowers him/her) to act upon his/her freedom. Clearly, distinctions often must be made; and, because they must, the matter of equity or justice comes inevitably into play. Justice demands that people should be treated differently if there are relevant grounds for so treating them. [30] To put it otherwise: distinctions should be made only on the ground of relevant differences, not irrelevant ones. Most Americans admit by now that racial segregation involved making distinctions on irrelevant grounds. The color of a young person's skin obviously has nothing at all to do with that person's "suitability" for any particular kind of education. Because that specific difference was irrelevant where the possibility of learning was concerned, there was no way of justifying racial separation. On the other hand, the creation of a therapeutic learning

---

[29]Howard Gardner, Frames of Mind: The Theory of Multiple Intelligences (New York: Basic Books, 1983).

[30]R. S. Peters, Ethics and Education (London: George Allen and Unwin, 1978), pp. 120-126.

environment for the emotionally disturbed can probably be justified; because, without such an environment, certain children might be immobilized, unable to learn how to learn. Similarly, it is probably unjust to deal with migrant children in precisely the way we deal with resident middle-class children. When one state arranged to provide such children with computerized records of their progress, distinctions were being made on the ground of what one can perceive as a relevant difference. We are also told by some that it is fair to categorize non-English speaking children and offer them bilingual teaching; because, again, their inability to understand English prevents them from learning to learn. Yes, there are differences of opinion, many deriving from varying conceptions of equality; and, yes, there is an emphasis on mainstreaming the different. Even so, the point remains: justice is served when distinctions are made on relevant grounds, and the value called equality is not violated, as it so often is when decisions are made for irrelevant reasons.

But, even as we consider the making of distinctions on appropriate grounds, we need to hold in mind some of the dangers that accompany any effort to categorize or label young people. We are all too familiar with the institutional and impersonal modes of labeling the young as in some manner deviant, whether because they are viewed as poor learners, slow readers, drop-outs, or discipline problems. This would not present the difficulties it does present, were it not for the fact that most of the children so categorized are poor or minority children from cultures that seem alien to the teacher's own. Throughout education, there are school people, often well-meaning, who distance and categorize without any awareness of doing so. They simply perceive human reality in the light of an unreflected-on conception of the "normal" and the "promising" and the "good"; and, often unwittingly, they become accomplices in the culture's stratification procedures, in the familiar allocation processes that keep the children of welfare clients, say, or the children of recently arrived Puerto Rican peasants, or the children of mountain people from the hollows, on the lowest rung of the ladder where they seem objectively to belong. What seems to be required, then, is not only attention to such principles as justice and appropriateness, but attention to the very enterprise of category-making. It is a matter of teachers beginning to think about their own thinking, to reflect on what they take for granted, to consider what accounts for their inability to see.

Because of the dominance (and persuasiveness of the meritocratic notion and old habits of' arranging things in hierarchies, many teachers are prone to construct' hierarchical realities in confronting their classrooms. Doing so, they are likely to freeze people into superior and inferior positions, and to treat them accordingly. Now, there is nothing about a hierarchy that is necessarily antithetical to equality; but equality is at the opposite remove from any unjust distribution of place and power within any hierarchy. The Jeffersonian tradition makes most people assume that individuals are somehow arranged "naturally" in terms of worth and ability; and it is difficult for them to realize that hierarchies of worth and ability almost never correspond to actual hierarchies of power. It is not as likely as people imagine that the "right" person ends up in the right place. More often than not, as we have discovered, it is the privileged person who is to be found in the right place.

Attending to this, a teacher might summon up the image of an academy boy in the 19th century or an Andover student of today, each probably guaranteed a place high up on the laddder of ability, if not success. Or the teacher might recall the faces of some of the more poised, civil, witty children in his/her own class and consider for a moment the manner in which privilege seems to create worth. Or the same teacher might, with the structures of technocracy in mind, consider how the highly analytic, highly cognitive students strike almost everyone they meet as promising, the "brightest and the best." Distinctions are continually made on grounds that appear, on the face of it, to be relevant in some prima facie way. But educators continually forget that relevance (like value and efficacy and power) is too often an unexamined function of the way they conceive their realities.

The actuality is that our efforts to offer what is suitable or appropriate for diverse children are undertaken within a context marked by multiple inequalities, "crystallized" privileges, inequities. Also, it is becoming a context characterized by a growing scarcity of desirable positions, inside and outside the schools--or, perhaps, by a scarcity of those positions this culture defines as desirable. John Rawls, for one, believes that any society that seeks to be just must transform its meritocratic aims and focus on "the essential primary good of self-respect." Educational resources, he has written, should not be allotted primarily "according to their return as estimated in productive trained abilities, but also according to their worth in enriching the personal and social life of citizens, including here the less favored." [31]

If Rawls' notion of justice as fairness were to be applied to classrooms, there would have to be a reconceptualization of much of what normally takes place. For one thing, the members of any class ought to be seen as members of a plurality, among whom rights and duties ought to be equally distributed. For another, each one ought to be seen as a distinctive person as well as a member--with his/her own life plan or project, with a story to tell, with a distinctive future to be pursued. The atmosphere of the class would be the kind of atmosphere that permits both communication and cooperation. Only then is it likely that a "confident sense of their own worth" may be sought for all those involved. Only then is it likely that those most favored (in the sense of being more self-confident, articulate, disciplined) will attend, not so much to their own quests for influence and position, but to the lived situation in their classroom and the benefit of all concerned.

The teacher in this kind of classroom has to resist his/her habitual categorizations, as he/she has to resist social and institutional mystifications and pressures to concentrate on "productive trained abilities" to the exclusion of all else. There is no question but that technical proficiency of some sort (as, for example, on the microcomputer) is required by everyone today. If it is made available only to the privileged, the inequalities in society at large will be effectively perpetuated in the schools, as they have so often been before. Moreover, those who are thought to be destined for purely routine or mechanical work will be abandoned to a variety of mystifications if they are deprived of opportunities to comprehend and to interpret, deprived of what has

---

[31] Rawls, op. cit., p. 107.

been called "high status knowledge," too often reserved for the few.

Even as we grant that relatively little can be done in schools to counteract the stratification that exists throughout society, we can still make somewhat problematic the schools' concern for training job-holders and consumers only. If teachers were to take seriously Rawls's stress "on enriching the personal and social life of citizens, including here the less favored," if they were then to go beyond such enrichment to the encouragement of critical reflection, it might be possible to stimulate more situated inquiry in classrooms. By this is meant the kind of perspectival sense-making that responds to personally felt questions, to the kind of problem-posing Paulo Freire has described.[32] The point of such sense-making would be to clarify and comprehend the situations students live individually and in common. It would be to conceptualize them in larger and larger contexts: the immediate socio-cultural surroundings; the institutional realities; the great technocratic systems that frame and sustain cultural life. Moreover, it would involve an effort to grasp aspects of the world around by means of a moral consciousness, the kind of consciousness that discloses values and brings them into the world. Values, as Jean-Paul Sartre saw them, appear in the world in response to perceived lacks, to an awareness of what is not and what ought to be.[33] Awareness of this sort is at the opposite extreme from merely calculative knowing, from an address to the world as given, predefined, simply there. It is the kind of awareness that is linked to freedom, the kind of freedom that involves the ability to look at things as if they might be otherwise.

Obviously, this approach to classroom life will not guarantee the elimination of so-called "deficits." Nor will it guarantee equality of capacity or any sort of sameness when it comes to learning styles. It may, however, enable people to understand that technical knowing is neither the only kind of knowing nor the

[32]Paulo Freire, Pedagogy of the Oppressed (New York: Herder and Herder, 1970).

[33]Jean-Paul Sartre, Search for a Method (New York: Alfred A. Knopf, 1963), pp. 91-115.

paradigm for all knowing. Technical or calculative learning may take on a kind of provisional quality as one mode of instrumental learning to achieve certain limited ends. If this is not separated off from normative thinking, from moral consciousness, it may no longer mystify or dominate in quite the same way. After all, the world as technically explained and analysed is not, necessarily, the world. To engage students in the various domains of the arts is to make it possible for them to realize this with particular clarity, especially if they are enabled to explore more than one symbol system, to look through perspectives that offer new vantage points on what has been presented as objectively "real." Equality of consideration demands this kind of diversification, as it demands regard for the integrity of many ways of seeing, including the ways of seeing of "the less favored" who are seldom even asked whether they see at all.

But what of excellence? Is there any way of reconciling the need to attend to excellence with the need to regard each person's integrity? Is there any way of introducing the value of excellence without thrusting teachers back to the competitive, overly individualistic mode? We might think again about a multiplicity of excellences, connected to the multiple ways there are of becoming a person. We might think of the various ways in which the qualities of mind may be displayed--studying history, painting pictures, cooking dinners, running day-care centers. What is suggested is that there is room for the expression of critical and creative capacities in the many domains of life; and it seems to be of moment for educators to hold in mind the normative or the "should" where the range of human activities are concerned.

At a moment when craftsmanship is at a low ebb in our country, when young people are continually exposed to deadening mediocrity in the media, when whatever constitutes "work" strikes so many as meaningless, it may be of particular importance to keep alive the notion of excellence, if it is linked to the sense of worth and self-esteem. The avoidance of the "should" under some rubric of benevolence has often prevented the poor and the less favored from reaching out towards possibility. When poor city children are, for instance, introduced to performing artists in their schools, one of the first things that impresses them is the degree of discipline required to become an

24

artist: the hours at the barre; the voice exercises;
the study of scripts.   It becomes important, in the
name of equality as well as excellence, to keep such
children in touch with the "should," if only to
acquaint them with a better order of things--for
themselves and those around.   It has been said that,
only when persons are able to conceive a better state
of things, do they recognize the deficiencies or
incompletenesses in their own situations and, perhaps,
take some action to repair, to learn, to transcend.

Finally,   attention may be drawn to still another
view of excellence, this one related to the notion of
a public space. It is adapted from Hannah Arendt, who
has explored what it signifies to live in a "we-
relation," to come together in authentic speech and
action, to summon into existence an "in-between,"
something of common and engaging concern.[34]   She has
written often of the erosion of the public space where
human beings can be together as free beings, appearing
to one another as worthy of regard.   She has written
about the impacts of mass society, of submergence, of
depersonalization, and contrasted it with a world of
truly human action and new beginnings. And then:

> Excellence itself, <u>arete</u> as the Greeks,
> <u>virtus</u> as the Romans would have called
> it, has always been assigned to the
> public realm where one could excel,
> could distinguish oneself from all
> others.   Every activity performed in
> public can attain an excellence never
> matched in privacy; for excellence, by
> definition, the presence of others is
> always required . . .[35]

It is a problem of action and speech, Arendt
suggested, this matter of excellence.   Through action
and speech people achieve their identities, even as
they come together with others to bring into being
something valuable--a durable common world.

Education,   clearly,   does not have the power to

---

[34]Hannah Arendt, <u>The Human Condition</u> (Chicago,
Ill.:   The University of Chicago press, 1958), pp.
181-188.

[35]Arendt, <u>op</u>. <u>cit</u>., p. 178.

change the social order nor to institute a truly public space. Nor can the inequalities that are a function of the post-industrial, capitalist society be totally eradicated by what is done in schools. There will remain insufficiency, polarities, confusions of ends. But there can be efforts to reconceive, to engage in reflexivity, to strive for quality and equality at once and a sense of what should be. Isaiah Berlin has spoken of the desire we have for a single intelligible structure in our worlds, and for a single end. He has described the profound disagreements that have always existed and still exist with regard to moral issues; and he has pointed to the likelihood that there exists no single overarching standard that might enable us to choose rationally between equally ultimate but incompatible ends.[36] What follows from this where equality and excellence are concernd? An ongoing effort to look at alternative possibilities, alternative ways of pursuing a life of integrity and decency and mutuality in a contradictory situation where transformations are always called for and there is a continuing need to renew. We, as teachers, are ourselves newcomers or ought to be. Emerging from a tradition of uncertainty and conflict, we are asked to keep the unease alive and to remain in search of openings, to pursue what is not yet. The "risk," the true risk is to become somnolent; the true risk is to despair.

---

[36]Isaiah Berlin, Against the Current: Essays in the History of Ideas (New York: The Viking Press, 1979), p. 69.

EDUCATION AND THE UNEQUAL SOCIETY:

THE QUEST FOR MORAL "EXCELLENCE"

Svi Shapiro

Introduction: Social 'Facts' and Social 'Meanings'

It   may   be   that   the   most   significant - and
exciting - recent   event in the attempt to   understand
the purpose and role of schools in western   capitalist
societies   has been the merger of marxist analysis and
the phenomenological perspective. The former, with its
emphasis on class, power, and the relations and forces
of   production,   has provided us with the means to   go
beyond formulations that interpret the present   nature
of   the school as simply a result of the irrationality
of   personal or organizational behavior (the notorious
'mindlessness' of Charles Silberman).   The,   by   now,
well-documented repressive,   coercive,   and stratified
nature   of schools is not preeminently,   the result of
an   unfortunate accident of history,   or   the   inhuman
dispositions of practitioners.   Schools, we have begun
to   recognize,   are a key element in the   reproduction
and   legitimation   of   a stratified society,   and   an
important   means   of   transmitting   an   ideology
underpinning   a   bureaucratic consumerist   capitalism.
The work of Antonio Gramsci and others has made   clear
that,   at   least   in   the west,   the   continuation   of
unequal   and exploitative societies rests less on   the
brute,   coercive apparatus of the state,   than on   the
development   of   a   shared   consensus   (hegemony)   of
aspirations   and beliefs.   Within such a   perspective
the   schools rather than the jails play a key role   in
maintaining an acceptance of the present   distribution
of power,   resources, and experiences. Schools are an
important,   if not the   key component in the operation
of social control.

Within such a context the marxist analysis of the
state has been especially useful.   Unlike the liberal-
democratic notion,   the state in capitalist society is
seen not as an entity that represents the popular will
of   the   people - arbitrating impartially   between
competing social and economic interests.   Instead, it
is   viewed   as existing to ensure   and   safeguard   the

27

present contours of power, wealth, and opportunity. This, of course, is not to say that it is entirely inflexible and unresponsive to the demands of subordinate groups or classes. Indeed, during periods of crisis the state will intervene so as to ensure the long-term survival of the system (e.g. the policies of the 'New Deal' or 'Great Society'). During such times reforms by the state may entail some shift of power or resources, but never so much that it will threaten the system in a fundamental way. Public education (as has been well documented by the recent 'revisionist' histories) has formed an important instrument for maintaining the illusion of the state's neutrality, as well as sustaining a belief in the extent and possibilities of liberal social change.

In the application of a marxist analysis to education the notion of ideology has been a key one. There is now a developed literature on the way in which the experience of school, primarily through the 'hidden curriculum' replicates the values, beliefs, moral and aesthetic judgments of capitalist society. In particular, it has become increasingly clear how the social relations of the classroom 'mirror' the social relations of production. The values and norms of the work place are shown to be an important factor in determining pedagogy and even curriculum.

Despite this understanding, the notion of ideology used by sociologists and historians of education generally contains a deterministic view of human behavior. There is, as Madan Sarup argues, an oversocialized view of man operating in the literature. Once the ideological constraints or imperatives of the capitalist organization of work are described, and their 'reflection' in the organization of the classroom noted, a robot-like response is assumed by those subjected to the ideology. Sarup writes that, in this view

'Society' makes people what they are, as they have no free will of their own. They are impelled by the ideas they have absorbed from their social environment, the family, the school, the factory . . . Actor-members are always regarded as passive; youth is accustomed to the social relationships of dominance and subordinancy in the economic system. This over-symmetrical view does not

sufficiently recognize that people have
perceptions of stratification and status
groups, that these perceptions vary and do
not always conform to the model of the
'scientific' observer.[1]

The same kind of determinism can be found in
other descriptions of ideology. Such a perspective,
for example, has resulted in the distortion of the
influential notion of ideological hegemony elaborated
by Antonio Gramsci. Thus, if a social class becomes
hegemonic it is not, as some interpretation would have
it, because it has succeeded in imposing its ideas and
beliefs upon society. Such an interpretation leads to
a view of hegemony as a phenomena of ideological
inculcation or indoctrination. It sees man as a
cultural puppet passively manipulated by the purveyors
of ideas among the dominant social groups. He is seen
as totally determined by his environment, or
thoroughly mystified, duped or indoctrinated by
ideology. Gramsci in refuting the deterministic
reading of Marx, asserts that ideology is 'the terrain
on which men acquire consciousness of themselves.'
Hegemony cannot be reduced to a process of domination.
It is a consensus on the direction of society formed
through a complex articulation of the needs and
aspirations of different social groups.

The struggle to go beyond a positivist,
structurally-oriented understanding of human behavior
has a long history. As Martin Bulmer suggests,[2] the
tension between social structure and social meanings
has been present in sociological work ever since
Durkheim enjoined us to 'consider social facts as
things', and Max Weber directed our attention to the
'subjectively meaningful' nature of social action.
And, as he points out, at least since Marx
distinguished between 'classes-in-themselves' and
'classes-for-themselves' the nature of men's
perception of society, social inequality, social
stratification and social class have been a central
philosophical and practical concern.

---

[1] Madan Sarup, Marxism and Education (London:
Routledge and Kegan Paul, 1978), p. 176.

[2] Martin Bulmer (Ed.) Working-Class Images of
Society. (London: Routledge and Kegan Paul, 1975).

In writing this paper the overarching framework is the concern of how it is possible to move towards a society in which human beings are less divided, stratified and unequal. Within this framework the issue of how we see ourselves in relation to others is of critical importance. The possibility of a collective social and political movement - the necessary requirement for radical reform in this direction - depends on overcoming the images of separation and inequality that divide those who, in reality, have common interests. In order to do this we must look at the way schools in our society help to place individuals in the class structure imbuing each of us with a belief about our respective abilities, potentialities and capabilites. We must also look at the way in which school teaches us about the overall structure of social relations in this society. School does represent to us the contours of the organization of our social world. It provides us with an image of the system of separations, continuities, oppositions, etc., that join or divide human beings in our society. In this context we must look too at the 'deep code' of the notion of educational excellence - a term that more often than not helps to sustain the separations and distinctions that are essential to a hierarchically divided society. It is, of course, through the acceptance (or rejection) of all these representations that man adopts a course of political action in the world.

In dealing with only 'social facticity' and not the phenomenological sense of human activities, i.e. consciousness, it becomes impossible to understand the social response to the contradictory experiences that permeate our lives. Few would deny, for example, that the notion of human equality is a central component in the belief system of this society. After all, it is a concept whose value is framed in the very founding document of the nation. And yet it is clear that nowhere are our declarations and actions more dissonant or conflicting. It would be difficult, for example to reconcile any such claim to equality in America with the fact that, according to recent reports of the U. S. Census, the top one percent of the American population received in one year more money than the poorest 50 million Americans (25% of the population); the richest 10% of Americans received more income than the entire bottom half of the

population. And yet, how do we begin to explain the
dissonance between the reality and our public ideals.
Can it be the results of wilfull disregard? Does it
reflect a confusion about the meaning of equality? Or
might it be the product of the mystification and
manipulation of our perceptions by those who have most
to gain from maintaining ignorance about the realities
of our social world? The answer may contain all three
possibilities. More profoundly, however, it might be
seen as a result of the construction of a particular
social reality arising from the experience of our
social relations and interaction. Such relationships
(at school, as well as at home or on the street)
provide the matrix within which human consciousness
shapes, organizes, separates, or aligns individuals
and groups of individuals. The consequences of such
separations or alignments - prestige, wealth, power,
etc. - appear to flow logically and inevitably as a
result of the meanings we impart to them. In short,
we construct a social 'reality' that appears to make
sense: a system of symbolic meanings that is
ontologically correct. Only through understanding and
engaging these meanings is it possible to intervene
and undermine the existing patterns of domination and
subordination in society. And only through the
joining of such theoretical activity to social
practice will it be possible to attempt the process
of radical political, social and educational reform.

Work and Reason: Schools and the Social Division of Labor

In pursuing the way in which the school in
capitalist society mediates and reinforces a
particular form of consciousness in regard to the
social relations of that society, it will be useful to
start with the contributions of the late French
sociologist, Nicos Poulantzas. For Poulantzas the
major role of the school is in relation to the
reproduction of the social division of labor between
mental and manual activities. His thesis helps to
more fully locate the school in the ideology of
capitalist society, and the production of a
consciousness apposite to social relations there, than
the more usual considerations involving the role of
'tracking', and the 'hidden curriculum'. It is not,
for Poulantzas, aspects of school practice,
curriculum, extra-curricula activities, organization,
etc., that may be class-biased, but the very nature of
school itself. School, he argues, as an institution,

is the living embodiment of the social division of
labor - and the beliefs, values, and practices that
are encompassed by it.

The main role of the capitalist school, he says,
is "not to 'qualify' manual and mental labour in
different ways, but, far more, to disqualify manual
labour (to subjugate it) by only qualifying mental
labour."[3] While schools divide students between
those suited to manual labour and those not, training
for the former does not really take place;

> The worker does not acquire his basic
> professional training and his technical
> skills in school (they cannot be 'taught'
> there), not even in the streams and
> apparatuses of technical education. What is
> chiefly taught to the working class is
> discipline, respect for authority, and the
> veneration of a mental labour that is always
> 'somewhere else' in the educational
> apparatus.[4]

In some respects Poulantzas' argument resembles
that of John Dewey's who, 50 years before, had stated
that the separation of education into vocational
training and the academic curriculum reflected (and
reinforced) the social division of labor inherent in
all class-divided societies. Poulantzas, however,
goes further. He suggests vocational training
programs (which in all countries are overwhelmingly
filled with the children of working class families)
are far less effective as actual programs of technical
preparation than as a means of reinforcing a
particular ontology. They legitmate the
differentiation between those with or without the
capability of engaging in 'mental labor'. In short,
most of what goes on in school via the curriculum does
not represent a direct training for work - but is
intended to locate an individual on one side or the
other of the mental/manual division of labor. Such a
division is at the heart of the unequal and
hierarchical social relations that characterize the

---

[3]Nicos Poulantzas, Classes in Contemporary
Capitalism (London: New Left Books, 1975), p. 266.

[4]Ibid., p. 266.

organization of work in capitalist society;

> The training of mental labour essentially
> consists, to a greater or lesser extent, in
> the inculcation of a series of rituals,
> secrets, and symbolisms which are to a
> considerable extent those of 'general
> culture', and whose main purpose is to
> distinguish it from manual labour. Once
> distinguished in this way, mental labour is
> to a great extent universally employable
> . . . Thus to say that a university degree
> in social science, literature, law or a
> certain baccalaureate, etc., does not offer
> openings that correspond to the
> 'qualification' that it represents, is not
> strictly correct, in the sense that this de-
> gree is not basically intended to guarantee
> this or that specialist knowledge, but
> rather to locate its bearer in the camp of
> mental labour in general and its specific
> hierarchy, i.e. to reproduce the
> mental/manual division.[5]

Poulantzas' concern with the division between
mental and manual labor stems from his attempt to
understand what he calls the "new petty bourgeoisie" -
that massive and ever-expanding group of salaried
workers who are involved in tertiatry-sector and white-
collar work. These include civil servants, human
services and education workers, and those employed in
commercial, insurance, accounting and banking
concerns. A key aspect of the class is its
relationship to mental labour. Such work, he argues,
is characterized far more by its symbolic and cultural
form than any real scientific or technical content;

> This mental labour is in fact encased in a
> whole series of rituals, know-how, and
> 'cultural' elements that distinguish it from
> that of the working class . . . If these
> ideological symbols have little in common
> with any real differentiation in the order
> of elements of science, they nevertheless
> legitimize this distinction as if it had
> such a basis. This cultural symbolism is
> well enough known for us not to have to

---

[5]Ibid., p. 268.

dwell on it. It extends from the
traditional esteem given to 'paper work' and
clerical workers' in general (to know how to
write and to present ideas) to a certain use
of 'speech' . . . and finally includes
ideological differentiations between general
culture and savoir-faire on the one hand,
and technical skills (manual labour) on the
other . . . Everything that needs to be
known in this respect is that which the
others (the working class) do not know, or
even cannot know . . . this is the knowledge
that matters, genuine knowledge . . . The
main thing in fact is to know how to
'intellectualize' oneself in relation to the
working class; to know in these practices
that one is more 'intelligent', . . . than
the working class, which for its part, can
at most be 'capable'. And to have the
monopoly and the secrecy of this knowledge.' "[6]

The school then, has as its central task the
mediation of the pervasive separation in our society,
between those who we refer to as professionals,
clerical or white-collar workers, from those who work
directly at the point of production (in factories,
mills, mines, etc.) - the 'manual' working class or
blue-collar workers. Schools not only mediate the
separation but legitimate the latter's subordinate
position in society's order of value. Even more
significant is its reinforcement of the notion that we
may successfully distinguish between those members of
society capable (through their 'brain work' ability)
of planning and administering, from the majority who
are capable of only execution and the following of
orders. [*] It is such a distinction that underpins
the autocratic organization of industry in which
workers are excluded from the perogatives of

---

[6] Ibid., p. 258.

[*] It is not suggested, however, that all white-
collar workers are involved in the process of planning
or administration. Such tasks are reserved for a
select and relatively small number of individuals.
White collar workers do, however, more closely
identify themselves with the planning or
administration component of the production process.

decision-making and administration (as well as being segregated socially - separate canteens for blue and white-collar workers, different entrances, bathrooms, etc.).

The individual psychic consequences of such disjunctures are well documented. Richard Sennet and Jonathan Cobb in their study of blue-collar workers in America [7] suggest that everything in the family lives of the workers that they spoke to is oriented to moving their children 'over the barrier' - to white collar work. Education (perceived as the key to this transformation), they believe, will not simply make their children different, it will be set against a character failing the parents see in their own youth;

> 'If you don't have them degrees, they're gonna treat you like you was nothing,' says a garbage collector to his children. 'I say to Sheila,' remarks an electrician, 'you do that homework or you'll wind up in the same boat like me . . . it's for your own good you got to study.' [8]

Sennet and Cobb argue that while 'crossing the barrier' from 'blue' to 'white-collar' work does bring its rewards - wearing a suite and tie, going downtown to the office commands a certain prestige among peers and parents - those are often more illusory than real;

> To get a white-collar job you must stay in school. Schooling is supposed to develop your internal powers, make you as a person more powerful in relation to the productive order of society; the move into white-collar work is in a way a consequence of your having become a more developed human being. Yet most of those flowing into white-collar work find the reality quite different - the content of the work requires very little mind at all. [9]

---

[7]Richard Sennet and Jonathan Cobb, The Hidden Injuries of Class (New York: Vintage Books, 1977).

[8]Ibid.,

[9]Ibid., p. 179.

The low-level, routine and bureaucratic nature of the
majority of the jobs ensures that for many of the sons
and daughters crossing the barrier into white-collar
work, the promised emotional gratifications are not
available. Work does not offer the kind of freedom,
control, interest or respect that was anticipated.
Yet despite the disparities in what they believe they
ought to feel as a result of being educated, and what
they experience directly in their new work, the
promise of white-collar work remains a significant
goal of working class life. It continues to represent
an important moral symbol through which one may claim
a superior position in the American class structure.
Education mediates a view of the social order in which
there appears to be specific kinds of distinctions
that separate those capable of planning and
administration (or, at least, who identify themselves
with those tasks) from those who appear able only to
execute. School sustains and reinforces the notion of
the social division of labor as the rational, or even
inevitable, form of human organization. Indeed school,
as we have seen, is the very embodiment of this
organization. The consequences of maintaining such a
view of the social order are profound in their effect
on the nature of experiences both inside school and
out.

Embedded in this division of labor is the
separation between 'culture' and 'civilization'.
While the latter comprises activities in the daily
round of existence (work, community, family, etc.),
the former is viewed as representing the
crystallization of man's imaginative efforts to grasp
the nature of our social and natural world. The
limited definition traditionally applied to culture
had its origins in the historical separation between
mental and manual activities. This separation was
underpinned by the division of society into social
classes. Those occupying the dominant social
positions applied a hierarchical value structure to
the activities performed. The practical and
functional were separated from, and relegated in
status to, intellectual and aesthetic concerns. The
notion of culture was attached to the latter
activities, while the former - the material
reproduction of society - assumed the character of a
commodity, engendered contempt, or sometimes
paternalistic concern. Education (as the process of
transmitting 'culture') reflected these ideas in its
abstract, scholastic separation from activity and

experience in the real world. Experiences that have provided the matrix for education are held not to occur in the world of work, of community, political life, or family, but behind the doors of special institutions. The organizing principles of academic knowledge continue to underline its separation from 'everyday' human experience and social reality - its compartmentalization and structuring, its abstractness, and the reliance on literacy and symbolic language. School itself, of course, represents the very embodiment of such experience. The activites of the classroom are almost always vicarious, symbolic and abstract - 'make-believe' activities in a 'make believe' world. Writing in Democracy and Education Dewey summarized the separation we have described in the following way;

> Of the segregation in educational values ... that between culture and utility is probably the most fundamental. While the distinction is often thought to be intrinsic and absolute, it is really historical and social. It originated so far as conscious formulation is concerned, in Greece, and was based upon the fact that the truly human life was lived only by a few who subsisted upon the results of the labor of others. . . It was embodied in a political theory of a permanent division of human beings into those capable of a life of reason and hence having their own ends, and those capable only of desire and work, and needing to have their ends provided by others. The two distinctions, psychological and political, translated into educational terms, effected a division between a liberal education having to do with knowing for its own sake, and a useful, practical training for mechanical occupations, devoid of intellectual and aesthetic content." [10]

While little remains of the notion of a liberal education devoted to "knowing for its own sake", where education is traditionally conceived of in its developmental (i.e. non-vocational) sense, it is sought, not in the world of our 'everyday' social

---

[10] John Dewey, Democracy and Education (New York: The MacMillan Company, 1969), pp. 260-261.

experience, but in an academic curriculum which
provides experiences sharply separated and
qualitatively distinct from it. Such experiences
contribute to a realm entirely distinct from those
contained by 'civilization'. The important
characteristic is the notion that the educational
institution (school, college, university) provides a
set of experiences not readily available to all, that
enables the graduate to command deference from his
social subordinates, not so much for what he can do
but, more fundamentally, for who he is. In the
extreme example, it is, to this day, quite enough to
have gone to Yale, or to be a 'Harvard Man' to claim
ones dominant position in the social order. What is
of essence here, is the type of person emerging from
these insitutions, not the vocational credentials he
carries. The hierarchical and unequal distribution of
educational experiences facilitates the unequal
distribution of cultural 'capital' and the
reproduction of the hierarchical division of labor.

In this sense, it becomes clear that calls for
'improved excellence' in education are little more
than disguises for demands that schools reinforce, the
distinctions between students as to their believed
capacity for intellectual and creative work --
distinctions that will divide those capable of
assuming planning and conceptualizing roles in the
hierarchy of work, from the rest. Certainly those who
are the most ardent proponents of 'excellence' in
education are frequently the ones who have most
severely criticized the notion of equality in schools
and have claimed that such tendencies have a
'levelling' effect. They argue that the demand for
equality in the treatment of students contradicts and
undermines the quest for excellence in education. The
proponents of programs for the 'gifted and talented',
for example, argue that in order to nurture excellence
among the young, we must ensure that the 'cream' of
our students can receive an education commensurate
with their abilities, rather than be compelled to
endure the mediocrity of their peers. Such arguments
rest on notions of excellence that are unquestionably
elitist. There is a strong implication that excellence
is the concern and pursuit of a minority. The majority, it may be assumed, are relegated to permanent mediocrity or worse. Of course, such a perspective is not
new. It is a sentiment that is reflected in all those
societies where elites have claimed a monopoly on vir-
ture, artistic or intellectual ability, leadership,

or some other human attribute. It is also true that claims as to the 'giftedness' of certain students, and not others, depends on a very limited determination of the kinds of educational experiences that constitute legitimate fields in the quest for excellence. Why, one may ask, must we limit the quest for excellence to a relatively small number of individuals who happen to show ability in a few specific areas? Indeed, why is school knowledge or curriculum arranged in a hierarchical fashion so that some kinds of curriculum experiences (the 'academic' subjects) are deemed to be more valuable or important than others?

It is clear that the nature of education in our society, reproducing as it does the social division of labor and the distinction between 'culture' and 'civilization', supports the disjuncture between a minority 'capable' of performing tasks that are personally as well as socially enriching, and the masses able only to engage in limited, routine, and often stupefying activities. But the true significance of mass education lies not only in its ability to legitimate the distribution of intelligence or ability along the lines of the existing class structure but, more profoundly, the validation of the division of labor through its legitimation of the very notions of intelligence or ability.

Education and the 'Normal' Distribution of Failure

In the organization of our society around values that have their origins in the social division of labor, schools have always been the primary vehicle for asserting the 'natural' inequalities and capacities that divide human beings. From our first day in grade school the message transmitted is subtle but persistent; human ability is unequally distributed. The distribution of intelligence among human beings (mysteriously) follow the points of a 'bell-curve' - only a minority of any population can be 'smart', the majority must fall somewhere between 'dull' and 'average'. Ability among children can only be a relatively scarce phenomenon (after all, teachers who award all their students A's would quickly be suspect). In assigning some children (a minority) to programs for 'gifted' and 'talented', we are, in effect, assigning the rest to programs for the 'ungifted' and 'untalented'. From our earliest placement in a high or low reading group in elementary school and pervasive 'ability' groupings of junior and senior high schools, to our admission to a prestigious university or a local community college, the message is unrelenting - come to terms with who you are, what you are capable of, and what your place is in the social relations of domination and subordination. Curiously, the mechanism that provides the foundation for the process of establishing the 'natural' inequality among students - our ability to accurately identify and quantify ability or intelligence - is frequently criticized, but rarely humbled. Testing is, after all, big business. Despite almost 20 years of research which has revealed the class biased, racist and sexist nature of standardized tests, we are still (to judge by their widespread use) infatuated by them. We remain convinced of our ability to 'scientifically' assess that most personal and unique of human attributes, intelligence. Nor are we prepared to admit the totally relative and subjective nature of judgements about who is 'bright' or 'dull', a 'good' or 'bad' student - that such judgements are rooted in social prejudices and societal conventions. We cling to the belief that grades represent some kind of objective statement of a student's capabilities (rather than how well a student's background has prepared him to play the classroom 'game'). On the basis of such dubious evidence the school assigns students to an 'appropriate' educational program. In the junior high school these may be 'suitable' ability groupings in the key areas of a child's educational experience - the academic curriculum. In the senior high school some form of tracking - 'advanced placement', 'college preparatory', vocational training or 'business' classes - is the norm. And, of course, in all schools there are the ubiquitous 'special needs' classes. While fewer schools now compel students to enter particular classes or programs they (or their parents) are 'gently' urged by teachers, administrators, and counselors to be 'realistic' about their expectations and capabilities. Such 'realism' ensures that entry into vocational programs, for example, is reserved predominately for the children of the working class.

In a society as rooted in notions of 'getting ahead' or 'looking out for number one,' there is, at best, an uneasy compassion for those who 'don't make it'. Our suspicion towards those out of work or on welfare may reflect on ambivalent feelings of responsibility toward the less well-off than ourselves. In the 1980's the consciousness of Americans is still shaped by Social Darwinism. There is thought to be a 'natural' inequality among individuals that (together with personality traits such as perseverence, competitiveness and aggressiveness) determines who will be the 'winners' and 'losers' in society. The responsible parent or teachers ensures that their child understands that success is a scarce commodity. Our gain must necessarily be somebody else's loss. That, though all of us may start life's race at the same point, we are destined to finish it at places that will differentiate us on a hierarchy of success or failure. In the final analysis the school drop-out has only himself to blame. While school teaches us the rules of the game (how to win, compete, etc.), it also emphasizes the penalties for those who stop playing.

Despite the corporatization of American life, the clear determination of our life chances by state policies, and the effects of structural shifts in employment patterns, income distribution, etc., school mediates and reinforces a petty-bourgeois mentality. The success or failure of an individual can be laid at the door of his or her personal ability, efforts or motivation. More than this, success or failure is not a collectively owned or shared enterprise, but 'belongs' to the individual. Our emphasis on the individual and his or her social mobility obfuscates the notion of social class in capitalist society. Thus, while the school may direct one individual rather than another towards a particular social position, the positions themselves are created by the system of production, and exist prior to their occupation by any particular individual or group of individuals. Even in a (mythical) situation of perfect mobility, social classes would not cease to exist, only there would be a more thorough displacement of individuals from one class to another. Our concern with the injustices currently associated with aspects of the distribution of success or failure among students (for reason of race, sex, or handicap) in no way undermines the class structure.

The notion of individualized instruction which has formed a cornerstone of progressive educational reform illustrates well this thesis. In defining the 'problem' or 'handicap' of a student as the individual's problem we adopt the quintessential petty-bourgeois perspective. Those who overcome 'their' problems become latter-day Horatio Algers, pulling theselves up by their bootstraps. Those who fail must blame themselves (for lack of persistence, ability, or the vicissitudes of fate). Individualizing instruction as the process for remediating the problem also embodies this value structure. It is an approach that isolates individuals from their peers. It emphasizes individual activity at the expense of group-work and support. Most importantly, success or failure at the task (like the problem itself) is seen primarily as the responsibility of the individual. In all of these ways individualization reflects the bourgeois commitment to individual effort or responsibility. Such a commitment reflects a culture whose central tendency is toward fragmentation of social activity and the isolation of the individual ego. In attempting to understand or explain student 'failure' through such means we adopt what William Ryan calls the ideology of 'blaming the victim'. Such an ideology defines the 'problems' of society in terms of the disposition, attitudes, values, or culture of those who represent society's deviants - the poor, unemployed, those on welfare, school drop-outs, etc. In defining the origin of problems as residing 'inside the skins' of individuals we may ignore the way in which the instructional process or social structure systematically generates such 'problems'. Thus, failure in the traditional school situation is not viewed as the result of an environment that systematically alienates and excludes a significant section of the student population. Instead, such students may be labelled 'learning disabled', 'emotionally unstable', or 'socially maladjusted'. We may see their problems arising from an indolent or apathetic disposition, broken homes, mental retardation, 'cultural deprivation' or other 'handicaps'. In all of these ways we are able to ignore the educational process that is often responsible for school failure. Just as the unemployed represent, for the most part, not an indolent group, but the product of economic policies deliberately designed to maintain a level of unused productive capacity, so schools are organized around the competitive principle which ensures a normal distribution of success and failure.

In the process described above, school both reproduces the class structure but, at the same time, ensures a consciousness which obfuscates the nature

of social relations in capitalist society. Such
consciousness facilitates awareness of the individuals
or agents within their class positions, but not an
awareness of the positions themselves. In short,
school contributes to a consciousness which 'de-
structures' the class system in capitalist society.
The traditional concern of social policy-makers or
educators with the social mobility of individuals or
groups is to miss the fundamental nature of social
classes in capitalist society. In education, for
example, the elimination or reduction of tracking,
introduction of 'culturally-unbiased' selection
procedures, implementation of 'mainstreaming', leave
untouched the underlying structure of inequality in
the U.S. Indeed, most of what has been at issue in
educational policy has concerned the relative
distribution of particular groups of individuals in
the social structure - not the structure itself. To
whatever extent policies result in redistributing
individuals or their offspring to different social
classes, it leaves untouched the existence of these
classes, and the resulting relations of domination and
subordination that pervade every relationship and
practice in our society.

Schooling and the Middle Class View of Society

In the last few years we have begun to understand
more clearly how schooling reproduces the social class
structure of capitalist society. In particular, that
there is some kind of 'correspondence' between the
experiences of school both via the organization of the
explicit curriculum, and through the informal or
'hidden' aspects of the school or classroom, and
those that characterize the occupational structure of
capitalist society. It appears that, in many
identifiable ways, classroom practices provide the
norms, values and attitudes (and, to an extent, the
skills) apposite to ones anticipated position in the
occupational and class structure of society. Such
positions generate personality requirements and modes
of behavior differentiated according to their location
in the structure of the social relations of
production. Those in the higher positions are
expected to exhibit the ability to work autonomously,
manifest self-initiated behavior, and display some
degree of creative problem solving. Among those in
the lower positions, control, supervision, and rigidly
defined activities are the norm. Such behavior is
mirrored in the classroom. Classes for the

43

academically advanced students are characterized by greater flexibility, and opportunities for independent and creative activity. Those of the 'less able' are characterized by stricter control, rote-learning, and more rigidly-defined activities.[11]

While much of the attention to this point has focused on the distribution of students to school experiences that are differentiated with respect to norms, values and behavior - mediating the reproduction of social relations in capitalist society (hierarchy, bureaucracy, sexism, etc.) - there is another aspect of the process that must not be overlooked. Students are not only 'trained' for their particular place in the class structure, but also acquire an image of the entire social order. Schools contribute not only to the specific psycho-social requirement of each persons role in the school system, but also provide a view of the totality of social relations in that system.

In their seminal study of social class imagery John Goldthorpe and his colleagues[12] suggested that the basic bourgeois image of society is a hierarchical one. According to this view, society is seen as divided into a series of levels or strata differentiated according to the life-styles and associated prestige of its members. The structure is seen as a relatively 'open' one, and given ability and the appropriate moral qualities such as determination and perseverence, individuals can, and do, move up the hierarchy. What a man achieves in the end depends primarily on what he 'makes of himself'. The dominant notion is of a social ladder that all have the opportunity to climb. The objective is to keep up a progressive improvement in consumption standards, and correspondingly, a steady ascent in terms of prestige and the quality of ones life-style. Such an image rests on a middle class social ethic which is a basically individualistic one - the prime value is

---

[11] The most influential formulation of this 'correspondence' theory is found in S. Bowles and H. Gintis, Schooling in Capitalist America (New York: Basic Books, 1976).

[12] John H. Goldthorpe, David Lockwood, et. al., The Affluent Worker (London: Cambridge University Press, 1968).

that set on individual achievement.

Such a perspective contrasts with what they
suggest is the traditional working class view. In
this the basic conception of the social order is a
dichotomous one. Society is divided into 'us' and
'them'. 'They' are persons in positions in which they
can exercise power and authority over 'us'. According
to the Goldthorpe account, the division between 'us'
and 'them' is seen as virtually unbridgeable - people
are born on one side of the line or the other and very
largely remain there. The social circumstances an
individual faces are those 'given' facts of life and,
apart perhaps from exceptional strokes of luck, these
facts have to be accepted and 'put up with'. To the
extent that purposive action can be effective, the
emphasis is placed on action of a collective kind
aimed at the protection of collective interests. A
prime value is that set on mutual aid and group
solidarity in the face of the vicissitudes of life and
the domination which 'they' seem to impose.

It is clear that school generates an image of
society congruent with the middle class perspective.
Students aware of their separation into tracks,
ability groups, etc., are encouraged to feel that
these are relatively open (given the appropriate
effort, etc.). That rather than representing
fundamental and insurmountable divisions, they
constitute a continuum of experiences which are
separated quantitatively rather than qualitatively ("a
slightly higher grade average and I could have made
Harvard"). The image of social relations in the
school is that of a hierarchy or a ladder of skills,
abilities and opportunities continuously open to the
possibilities of upward or downward mobility. It may
be that the decision in England to replace the system
of separate secondary schools (the college preparatory
Grammar Schools, and the vocationally oriented
Secondary Modern) with their clear purposes of social
class formation, with the American-style comprehensive
high school, represents an attempt to undermine
traditional working class imagery and replace it with
the less conflictful middle class view of the social
order. In the United States the early imposition of
common institutions of public education surely played
their part in the development of a uniquely
impoverished form of working class consciousness, and
the widespread acceptance of a middle class version of
social relations.

Despite the schools attempt to generate such a view of the social order it is significant that it is an image that continues to be rejected by an important segment of the student population who continue to view school through dichotomous 'lenses' as a struggle between 'them' and 'us'. Such students often reject the individualistic mode of adaptation opting instead for the bonds of group or peer solidarity, and forming a sub-culture within the school as a method of defending themselves against the attacks of the dominant institutional structure.

Politics and Economics -- Competing Moments in the Formation of Consciousness

In this paper we have focused on the role of schools in developing a consciousness apposite to the social relations of capitalist society. Within this consciousness are embedded notions that support and reinforce the forms of social inequality and human division that characterize this society. Like others concerned with developing a critical understanding of education, schools have been viewed as a vehicle for inuring individuals to their differentiated positions in the distribution of society's resources, culture and experience. Schools, I believe, mediate and reinforce this distribution, validating and legitimating the result. More than this however, I have argued here that schools provide an image of the nature of social relations in capitalist society - providing individuals a view of the continuities and disjunctures in the social order. Within this image we have noted the separation between manual and mental labor, the distinction between the activities of 'culture' and 'civilization', and the destructuration of the concept of social class. It is my belief that the world-view engendered by these notions obfuscates the true nature of social relations in capitalist society - leaving in its place a view of society pervaded by inequalities the apparent nature of which 'disorganize' rather than join together those who are most oppressed and unfree.

In this paper we have viewed schooling primarily in the context of reproducing the social relations of production - the transmission of an ideology that is apposite to the 'culture' of work in our society. Such 'economic' socialization is, however, only a partial description of the school's ideological function. Education, it must be remembered, is a

46

component not of the economic 'infrastructure' but of the state 'apparatus'. This is a confusion that is prevalent among many of those who have proposed a critical view of schooling in the U.S. While schools do clearly mediate and reinforce a consciousness that underpins the nature of social relations in the sphere of work, it must also provide experiences that mediate the _political_ nature of American society. We may better understand this separation in the realms of socialization by looking at the divisions in human existence described by Marx in his early writing. Shlomo Avineri suggests that for Marx, man in modern society possessed two kinds of identity - that associated with 'civil' society (the economic order), and that within the 'political' domain. In the former, man behaves according to his egotistical needs and interests, relating to his fellows according to the criteria of the market place and the division of labor. Some of its effects we have explored in this paper (inequality, hierarchy, etc.). Within the 'political' domain - the arena of the state - man takes on the role of citizen. He is expected to develop a sense of universal attachments and obligations, and to recognize the claims of equal considerations, rights and opportunities. Such notions are embodied (though only formally) in the institutions of the state where all, at least in principle, may invoke the equal claims of citizenship (one man, one vote; trial by a jury of ones peers; equal access to public institutions, etc.) Of course, for Marx, despite the development of the state in capitalist society, 'political' emancipation does not ensure 'human' emancipation; "The existence of the state as a _separate_ sphere of universal attributes shows that all other spheres have been abandoned to particularism and egoism." It is important to understand that the contradictory tendencies described are the inevitable result of the functioning of capitalist society. The state, as Bertel Ollman argues, is "an illusory community as well as the

---

Shlomo Avineri, The Social and Political Thought of Karl Marx (London: Cambridge University Press, 1968).

Ibid., p. 47.

47

instrument of rule in class-ridden society.[15]   All
classes strive for political power in order to
represent their special interests as the 'general
good'."

It is my belief that public schools occupy a
unique position in the institutional structure of
capitalist society. They contain, at one and the same
time, the 'economic' and the 'political' moments of
bourgeois ideology. As such they not only provide
experiences necessary to the formation of a
consciousness apposite to ones role in the social
relations of production, but also experiences that
mediate and support the notion of the universal values
and communal ties associated with the state. This is
reflected in the public schools' obligation to provide
equality of access to the progeny of all citizens,
while dispensing differentiated forms of knowledge and
unequal educational experiences to these same
individuals.

Despite the lack of a sustained assault on
bourgeois values (hierarchy, profit, inequality, etc.)
in liberal capitalism, it is also clear that such
societies do not function with entirely acquiescent or
pacified subordinate classes. The universal and
classless values associated with the ideology of
citizenship frequently form the springboard in the
demands for a treatment of human needs that transcends
the criteria of the market place. Public education, I
believe, perhaps more than in most areas of our public
life, embodies this struggle between the competing
notions of community, universal responsibilities and
collective obligations, and the egotistical and
unequal imperatives of the economic system. It forces
us to confront daily the conflicts and contradictions
between the vision of institutions rooted in human
values, justice, dignity and mutual consideration, and
the reality of a world distorted by the commodity
values of the marketplace. Yet despite the chronic
reminder of this unfulfilled vision, the present
reality must leave us far from sanguine. While our
world so desperately demands the fostering of an ethic
that recognizes the importance of human
interdependence and cooperation, the school continues

---

[15] Bertell Ollman, Alienation: Marx's Conception of
Man in Capitalist Society (New York: Cambridge
University Press, 1976).

to emphasize an entirely opposite behavior. We award nothing to the group or collectivity for its accomplishments (with the notable exception of team athletics where cooperation is required to vanquish the opposition). As we have seen, the assessment and recognition of excellence and, indeed, of almost all school activity is still an isolated, individualistic and competitive affair. Against such practices education concerned with the need for a more just and humane society will have to propose a notion of moral 'excellence' -- one in which sharing and solidarity rather than separation and superiority become the hallmarks of the educational system. In the quest for a society without exploitative social relations and without the usual form of hierarchy, domination and subordination, incorporating such an ethic into the educational 'agenda' must be regarded as nothing less than our vital and inescapable responsibility.

THE CALLING OF TEACHING

William A. Arrowsmith

Let me plant firmly here at the outset the single most powerful description of education and teaching I have ever encountered. The author is Friedrich Nietzsche in a little work dedicated to his own greatest teacher, Arthur Schopenhauer:

> How can we ever know ourselves? How can a man know himself? He is a dark and hidden thing. The hare is said to have seven skins, but a man may remove seven times seventy skins and still not be able to say, this is you as you really are. Besides, it is a dangerous thing to dig down into one's self in this way: to descend directly and violently down the shaft of one's own being. A man could injure himself by so doing in such a way that no doctor could ever cure him. But let the young soul ask itself looking back on its life: What have you truly loved until now? What has drawn upon your soul? What has at one and the same time mastered it and made it happy? Consider these objects of your veneration. Perhaps they will reveal to you through their being and their sequence, a law, a fundamental law of your true self. Compare them; see how one complements, extends, surpasses and transforms the other. See how they form a ladder on which you have climbed up to yourself so far, for your true self does not lie hidden within you but far above and beyond you, or at least beyond that which you usually considered to be your true self. Your true educators and teachers, your shapers disclose the true original meaning and basic material of your being. Your teachers can only be your liberators.

What have you truly loved? What mastered your soul? What made it happy? The emphasis is characteristically Nietzschean, in its active complexity upon discipline, upon love and joy as

51

essentials in the soul's liberation, which for Nietzsche education meant.

Even more fundamental perhaps is the insistence and answer to Freud before Freud actually wrote, that self-knowledge lies not within but beyond. If we only come to know ourselves by realizing ourselves, by surpassing or transcending ourselves, by growing, we at last make ourselves comprehensible, intelligible, and manifest. In this high sense, education and teaching are metaphysical acts.

Metaphysical acts involve intangibles and fundamentals. They return us to first principles and ultimates. Ultimately the questions "What shall we teach and what is education?" are metaphysical queries about the nature of man and human destiny. Even if a teacher never asks the questions, what he does every time he teaches or gives an assignment presupposes them, presupposes in fact that they have been answered, if not by him, then by those who taught him: by society, tradition, or the culture. All educational reform that aims at more than face-lifting requires that such questions be raised, and, if possible, answered. Any project of renewal requires us to return to our beginnings, to reconsider our sources. Why do we teach? What do we teach? According to what definition of man do we want our students to become what they will become? What now-- in an age when all definitions of the species are up for grabs--what now is an acceptable and possible human fate?

Teaching in this sense is a fatal act, and we must, for the sake of those we teach, for the sake of all of us, know what we are doing. Otherwise we are doomed, doomed in any case to go on doing what we are doing now, teaching merely disciplinary skills as though they were identical with liberal education. Doomed, that is, to what Charles Silberman has called all too aptly, "the pervasive mindlessness of the academic world." The antidote to that mindlessness can only be, I think, a renewed awareness of the metaphysical implications of teaching. As the sad pedagogical history of the sixties shows, most acade- mic reform is transient gimickry. New professorships, team teaching, special award incentives, cluster colleges--unless these things are grounded in a shared sense of mission, unless informed by a tangible educational ethos, these reforms are, for

for all their showiness, nearly useless.

Where then does the reformer take his stand? Above all, I believe, on those structures and assertions in which institutional mission is most clearly involved. In a teaching instiitution, for instance, the chief aim should surely be to assign the deepest pride of place to teaching. The teacher should have no doubts whatsoever about the dignity and the reward of what he does. Everything in the institution's structure and operation should conduce to make him proudly conscious of himself as an educator rather than as an apologetic part-time scholar.

Most American universities are primarily teaching institutions, yet in almost every one of them the teacher is in fact a second class citizen. By teaching milieu, I don't of course mean one in which scholarship is not honored, but I do mean one in which scholarship is not honored at the expense of teaching. But I was speaking of this metaphysical aspect of teaching.

My second text for this is Plato, that famous passage in the Symposium where Aristophanes give his great account of love. We were once, he says, integrated; we were both sexes in one, in a single globular body. This primal happiness of ours made us arrogant, and so the god cut us in half. We became half creatures, tallies of men and women, and when a tally meets its counterpart, it falls in love and cannot bear to be separated. And these lovers, Aristophanes goes on, could not tell you what it is they want from each other, for none of them could believe that his pleasure and desire to be with the other could be accounted for in simply sexual terms. No, clearly it must be "something else" (allo ti is the word in Greek), allo ti, something else, which the soul desires, something which it cannot explain except in riddles. Suppose, he goes on; suppose that the god Hephaestus came and asked these divided lovers what they so desperately desired from each other. He offers to fuse them for eternity in a common life and a common death. And, concludes Aristophanes, "surely no lover would be so mad as to refuse what he had always wanted. To be fused, and from being two, made one. "The reason for this of course, is that originally we were fused," he goes on, "and this longing for completeness, for <u>allo ti</u>, this transcendent something, this metaphysical X which is greater than sexual pleasure, and of which sex is only the sign, is Eros, or love."

The teacher I would like you to suppose is just such a Platonic tally, and teaching itself is a metaphysical enterprise in pursuit of some intangible and final X, an enterprise which resembles love. Now it is his vocation for this enterprise, this metaphysical passion, that mark him as a teacher and not just another professor. Professors, it seems to me, do not really have vocations. They have professions; they have posts; they have jobs; they teach French or Latin or biology. But insofar as they teach students, they are potential teachers in the true sense. Insofar as the pursue <u>allo ti</u>, a worthy <u>allo ti</u>, no matter whether they teach calculus, or sociology, or Coptic, or Baroque opera, they are the actual teachers, the true-blue/Nietzschean article. They are liberators and lovers of the species. In any university they will always be the smallest minority, but they are almost certainly the only truly educational force around and probably the only metaphysical show in town.

I am talking, of course, transcendentally; I think that is what the subject requires. I am not, need I say, concerned here with the teacher as a diffuser of information or a knowledge conductor. As such, he is useful and necessary because he carries the bulk of the teaching load. I am concerned rather with what he might be if he were freed by inclination and institutional structure to be what he wanted to be. He may very well have no interest in the kind of teaching that concerns me here, and he may wish to be precisely what he is. But as such, he is not designed for <u>allo ti</u>. Not for "something else"--anything but-- rather, for the same old thing.

Specifically, what are they like, these teachers? How could we recognize them? What is the family likeness? Begin with that vocation of theirs, that metaphysical passion, <u>allo ti</u>. I call them Platonic tallies because I have in mind the greatest tally-teacher of them all, the Platonic Socrates. By educator I mean a Socratic teacher, a visible embodiment of the realized, or realizing, humanity of one's aspirations, skills and scholarship. I mean men and women ripening into such realization as Socrates

54

at the end of the _Symposium_ comes to embody, thereby guaranteeing his own definition of love.

This Socratic teacher is what he knows, and what he knows is secondary to the passion for knowing and even the purpose for which the knowledge was acquired. The knowledge looks beyond itself; it acknowledges humbly a limit to knowledge. He says what he knows, and the student thinks, "This man or woman has <u>seen</u> these things." The student recognizes, let us hope, that this is a vision and understands that the vision is the result of painstaking submission to facts beyond the author's control. The teacher's submission to the necessary is perceived rightly as discipline, and this controlled knowledge emerges as earned authority.

But his embodiment is not total; indeed, it is necessarily deficient, partial. This is why the teacher is a tally. His incompleteness matches and responds to that of his student. They are complementary, though at different levels, perhaps. The teacher is the custodian of a test, or a body of knowledge, or a tradition to which he stands as an apprentice. He needs, like the platonic lover, what he does not have.

The passion for surpassing ourselves, for transcendence, is founded on the conviction of being imperfect. If we were perfect beings, we would never love. Eros begins in want. This incompleteness, then, is actively and powerfully present in this kind of teaching. It is what draws the teacher to the texts he professes in the hope of achieving a greatness he sees in them. He exhibits in generous measure, then, the hunger for greatness, human greatness, a greatness which he covets because he does not have it, not wholly, a greatness which he hopes to acquire at least in part for himself and others by study and emulation.

Combined with the hunger for greatness is a belief in meaning, in an earned order implied by greatness, for greatness is a victory over the turbulent disorder of the moral world. The hero, as Nietzsche knew, justifies human existence. He may be the only justification. The one habit which Achilles and Oedipus cannot kick, the habit the species cannot kick, is meaning. We are responsible for our meanings.

The teacher stands upon tiptoes, then, toward his texts and the humanity they embody. These texts are his teachers. They tell him who he is or give him that trajectory toward the self he hopes to become. It is because the teacher exemplifies this passion for fulfillment that he can influence others. When the teacher is successful, the student contributes a correspondingly radiant hunger for becoming.

I speak of course of an ideal student, the tally of his teacher. But even the ordinary student may feel the remote contagion of these texts passing from person to person, from teacher to student, from peer to peer. The teacher impersonates a great humanity which he has the knowledge to understand and the human capacity to interpret in a compelling way. Upon the power of his impersonation, a student's human fate may depend. This kind of teaching is a fatal business.

I spoke earlier of this teaching as an activity resembling love. There is in it, or should be, a sense of compassion and care; a care for the species, for what it might be, for the young, for their fulfillment. Insofar as teaching is a profession, it is one which was founded not on a body of methods or disciplines, but upon service, on an inspiriting ethos of presumably efficient love. In theory, at least, teaching is unselfish; it claims to foster. Now, of course, the pretense of service has vanished almost as completely as it has vanished in law and medicine. The modern professions embody a reciprocal exchange of benefits between patient and practitioner with the balance of benefits steadily tipping toward the practitioner. Teaching becomes increasingly a matter of contractual relations, of measurable social utility, of quantifiable ends, of marketplace services. And as it does, the odds against the kind of teaching I am describing steadily worsen.

But the vocation of teaching will not disappear, for the simple reason that we cannot do without it. We can no more do away with it than we can do away with personal influence, of which teaching is the most obvious example. As soon as someone with a complex vision cares deeply enough to communicate it, and somebody else is prepared to listen; as soon as two or more human beings combine to pool their skills or to surpass themselves in concert, the vocation of teaching returns. As a vocation.

56

The universities and colleges, it seems to me, are likelier to provide the right circumstances and the setting than the marketplace or the streets. In a talk of 10 years ago called "The Future of Teaching," I said that the universities were about as uncongenial to teaching at present as the Mojave Desert to a clutch of Druid priests, and I don't think they are a great deal more congenial now. If they are still uncongenial to teaching there is no inherent reason for their being so. The very fact that they are charged with the responsibility to teach the young means that something of educational importance can still happen. The teaching college, the teaching university, is where it could most easily occur. With care, it can.

I have talked of teaching as an activity resembling love. The process I have in mind is one which the Greeks first defined and which we have never bettered. You will find it implied in the relation between Achilles and Patroclus from the Homeric poems in the 5th century, the supreme teacher-text. The ancient account which best articulates that process is Plato's <u>Phaedrus</u>. What Plato gives us, in essence, is an account of love which is a metaphor for all dynamic human relationships in which personal influence is central and mutual growth is the dominant ideal. Examples would be the relation of lover to the beloved; of teacher to student; of leader to led; of politician to constituency; dramatist to audience; priest to congregation. But the model is unabashedly erotic, perhaps because in all of these activities, as in Plato's idea of love, <u>allo ti</u>, this metaphysical completion of the incomplete nature of man is so central.

This is Plato's account: a lover imputes to his beloved qualities which idealize her. He aims, as it were, over her head. He does not do this because he is unobservant or criminally stupid, but because he loves what is godlike in her. He loves her for what he sees in her at her best, becoming better. He loves her for that self which lies, as in Nietzsche's example, beyond her. Now this act of loving respect forces her, if she responds, on to her tiptoes. She is forced to rise simply to meet her lover's expectations. As for him, he has already had to stand on tiptoes too, and now she imputes to him, in turn, the divinity of his nature, forcing him to rise.

And so in a steady accelerando of ascending and criss-crossing admiration and wonder, they compel each other to rise toward the height of their natures, and by so doing to reveal what is divine in themselves and in the species. This is the godlike happiness, the eudaemonia of these Platonic lovers. Steadily, in loving rivalry, they surpass each other and themselves. They realize themselves; they are revealed. It is this erotic dynamic which, to move from the Greeks, I think controls Shakespeare's Antony and Cleopatra.

Antony's death and final nobility (I am convinced this is Shakespeare's dramatic premise) provokes and challenges Cleopatra to a matching nobility which culminates in those great lines of hers as she too rises: "Give me my robes, put on my crown." And then, after she puts those things on, the action nicely italicizing the words that are about to come, she says "I have immortal longings in me," by which she means that she becomes, as she says, "all air and fire," leaving her other, her mortal, elements behind. She reveals, competing with Antony, a divinity nobody could have predicted in her or in him--one which the level-headed, factual, cynical Caesar, the one-dimensional politican, incapable of any level at all except a flat dead level, cannot begin to grasp.

At least in essentials, this seems to me the dynamic that governs all the diverse activities--religious, political, artistic, pedagogical that comprise personal influence. The tension implicit is profoundly personal, profoundly reciprocal. I stress reciprocity. It is a modern idea, or a lately popular one, that teaching is a unilateral activity involving the teacher and the taught, flowing downward. Obviously, the teacher must know more than the student or he is not entitled to teach. But the activity is cooperative, since what brings student and teacher together is not only what the teacher knows and the student does not, but what neither student nor teacher yet knows. They meet to enlarge themselves; they meet as, presumably, these Platonic lovers might: in order to grow, to become by mutual definition what they only incipiently are. There is no teaching worthy of the name in which the teacher is not also taught; otherwise his only motive would be benevolence, and benevolence, it seems to me, is insufficient to explain what takes place in teaching at its best.

The teacher, Nietzsche said, was a liberator, but he liberates himself by teaching. All the virtues and all the vices are taught by direct personal contagion and propagation. There is no way of teaching honesty except by being honest. You cannot, except by evincing courage or freedom, make another person courageous or free. But any increase in his freedom and courage is returned to you as the enlarged freedom demanded by what you and he have jointly become.

What is true of the virtues is true also for understanding, even of a vision. If I struggle to articulate my vision worthily of your attention, then your attention will help me to see what I could not see before I began to articulate. My understanding as a teacher is dependent upon what you, as a student, genuinely grasp of what I say, and upon your heightened demand that I speak more clearly, more comprehensibly, when I speak again. It is this cooperative quality, this sharing of a fatal purpose, that confers on teaching of the apposite sort the status of calling or vocation. We cannot do it alone. Why? It is hard to say. We are social animals, we cannot speak for others. Only they can do that, and what they say inflects our behavior and thence theirs. Our affinities and hatreds reveal to us, in part, who we are. I can learn French, if I must, from a Berlitz-trained machine, but only this criss-crossing, irritable, reciprocal commerce with other bewildered and emerging creatures will tell me what it is to be a man.

This cooperation is why I believe the inspired teacher literally disappears when the fit is on him, disappears as a personality. He has transcended himself and his own petty, parochial reality. This only occurs, it may be, at moments of full intellectual operation, but it happens. It may be as John Jay Chapman suggested, that man's brain is so constituted that in the moment of its full operation the man himself disappears. The penalty for this kind of fit is that such a man is defenseless, innocent. He no longer knows how to protect his own interests because he has lost his sense of them; he is volatized as simple influence. Such teachers are rare but precious. They need all the protection they can get. But they do exist.

Let me close by remembering one of them, a colleague and friend of mine a decade ago; he died

last year. I knew him as a good man, a decent man. I
never knew the full extent of his personal influence
and power until a student sent me a letter she wrote
him when he decided in anger and the conviction of
failure to leave his teaching post.   Her letter, it
seems to me, is one of the finest statements on
teaching, teaching as a vocation, that I know. It is
first of all a letter that could not have been written
unless she had been as touched and changed in her
encounter with this teacher as the letter reveals her
to be.   But she also writes as the student of a great
text. Again, it is Plato and the Greek tragedians you
will hear, doubly apprenticed and unmistakably
fulfilled.   Between her teacher and her text, she has
managed to say more than she ever could have known she
might say a year before.

This is a part of her letter.   It is, I am
afraid, embedded in a context, and I cannot, without
going into context and personalities, do more than
give you passages in somewhat discontinuous style.
This is the letter she wrote him:

In a classroom, dear gifted idiot man,
you   never lose,   not once,   not even
partially. You don't waste one minute, and
you don't miss one blockhead.   I know
whereof I speak better than you ever will
because I've thought more about how to teach
than you ever have.   I'm not a gifted
teacher, I am just a good one. And I'm here
to tell you how much effort and revision and
thought it takes the rest of us to develop
techniques for what you can do unerringly,
invariably, unselfconsciously, in spades
redoubled at slam.   You've never had the
faintest notion how to know what a student
is or what you are making him become.   You
just project what you are and what the work
at hand is.   It is only because of what you
are that you can be so criminally innocent.
One reason that you think you have failures
is that you habitually overestimate what you
had to start with.   That just happens to be
inspired teaching technique.

I deliberately overestimate the worth
and capacity of my students because too much
time and too many terrible failures have
shown me that no human motivation is

stronger than the desire to vindicate the confidence of those who happen to think well of you. My standard way of stopping a cheater is to tell the local yahoo blabbermouth that the cheater in question has a much better mind than he thinks he has, and it puzzles me that this bright, attractive young man seems to think that he is incurably stupid. Blabbermouth invariably says, 'But he is a discipline problem and he cheats,' and I say, 'I can't believe it; in my class he is well-behaved, a gentleman, and he seems to be responsible.'

Within 48 hours the cheater has heard it from four different sources and with embellishments and refinements. It never fails; the little bastard becomes so anxious to preserve the illusion that he begins to cheat with finesse and imagination. From there it takes just a little practice and persistence to nudge him into some real production. If that doesn't work, he learns to be genuinely ashamed of himself when he is being sleazy, which is only learnable from those who project confidence in his respectability.

I can shrug, however, I'm not seeing these rats for the first time. I would just as soon persecute, humiliate, insult, despise, if it were useful, which it isn't. What I do is a planned and practiced technique, and I have listened to your tirades and watched your students react. For all that gorgeous baroque invective, you have never in my hearing nicked a one. I'd have noticed, believe me. So you bully, wheedle, harangue and make demands of your students, not of what they aren't, but of what they ought to be, which couldn't be better for your students, but which is hard on you. I've seen you move real garbage about four degrees in the right direction by sheer force of that conviction. That's not rabbit-out-of-the-hat magic, it is an old fashioned prodigy, and I am frankly dazzled. You not only fail to realize what you've done, you actually think you are down six

61

and moan about futility.

I despair of communicating to you the depth of gratitude from which the enthusiasm of these students comes as a secondary effect. Never mind, just take my word that it is warranted. So your Philistine may still be a clod. He's not only never going to be hostile to your concerns, he will defend them against the other Philistines, which is something he is equipped to do and you aren't. Suppose you had the Philistine politician's awesome energy and killer instinct working for you. He may be hopeless by now, but he would have had that instinct for decency if anyone worth not disappointing had ever expected it of him. He might have had a dim notion that Greek tragedy is worth promoting if a teacher like you had ever done him the unwitting kindness of expecting it to stand his hair on end. I've seen a potential Philistine or two walk into your classes. I've yet to see one walk out. You know not what you are--to coin a phrase--you know not what you do.

FREEDOM/RESPONSIBILITY

The 'cultural crisis' of the 60's and 70's aroused strong fears that society would have to choose between chaotic anarchy or authoritarian control. In one sense the conflict was no more than the latest manifestation of an antinomy which is at the heart of American society and culture; the contradiction between the unbridled egoism of the capitalist ethic and democratic notions of universal social responsibilities and obligations. During this time schools have been a pivotal focus in those concerns. The public's fears are expressed time and again in their demands that schools more effectively regulate and discipline the lives of students. Individual freedom for the young is, for many, no more than a dangerous indulgence. Rejecting the notion of an irreconcilable duality, the conference sought to address how we could affirm our commitment to individual freedom along with our strong concern for social responsibility. It asked what were the limits of liberty and at what point does social responsibility stifle individuals.

In his paper Kurt Baier approaches, analytically, the meanings of individual freedom and social responsibility in the context of schooling. He considers the society's responsibility for and to the schools as well as the school's responsibility to the society. Among its responsibilities, he notes that the school must provide for the socialization of the new generation. Society, on the other hand, is obliged to ensure that children should have equal access to the social instructions which transmit society's culture; particularly those which transmit those skills and qualifications whose possession is required to enable people to live worthwhile lives. Baier asserts that the right to individuality or self-realization is at the core of the right to individual freedom - though in no sense, he says, can this be considered a 'blanket license' to develop whatever faculties be in us.

For Kurt Wolff the central responsibility of the teacher today is to arouse in students the desire to learn critically. To Wolff this means to learn the human tradition so that we understand how human societies have fallen short of being good societies - to see, in particular, that the global society of which we are a part 'is the most endangered and the most dangerous of all.' In this context freedom is the necessary condition for discharging such a responsibility. It demands that the teacher not be limited - through subjective or objective restrictions - from educating critically. It depends on a personal willingness to engage in such activity with all of its risks, as well as the capacity to fight social and institutional infringements.

63

FREEDOM AND RESPONSIBILITY IN THE SCHOOL

Kurt Baier

My assignment today is to address the problem of how to reconcile the claims of individual freedom with those of social responsibility. At what point must liberty bow to responsibility? When do claims of social responsibility become so demanding that they stifle individuality and should they then be resisted? To whom, and for what, are schools, students, and teachers responsible? What can schools do to promote responsibility on the part of teachers and students? On what grounds does such responsibility rest? Which dimensions of freedom should schools promote, which restrain? What should students and what should teachers be free, what not free, to do? And finally, what rationales underlie the various rival answers to these questions?

These are weighty and intricate problems. To give detailed, practically useful and sound answers to any, let alone all of them one would need to have much greater knowledge of our school system than I possess. I therefore take my task, as a moral and social philosopher, to be not so much the formulation of such detailed answers which you would have no good reason to have confidence in, as, rather the clarification of some of the conceptual and moral difficulties which underlie these problems. In my talk, I shall therefore concentrate on those difficulties to which the methods of the philosopher, rather than those of the social scientist can be applied.

The normative problems in the formulation of suitable policies for schools cannot be answered without a clear understanding of the role and function of schools in a democratic and pluralistic society such as ours. I therefore begin with a brief description of how schools came to have this role and function. Next I explain the idea of social responsibility and give some tentative and partial answers to questions arising out of the commitment to social responsibility. The answers to one of these questions raises in acute form the conflict between social and individual responsibility, and I end with a few clarificatory remarks about this issue.

65

1.   The function of the school. A society is a
relatively long-term, large-scale organization for the
promotion of the interests of its members. Its
institutions determine a large number of positions or
roles which are occupied by different persons in
succession without thereby themselves undergoing any
change. A policeman, a teacher, a magistrate, dies or
is dismissed or moves to another city, and another
takes his place playing exactly the same role and
performing exactly the same function as the one before
him. But since a society caters to the needs of its
members, it must, if it is to continue, cater at least
to their most fundamental needs and regulate their
interaction. Every society must arrange for
collective decision-making, both in the political and
the economic domain; it must regulate the sexual and
reproductive behavior of its members to ensure the
continued existence of the society; and lastly, of
most concern to us here, every society must make
provision for the socialization of its new members,
that is, the transmission to them of the society's
culture.

There are at least three importantly different
aspects of a culture all of which should be
transmitted, though not necessarily in the same way or
to the same degree to all the new members. The first,
to which we in this country pay most attention,
concerns the know-how which the society has succeeded
in amassing, that is, the knowledge of how to attain
a variety of ends or goals, which are commonly adopted
by large numbers of people: how to build a suitable
shelter, how to cure the sick, how to improve the
ability of getting and transporting things from one
place to another, say, by building vehicles or
bridges, or how to kill people. In advanced societies
such as ours, the know-how is continuously improved
and increased by the advances in the applied sciences,
such as agriculture, medicine, and engineering.
Since it is now virtually impossible to keep such
advances secret for long, we can pass on to the next
generation also the advances made in other societies.

The second aspect of a culture deals with what,
by contrast with the know-how, we may call "the know-
what". This aspect contains a society's, as it were
"official" answers to the question of when, that is,
under what conditions, to try to bring about and when
to try to prevent those states of affairs concerning
which the know-how tells us how to do so. In

66

democratic societies, these official answers need not be uncritically accepted, but may be and often are subjected to critical scrutiny by our religious, social, legal and moral reformers, as well as other types of pundits. These reformers play, with regard to our traditional guidelines concerning ends or goals, the same sort of role as, say, agricultural science plays with regard to the traditional know-how handed down from one farmer's generation to the next.

The first two aspects of our culture thus are "practical" in the sense of specifying suitable intervention in the natural course of events, whether in regard to means or to ends. The third aspect is not practical in this sense. It is concerned rather with those human beliefs, activities, and artefacts, by which our lives are enriched and rendered flourishing, worthwhile, happy, or fulfilling. Socializing the new generation also includes acquainting them with, and teaching them to appreciate, the relevant contributions of their own culture and, in "open" societies, also those of other cultures. In this field belong the arts, the religions, the games and sports, the hobbies and all those other activities, now often called "auto-telic", which are engaged in for their own sakes, rather than merely as a way of making some difference to the expected course of events.

In primitive societies, the culture is passed on to the young in the context of the family, simply by letting the children participate in the activities of the adults. Transmission is effected by "on-the-job" learning, perhaps also by a certain amount of training by adults. But as knowledge advances, parents become less and less able to cope with the task of transmitting the most important parts of the culture. At this point a new class of professional culture-transmitters springs up. The Greek sophists were among the earliest such specialists. To begin with, such teachers and schools in which they do their teaching were accessible only to the upper classes who could afford to send their children there. As long as the culture is simple and unified, there is little problem about the content of such teaching. All agree on all three aspects of the culture, including know-what. In Europe, during the Middle Ages, such questions concerning appropriate ends were debated within the Church and authoritatively settled by Church Councils or by the Pope. Such authoritative decisions were then enforced more or less effectively and ruthlessly for the whole of Christendom. When the Cathars proclaimed all material things and social life to be evil, they were brutally suppressed (in 1209) in a crusade inspired by Pope Innocent III (1160-1216), the inventor of crusades against Christian heretics and enemies of the Papacy. After the unity of medieval Christianity was ruptured by the Reformation, a new type of problem arose. Thus, in England, in the seventeenth century, both Anglicans and Presbyterians insisted there should be only one religion for the whole political realm--though they differed, of course, on which religion that should be--and used the schools as instruments of their policy of religious territorialism. Congregationalists and Baptists urged, on the contrary, that Christians within a given political realm should be free to form their own congregation and their own free church, as well as to adopt their own doctrine. As this third view prevailed, religions began to compete with one another, like businesses, in the market place of religious ideas, and parents became free to send their children to a school which taught their preferred religion.

A further important change was brought about by the Industrial Revolution. It created conditions of work which greatly reduced the opportunity of the family to socialize the children in any way. Under the new conditions, the father--and quite often also the mother and some of the children--left the home early in the morning to work in a factory and came home too late and too tired to spend any time with their children. The government then began to set up public schools to take over from the family the educational task no longer performed by it.

Short and oversimplified though this sketch is of the changing ways in which societies transmit their culture and of the rise of the school as a social institution, it throws some light on the function of that institution. Clearly, its minimal function is the transmission, by specialists, of that part of the culture of the society which I have called its know-how. Probably not many people would object to including among the functions of at least some schools

_____

Sir Ernest Barker, <u>Oliver Cromwell</u>, Cambridge University Press, 1937.

also the transmission of the third aspect for which in most contexts--not in anthropology and sociology--the word 'culture' is reserved: music, literature, and painting. But there is, I think, widespread opposition to having the second aspect of culture, what I have called the "know-what", taught in schools. For such teaching would have to include, indeed concentrate on, moral education. But since our schools can no longer claim authority to control the religious and moral opinions of individual instructors, parents who treasure their right to indoctrinate their children in their own morality tend to oppose, as insufferable indoctrination by the teacher, any program of moral education which may subject to rational scrutiny and so may call into question the religious and moral doctrines the parents believe in. I shall return to this point shortly.

To these primary functions of the school, we must add another closely related one, namely, the preparation of the students for their eventual roles in society. The school not merely transmits to them the society's culture: it also classifies and pigeon holes them, so that they can be shunted into one or other of the niches in the social order for which the school has found them best suited. The school must therefore provide opportunities for students to exhibit their inborn and their learning abilities; it must channel them into learning paths suited to their already demonstrated talents as well as to the society's needs; and finally it is required to certify the students who have reached the appropriate standards of excellence. This last set of functions generates important conflicts of interests. Parents, of course, want to see their children in what they regard as prestigious and rewarding positions in life. But these are, to a considerable extent, also in our society, dependent on schooling. Thus, if a person is not admitted to medical school, he is denied the license to practice as a physician, a way of life many parents and students regard as one of the most attractive, rewarding and respected. Hence some parents, especially those who think that their children are especially gifted, favor "tracking" in order that they not be held back by their duller school mates, while those parents who fear that their children are not especially gifted, tend to oppose it, in the hope that their progress will be speeded up by contact with their brighter school fellows or that if they bloom later, at least they have not been relegated from the beginning to a track of inferior promise.

The functions I have mentioned so far are what might be called "assigned" functions--the tasks society imposes on the schools. With regard tc all such functions we can, should, and do ask whether society ought to assign them to the school or whether it would be better to assign them to other agencies, say, the parents or the peer group or the employer or whoever. There is, however, also another sense of 'function', one current in the social sciences, in which the function of something is simply what it regularly does or brings about. In that sense, polluting the air is one of the functions of a car.

Cne of the important current functions of the school in this sociological sense, is its role in courtship, sexual experimentation and selection of a long-term sexual and reproductive partner. This aspect of adolescent life, until recently firmly repressed and postponed as long as possible, seems to assume ever larger proportions in our schools and to begin ever earlier in a young person's life. This raises the question of whether this is an undesirable function for the school to perform or whether the school is an acceptable context for this important phase in our lives. Of course, the question may be idle, for possibly we can do nothing tc prevent the school from performing that unassigned function. Supposing, then, that this function is either desirable or else unavoidable, should society assign to the school also the function of providing the relevant teaching? Should children learn the facts of life from their teachers in class or should they learn them from their parents or perhaps from their peers? Of course, if, as is often claimed, very few parents discuss sex with their children, our question reduces to whether children should learn about sex from their peers or from their teachers. I shall return to this later.

Among the most worrying of these unassigned and clearly undesirable functions of the school is the introduction of children to the drug culture and to crime. If it is true, as many people believe, that addictive habits are particularly hard to shake when they are acquired at a tender age, then it would seem that the school should be prevented from performing this unassigned function.

70

2. The currently assigned responsibilities of teachers, schools, and students. Perhaps I have said enough about the social context in which the school functions, to begin the discussion of the questions of primary concern to us here, namely, our commitment to both social responsibility and individual freedom.

When, in this context, we think of social responsibility, we can mean either the society's reponsibility _for_ and _to_ the schools or the school's responsibility _to_ the society and _for_ certain results. Since the questions are interdependent, it is important to clarify and distinguish them.

Let us begin with the responsibility of the school. The school is responsible _for_ certain results, namely, the socialization of the new generations, in the sense in which a secretary may be responsible for office supplies. I shall speak of this sense of 'responsibility' as task-responsiblity, meaning roughly the duty to perform a task. When I spoke of the assigned functions of the school, I meant roughly the same thing as the task-responsibilities of the school. But the schools are responsible for the results in these matters also in the sense in which the secretary is the one responsible if the office supplies run out. He is, in other words, answerable for his _failure_ to see to it that there were enough supplies; he is responsible = answerable for his failure to discharge his task-responsibility. This implies that there is someone _to whom_ he must answer-- to whom he must explain why he failed. And if he has no exculpatory explanation, that is, no justification or excuse, then that person can hold him responsible, that is, impose on him that to which he is then liable, which is anything from a reprimand to being fired. Similarly, schools are answerable for their failure to discharge their task-responsibility.

But who is the person or persons to whom schools are answerable? Is it the students or the parents or the superintendent or the board of education or the secretary of education or society as a whole? Some people have argued that it is the students. Recently, a student who had passed through his high school without learning to read and write, sued the school. He argued that they were responsible for getting him the minimal training a person should have, which included literacy, and that they had (culpably) failed in this reponsibility and so were liable for the loss

71

he suffered.

But this is far from obvious. To get clearer about it, we must distinguish two senses of 'responsible to'. If I promise to look after your ailing grandmother while you are away, then I have an obligation to you and to her. But these are not two different obligations: they are one and the same obligation, though there are two different senses of 'obligation to'. In one sense, my obligation is to you because you are the person to whom I am answerable if I do not discharge the obligation and because you can hold me responsible, i.e., impose whatever it is I am liable to: reproaches, loss of friendship, perhaps damages. In another sense, the same obligation is to your grandmother because she is the intended beneficiary of my obligation. I must do something for her, if I am to discharge my obligation to you. If I have not discharged the obligation and you do not hold me liable, that is the end of the matter. The grandmother has no recourse. I don't have an obligation to her in that sense.

A task-responsibility is like an obligation or duty. It is something one is morally required to do. It implies a responsibility to someone either in the "answerability" sense, i.e., the sense that she is the person to whom one is answerable and who can release one of the responsibility and can impose that to which one is liable if one has no excuse, or else in the "beneficiary" sense i.e., the sense that she is the beneficiary of the performance of the task. It is clear that schools are responsible to their students in the beneficiary sense: students are the intended beneficiaries of the schools's performance of their task-responsibility.

But who are the schools responsible to in the answerability sense? Clearly, from the fact that the school's benficiary responsibility is to its students, it follows neither that the schools are responsible to them also in the answerability sense, nor that they are not. If a teacher neglected her duty, failed to show up for her classes or regularly forgot to grade her students' essays, or if she was grossly incompetent at doing these things, then her principal could and should reprimand or even fire her, if after properly examining her case he finds her guilty of failing in her task-responsibility. This shows that the teacher is answerable to the principal, because he is entitled to impose on her what she is liable to. Similarly, if the school as a whole fails in its task-responsibility and the principal does little or nothing about it, then the superintendent can, after due investigation, reprimand or fire the principal or the teachers or both.

Well, then, is the school, that is, the teachers and the principal, answerable also to the students? Of course, a student has a right to complain to the principal about a teacher if the latter has failed in her task-responsibility, just as the grandmother in the previous example can complain to my friend if I fail to look after her during his absence. But if only he can impose on me whatever I am liable to, then I am task-responsible and so answerable if I fail in my task-responsiblity, only to him and not to her. Similarly for the student. If only the principal or the superintendent can reprimand or fire the teacher after they have carefully examined the complaint, then the school and the teachers are not task-responsible to the students, that is, answerable for failing in their responsibility to them. The teachers are responsible to the principal, and the school is reponsible to the principal.

But what if the student takes his case to court and wins damages? Does not this show that he has a right to his basic education against the school? And does not this show that the school has a correlative task-responsibility for that education and so is answerable to him for any failure in that? I think not. For if the teacher, the principal, the board, the superintendent and so on up to the secretary of education, or even the President, were directly answerable to the student, the student would not have to take the case to court, but could himself investigate the wrong-doing of the teacher and the principal, and so on, and could impose on them whatever it is they are liable to. That he does have to take the case to court, shows that the teachers, schools, superintendents and so on, are answerable not to the student but to society. But it shows also that they are responsible to society not only by way of the various links in the ascending chain of the educational hierarchy, but also by way of the law which expresses the will of society as formulated by the legislature and interpreted by the judiciary.

We can give a few partial answers to some of the

73

questions raised in the beginning.   First: To whom,
and   for what,   are schools and teachers   responsible?
Their prime responsibility is for the socialization of
the   young.   The   teachers   are the   troops   of   this
battle.   They do the actual fighting.   The schools are
the quartermasters of this army.   They are responsible
for   supplies.   Principals,   superintendents,   school
boards   and secretaries of education   are   responsible
for overall strategy, recruiting of troops, and so on.
Who are they responsible to?   Well, in the beneficiary
sense,   their responsibility is to the students: for
the students clearly are the intended beneficiaries of
the   school's   primary   task-responsibility.   In   the
answerablility   sense,   the   teachers   are   responsible
that is,   answerable to society,   both by way of their
subordination   to   their immediate   superiors   in   the
educational hierarchy and, like everybody else, by way
of the law, as the ultimate agency of recourse.

Second: To   whom   and   for   what   are   students
responsible?   Students in their role as students, are
task-responsible   for   the completion of   those   tasks
which their teachers set them, and they are answerable
to   these teachers for failing to perform these   tasks
without   adequate excuse.   The teachers can lay   down
what   students are liable to for such failures,   which
ranges from a reprimand to expulsion from the   school.
While   they   are minors,   children   are of course   also
task-responsible for any tasks which their parents may
set   them.   If among these are also the tasks set   by
the   teachers,   then students are also   answerable   to
their   parents   for   failing to perform   their   school
tasks.   But this is so only to the extent that parents
back the schools,   and as long as children are subject
to   the   parents' authority and so is   only   in   their
capacity   as   children,   not   as   students.   Adult
university   students   are   not   answerable to   their
parents,   unless   there   is   some   quasi-contractual
relationship   between   them,   as when parents pay   for
their grownup children's university education.   It is
often understood between parents and children that   in
return   for   financial aid they are answerable to   the
parents for failure to attend to their studies.

Are   students responsible, i.e., answerable   to
society?   Again,   the answer is No,   unless there   is
some   quasi-contractual   agreement,   as when students
receive   scholarships or other similar   benefits,   the
award   of which gives society or their representatives
the authority to terminate the benefit if the   student

fails to complete the tasks set him by his teachers. But, apart from that, I do not think students in our society (are taken to) have any special responsibility to society. Our society makes these educational opportunities available to the young, but it does not impose duties on them to use them as best they can or to perform services for society with the skills they have acquired. Some other societies do impose such duties and responsibilities.

One further sense of 'responsibility'. So far we have been concerned mainly with the questions of what schools, teachers, and students are task-responsible for, to whom they are answerable if they fail in their task-responsibilities, and what they are liable to if they can produce no exculpatory explanation for their failure. Among the task-responsibilities of the school is also the task of ensuring that teachers and students know the task-responsibilities of their respective roles, so that they can discharge these responsibilities if they want to. There is, however, also the further and quite different task of turning teachers and students into responsible rather than irresponsible role-players, that is, persons who take their task-responsibilities, or at least those of their roles, seriously rather than lightly. This further task-responsiblity is concerned with the inculcation, not of know-how or know-what, but of suitable motivation.

Schools are supposed to tackle this further task by trying to inculcate a strong "sense of responsibility" in their students and perhaps also their teachers, that is, a strong disposition to do what they recognize as involved in the discharge of their task-responsibilities. One popular method is to let students "run things" themselves, to involve them in curricular planning, in grading, or in student government. By this device students are supposed to learn not only what to do and how to do it if they want to, but also to recognize what they must be willing to do if they are to achieve certain things they regard as desirable, and so to come to be willing to do these things. The theory is that being assigned certain important task-responsibilities, that is, certain "responsible" (rather than routine) tasks, makes one a responsible (rather than irresponsible) person. It would be interesting to have more empirical data about just what kinds of task-responsiblity are most likely to produce responsible persons, or about other methods to achieve that important end.

3. Responsibility to parents. So far I have talked only about those task-responsibilities of schools, teachers, and students, which are actually recognized in our society. We could, however, raise the further and more difficult question of whether some of these actually recognized responsibilities ought perhaps not to be recognized, and whether some that are not ought perhaps to be recognized.

Should schools be responsible to parents? Well, plainly, not in the beneficiary sense, at least not as far as the school's primary function is concerned. (Where schools secondarily function e.g., as day nurseries, their responsibility, in the beneficiary sense is and ought also to be to the parents. But as far as the primary function goes, their responsibility in the beneficiary sense is surely, only to the students.) But now we can ask whether, in the answerability sense, schools ought perhaps to be responsible to the parents. Should parents sit on school boards? Should school boards be merely advisory or should they have powers of educational policy-making?

To get clearer about these questions, we should distinguish between two very different functions of the educational, that is, the "education-delivery", system. Like an army, such a system "marches on its stomach" and can deliver its punch only with the help of many other supplies. It not only hires and trains the teachers--the "troops" who perform the actual teaching--but also provides the other wherewithal required for the teaching/learning process to take place. School boards in charge of the various battalions in this army may thus concern themselves with two very different sorts of issue: with what is to be taught and how it is to be got across to the students, but also with how the costs of this activity are to be allocated to various sections of the community and indeed with who is to get how much of the educational pie. The first would seem to be an educational, the second a political, perhaps a moral issue.

Consider, then, the first issue, what is to be taught and how it is to be got across. Reverting to our distinction between three aspects of a culture,

76

the know-how, the know-what, and culture in the narrow sense, it seems that, as far as the first and perhaps also the third aspects go, there is little reason to grant parents a vote on the school board. For presumably on these educational questions, teachers and the educational establishment are better qualified than parents to make sound decisions. There is, of course, no reason why parents, and for that matter students, should not participate in the board's deliberations on such educational issues. They may have original and helpful ideas on such matters, although again teachers through training and experience will presumably be better qualified than parents or students to gauge the usefulness of such concrete suggestions.

The problem is much less tractable in the case of the second, the know-what, aspect of our culture. Until not so long ago, such teaching occurred both within the family and through religious instruction in the school. With the growth of religious tolerance, the decline of religious territorialism, and the disestablishment of the Church, religious teaching disappeared from public schools. Hence moral as well as religious education became the exclusive responsibility of the parents. This has tended to increase tolerance, pluralism and, perhaps, indifference not only on religious but also on moral matters. It seems that the fiercely guarded right of parents to indoctrinate their children in the religion and morality of their choice now goes unexercised quite often and thus many children receive no systematic moral teaching at all. The consciences of such children seem to be unevenly developed, uncertain and weak on many issues, and often formed decisively by the strong emotional pressures of their peer groups rather than by their own or anyone else's rational thinking.

If we thus assume that a significant proportion of children do not now receive from their parents or their Churches any systematic religious or moral education--where that includes sex education--and that this leaves an undesirable void or worse, where firm and sound guidance is needed, then this raises anew the question of whether moral education, at least if it can be of a religiously neutral kind, should be introduced into the school curriculum, and whether parents should have a say in settling this problem, in shaping what should be taught in such courses, and just how it should be put across. Clearly, in this domain, it is not plausible to argue that teachers and the educational establishment are better qualified than parents to provide sound answers. At the same time, it is not clear how teachers are to teach a subject in which they cannot claim <u>any</u> expertise, where they may strongly disagree with the views of some parents, and the parents with one another. It should be apparent, even after these few words, that this issue is too complex and rests on too many uncertainties to be profitably examined here.

4. Responsibility for general education. Even more difficult is the problem of the second function of the educational system, the determination of who gets what schooling and who pays for the provision of such education. The solution to this problem must take appropriate cognizance of a large number of important normative principles which are in competition with one another, including the principles emphasized by the organizers of this Conference: social responsibility and individual freedom. How do they enter into our question?

Our society is organized on the basis of the division of labor. This greatly increases our efficiency and so our ability to satisfy our needs, but it also tends to increase inequality among the members of our society. For different types of work, involving different kinds of skill, tasks, and conditions of work, mean different prospects of life. A physician, a business executive, a professional soldier, a teacher, a trucker, or a coal miner must expect to lead very different sorts of lives. Some persons have such a fortunate mix of talents, tastes, and upbringing that they would not desire a different walk of life from that for which they have been fitted. But for many this will not be so. Some people insufficiently equipped for a given career, say, a doctor's, might still rather be doctors than what they are actually talented for. This brings home to us the importance of the principle of fair equality of opportunity. For our society also subscribes to the principle of task-assignment on the basis of merit. That is to say, the available jobs should be given to those competing for them solely on the basis of the job qualifications they have actually acquired. Race, creed, pull, sex, and age are irrelevant to job performance and are therefore improper considerations. An enormous amount thus hangs on education. It is now widely believed that people are in all probability born with different talents and tastes whose full development depends on suitable environmental influences, among the most important of which is the education provided by one's society.

But then it would seem that society does not adequately discharge its task-responsibility to all its members if it does not provide equality of educational opportunity. Only if it does, can differences in job qualifications reflect merely innate differences in talent. If society provides greater educational opportunities for those, say, who live in the affluent suburbs than for those from slums of the cities, then it does something similar to what caste societies do: it condemns some, especially the poor, to the status of unskilled laborers, even those who have the innate talents which would enable them, if they had access to proper schooling, to acquire the qualification necessary for the more rewarding occupations. It would seem, then, that children should have equal access to the social institutions which transmit society's culture and particularly those which transmit those skills and qualifications whose possession is required for those positions in society which enable people to lead worthwhile lives. Thus children should not be excluded from schools on the basis of color, creed, or sex.

But what about innate talent? If it is true, as seems to be the case, that different people are born with a different mix of talents and with different degrees of ability in the talents they do have, at least in the sense that the same amount of training yields unequal results, how are society's resources to be allocated? There is not merely the problem, analogous to that in the area of health-delivery systems, that to maintain an equal level of health, different people require very different amounts of medical resources, hence there is the problem of whether everybody should receive the same amount of medical resources or different amounts to meet his individually different needs? There is also the further problem that for some of the best positions, say, that of a physician, qualifications could be raised to any desired level. Patients may be thought to benefit the higher the qualifications of the licensed physicians. But since there is a limited number of such positions, only a limited number of people can fill them. Thus, those who are competing

79

for them are interested in having a better starting
point than their competitors. Parents who want their
children to be doctors have an interest in seeing to
it that not too many others have the necessary
qualifications. By contrast, no one has an interest
in others being less healthy than himself. But in the
field of education, many have an interest in keeping
others from being suitably educated. This raises two
very difficult questions: whether people ought to be
permitted or forbidden to improve the starting
position of their own children by sending them to more
expensive and presumably better private schools, and
whether all students attending public schools should
receive the same amount of public resources for their
education irrespective of their innate talents, or
whether the resources should be expended so as to
yield the same educational results, more being spent
on the less gifted, or whether on the contrary more
resources should be spent on the more talented, to
enable them to excel even more. Of course, these may
not be the only alternatives. One could maintain that
the social resources should be spent so that all,
whatever their endowment, would reach a certain
minimal level of all-round competence, that beyond
this each person who wanted to and was capable of
profiting from it, could lay claim to an equal further
amount for higher education, and that beyond that,
those sufficiently talented could, if they wanted to,
receive free or subsidized education in those fields
in which they had earlier demonstrated outstanding
talents. This last solution has a certain
plausibility because while a strong case can be made
for bringing all, even the less talented, to a minimal
level of all-round competence, an equally strong case
can be made for devoting more than average amounts to
the training in some fields of the specially talented.
The rationale for the latter is, of course, that all
may benefit more from such an unequal allocation than
from an equal one.

Fortunately, when the organizers of this
Conference raised the problem of how to reconcile the
claims of individual freedom with those of social
responsibility, they don't seem to have had in mind
this difficult conflict between the social (that is,
society's) task-responsibility for equal educational
opportunity (equal social expenditure for education)
and individual freedom (the individual's right to buy
more education for himself or his children than is
available to the next man). What they had in mind

80

were primarily the claims of social responsibility, that is, of the individual's answerability to society in educational matters and his individual freedom to do as he pleases in matters of education. Let us, therefore, look briefly at the rights of students and teachers in the context of the educational process. What should students be free to do in schools on the ground that the denial of such freedom would stifle their individuality? Are there any comparable freedoms for teachers? And how are such claims to be weighed against the task-responsibilities of their roles?

Individuality is plainly something highly desirable and worthy of cultivation and protection. We want to be ourselves, different from others, not mass products. However, the right to individuality or self-realization--which I take to be the core of the right to individual freedom--is not a blanket license to develop whatever might be in us. No one in his sense would want to claim that if it is in someone's nature to be a mass murderer, a rapist, a con man, a child molester, or a jew baiter, then it would be wrong for teachers not to bring this part of his nature to full bloom. Freud has tuaght us that children are little savages whose socialization and civilization require not only the unfolding of their natural talents and tastes but also the transformation, sublimation, perhaps curbing of some of their innate tendencies. Even if all things considered formal moral education should not be included in the school curriculum, it is plain that schools must give implicit moral training to their pupils. For the partly cooperative, partly competitive enterprise of educating and being educated takes place in an orderly context of regulated interaction between persons who have and exercise authority and persons who recognize and submit to that authority. Such informal and implicit moral training concerns school discipline and its limits, learning to submit to the teacher's authority, to respect him and trust his judgment, but also to ask him probing questions and to subject his opinions to critical tests before accepting them. And it involves also, much more generally, self-discipline, respect for other pupils, considerateness and fairness in competition with them, learning to empathize and sympathize, learning to look at what is happening through other people's eyes, noting and appropriately responding to others' self-centeredness, callousness, cruelty, or meanness, as well as to their generosity, truthfulness, loyalty, or trustworthiness, and learning to detect these vices and virtues in oneself. If the teacher uses his authority to curb the students' obstructive, aggressive, disruptive, or destructive behavior, in a way which helps the pupil to see that she is doing what she herself resents in others when they do it to her, or disapproves of when they do it to her friends, then such constraint cannot be considered a stifling of the students' individuality.

If, on the other hand, the teacher, in teaching a subject, does not allow students to solve the problems he sets for them in any way except the way he has followed himself; if he insists on getting back the answer he has spelled out without allowing any variations even if they are inventive or show that the student is trying to think for herself, then that is stifling the student's individuality.

The distinction I am trying to draw is one that is often made. It is between laying down and enforcing clearly defined rules of conduct necessary for a smoothly working learning process and allowing the learning process itself to be flexible, leaving the maximum room for student exploration, experimentation, initiative and innovation. The teacher may and should use his authority to enforce the rules of conduct governing the behavior of students towards one another and the teacher. But he should not discourage students in matters of intellect. He should encourage them to attempt different and new ways of finding solutions to the problems posed to them.

My suggestion is that there is no deep conflict, in the context of the teacher-student relationship, between social responsibility and individual freedom or individuality. The social responsibility of the teacher, though not that of the school and the educational hierarchy, is very limited. It is the task-responsibility of teaching the students the subjects of the school curriculum. In that role he is not infringing on the student's individual freedom or their individuality if he maintains discipline, that is, enforces the rules of discipline which are necessary for the smooth working of the teaching/learning process.

There may, of course, be considerable differences of opinion about just what these rules are--whether the pupils must sit still at their school desks without talking to one another, or whether movement, talk, play, and other activity is compatible with the learning process and so permissible. These details should, I think, be worked out by teachers, whose experience with children of different ages and backgrounds provide them with the empirical evidence required for the answer. What is important is that there should be no constraints which are not needed for or at least helpful in making the teaching/learning process successful, that the pupils should know the rules, that the rules should be applied equally and fairly to all of them, and that the pupils should, if at all possible, be made to see their importance for the success of the teaching/learning process. All this is said on the assumption that children already have a minimal motivation to learn. I have no constructive ideas about those schools where children arrive in the morning filled with frustration, aggression, and resentment, and where the teacher must spend most of his time coping with their rebellion, alienation, and anomie. In such conditions, schools are little more than prisons in which children are locked up and incapacitated for several hours of the day so that they are prevented from plaguing their mothers or the adults who would otherwise have to share the streets and neighborhoods with them. With regard to such schools, there is little point in discussing the niceties of where the school's authority infringes on students' individuality or their freedom.

Finally, it is clear that a parallel distinction applies to the question of the individual freedom of teachers in relation to their answerability to their principals and to the higher ranks in the educational hierarchy. There must be rules of discipline for teachers, telling them clearly what their duties and responsibilities are and how these rules will be enforced. Obviously, teachers must be required to keep to their timetables, to give their assigned courses, to grade students papers, to talk to their students also out of class time, and in general to carry out their part of the educational plan built into the school curriculum. Duties and responsibilities such as these do not infringe on the individuality or the freedom of the teacher. In intellectual matters, by contrast, the school authorities should be flexible and should encourage the teacher to find his own way of presenting the material, design his own courses within the confines of the general plan, experiment with new techniques provided there are good reasons for thinking that these innovations might succeed better than the officially approved methods, and so on. Of course, in such experimentation, the teacher must exercise judgment and responsibility. And if the school authorities have reason to think that his innovative techniques are harebrained, they should try to convince him of this and if he is unreasonable and stubborn, they may have to warn him against using such techniques and perhaps fire him if he persists. It is in this intellectual area that the teacher's responsibility to the school authorities may sometimes conflict with his individuality and his legitimate individual freedom.

RESPONSIBILITY AND FREEDOM IN THE SCHOOL

Kurt H. Wolff

A sequel to a recent session of a graduate
seminar made me realize that one of the teacher's
responsibilities is to be aware of students' feelings
in class. I returned to my office after that session
when a student, who had presented a paper in the area
of the philosophy of science, knocked at my door; as
soon as she entered I noticed that she was upset. She
"felt stupid," she said, because a term she had not
understood was so easily made clear by a few words of
explanation -- it was a household word to students of
philosophy, which she was not. But there was more:
"such a competitive spirit in the class"; she reminded
me of a student who in today's meeting had sharply
objected to another's interruption. This I did
remember -- as I did my twinge because I myself had
not insisted that people be allowed to finish what
they were saying. My visitor, now calmer, continued,
however: she led that competitive atmosphere back to
the very first session, when I had answered a student
in an overhasty, brusque manner.

There -- I had been teaching for many years, and
still such a thing could happen -- and how many times
had it happened before? Maybe I had even been told
about it by a student but had forgotten or suppressed
it; or I hadn't been told, and if I hadn't, it might
have been for all kinds of reasons: perhaps the
students didn't care, or they just accepted teachers
and classrooms, or they didn't have the courage to
confront me, or they made their peace with the sort of
person I was -- whatever. In any event, I hadn't
known and I didn't know but I should have known.

Clearly, or so it seemed to me, my failure to
notice what had been going on was irresponsible, a
failure of responsibility; I did not meet my
responsibility as a teacher. I failed to respond --
to my students, to my position as teacher, to the
demands of the classroom and of education. For
"responsibility" means the responding, proper to a
given situation and type of situation, to given people
and types of people; what "proper" is being determined
by the role, the rights and duties, of an individual

85

and type of individual. For instance, the teacher is responsible, or acts responsibly, by responding to the people he or she is typically associated with -- students, colleagues, administrators, parents, etc. The student who visited me made me aware of having fallen short of one of my responsibilities, the responsibility of not hurting my students, of being sensitive to them, aware of the "atmosphere" of the classroom, noticing its tendency to deteriorate, anticipating and preventing such deterioration.

This is a very general as well as largely formal statement of a teacher's responsibility; the only thing substantive was my violation. On the other hand, the setting in which the incident had occurred was quite specific: not all responsibilities in a graduate seminar can be generalized to all teaching situations. I thus have two tasks here -- aside from my other theme, freedom: to flesh out the responsibility of the teacher of graduate students, and that of other kinds of teachers, from undergraduate to elementary school. A third task is complementary: to articulate the responsibilities of different kinds of students. But teachers and students are not the only types of people or roles typical of the institution of teaching; obviously -- and I mentioned it before -- there also are parents, school officers other than teachers, and relevant public officials. Neither the time at my disposal on this occasion nor my knowledge allows me to discuss all of this. I feel least incompetent in an effort to clarify my thought on the responsibility of the teacher of graduate and undergraduate students and on the responsibility of those students themselves. I hope, of course, that this will stimulate others to test what I have to say against their own competencies in order to find out whether it can be applied, with whatever modifications may be necessary, to the analysis of their teaching situations.

What I am going to offer comes from my long teaching experience and is bound to reflect it. It is a talk to colleagues, with colleagues, most of them in other types of schools, and it will lead, I hope, to talking together so that we can perceive more clearly what is the case.

In order for you to learn something about the basis of my reflections so that you can see where I come from and can judge better what I am going to

submit, I'll say that I have taught for more than
fifty years -- as a teenager tutoring younger fellow
students; after leaving Germany in 1933, at two
boarding schools in Italy, first in one founded by a
fellow German Jewish refugee for refugee children,
both boys and girls, then in an Italian boarding
school for boys; after 1939, in this country, a year,
during World War II, at a small coeducational Quaker
college, then for 14 years at Ohio State, and since
1959, at Brandeis; in between, I was a visitor for a
year at the University of Rome, and for a semester
each at the Universities of Freiburg, Frankfurt, and
Paris.

What the painful incident I reported made sharply
clear to me is what had struck me on and off and with
increasing force for a long time: that a prerequisite
of good teaching and learning is that there be no
problems in the relations between students and
teacher. That is, if there are problems -- tensions,
questions about those relations, distrust, suspicion,
disrespect, feelings between students or a given
student and the teacher which are irrelevant to the
matter of teaching and learning, no matter how
important they may be personally -- there are just as
many impediments. It is tempting to say that the
teacher's first responsibility is to create
confidence, and I think this is desirable. But I also
think that it is far more important for the teacher to
arouse the wish to learn and, moreover, to learn
critically, in which case confidence comes by itself.
To this responsibility for critical teaching and
learning I shall come back because I believe it is
more urgent than any other. It follows that
confidence is to be wished for if it flows from or is
combined with this prime responsibility -- but after
all, it may not: a teacher may inspire confidence but
no spirit of critical learning -- by being a mother or
a father, soothing, a good chum, or just somebody
acceptable or at least accepted. In my experience,
the best classes have been those in which we all, the
students and I, were engaged in a collective
enterprise of learning and exploring. I trust that
all teachers can recall such marvelous meetings. What
happens then is that both students and teacher are
transformed from the persons they ordinarily are into
persons exhaustively identifiable as seekers after
what to the best of their consciousness and conscience
they cannot help but believe to be true. I think this
is the ideal of the teaching situation, of teacher and

student and their cooperation -- but it is the ideal, and in reality is rarely approximated. When it does happen it is wonderful and makes teaching worth its less positive characteristics.

In fact, this ideal goes beyond teaching, and in two senses, one more radical than the other. The less radical sense is that on such unusual occasions something that I am almost always aware of strikes me with special clarity: that at this time in our history, "teacher" is a title of colossal arrogance. I may know more about certain matters, such as sociology, than some or even all of my students, but they know more than I do about certain other matters, above all about their own outlook, mood, understanding of our world and time or their bafflement by them. But all of us share in the ignorance concerning what we may reasonably expect of the future, although there are very great differences in the awareness of such ignorance and in the scope of that future, the latter if only because of our differences in age. Obviously, I don't think of a teacher as a mere purveyor of information; if that were the only function, a machine or printed material would be faster and cheaper. I rather think of the teacher as a learner with students, the main difference between the two being that the teacher is more experienced, which is to say more keenly aware and knowing more than they of the glories and the miseries of the world. I fear that at this time in human history, the teacher should try to convey the glories by wishing and trying to make the classroom the occasion on which the marvelous meetings I have alluded to may take place. But then there is the second, more radical sense in which such a meeting goes beyond teaching, and this is that it cannot be brought about even with the best of will and intelligence -- at least not according to my experience. It is more like grace.

So much, or so little, about the prerequisite of good teaching and learning which is that there be no problems in the relations between students and teacher. I have indicated already what I mean by good teaching and learning, at least here and now -- but that, after all, is where we are: to arouse in the students the desire to learn critically. To learn what? And why critically? To learn the human tradition and the human traditions -- a few aspects of a few of them: history, and not just Western; natural

and social sciences; humanities, again not just
Western -- for our traditions distinguish us from
other animals. And why critically? Because in
comparison with what we can visualize -- and we can
visualize it precisely because our traditions have
taught or at least can teach it to us -- because in
comparison with what we can visualize, all human
societies have fallen short of being good societies,
and our own, not the United States alone but our
global society, is the most endangered and the most
dangerous of all ever. It is so dangerous because by
virtue -- or I should say, by vice -- of certain of
our traditions, above all the uncontrolled if not,
precisely, uncontrollable development of technology
which is not sufficiently contained and accompanied by
a corresponding development in intelligence and
morality, this global society has the knowledge needed
to obliterate itself. For the first time in human
history, humankind has the capacity to end its life,
along with the planet on which this life flourished,
and it often seems tempted by this new facility, this
novel opportunity: sometimes it looks as if the
possibility invited its realization by its mere
existence.

    If this is where we find ourselves, it obviously
has a consequence for the teacher's responsibility:
it is that whatever the tradition may be that the
teacher is teaching, it must be taught critically.
For it is true that we are our traditions; but it is
also true that our traditions have brought us to our
unprecedentedly critical situation. The teacher must
practice and teach critical thinking; the two terms,
critical and thinking, are equally important; here, in
fact, I use them to mean the same thing; toward the
end of my remarks I will say something about thinking
more generally and thus be able to make my present
argument clearer. Students have to learn to think,
and here to add the word "critical" is really
redundant, because not to think critically is not to
think at all but to engage in some other activity,
such as recollecting, wondering, dreaming, fearing,
despairing, being happy or hopeful or skeptical or,
the worst caricature of thinking, regurgitating what
has been learned by rote. (Let me make clear that I
don't rule out rote-learning, for I see a place for it
as a means to facilitate thinking, to acquire some
knowledge about which thinking then is possible.
Rote-learning is deadly only if it is taken to be
thinking.) Another way of talking about the teacher's

foremost responsibility is to say that he or she must impart to students a critical attitude toward tradition, instead of an uncritically accepting one. This is by no means to impart a disrespectful, let alone a cynical attitude, but rather an ambiguous one, for the more deeply we respect a tradition, the more deeply we must criticize it in the light of what it has led to or has at least not been able to prevent us from arriving at; and if we didn't care, we wouldn't bother to criticize it, just as we wouldn't criticize ourselves and those we love, including our students, if we didn't care for ourselves and them.

But are we _free_ so to teach, so to discharge our responsibility? You can see by this question how intimately related responsibility and freedom are. There are all kinds of restrictions on our freedom so to teach, and I am sure all of us here or anywhere else have experienced one or more of them -- or are experiencing them. The first freedom necessary to be a teacher in the sense I have suggested is that the teacher _himself_ or _herself_ can and wishes to think critically. That is, the first restriction of this freedom may lie in the teacher's upbringing (an external condition) or personality (an internal condition) itself. This is the most serious restriction of freedom, above all because the teacher may not know it, and because there may be reasons other than lack of contact with those who might alert him or her to it, such as the lack of any idea of thinking critically or fear of it or doubt of its possibility or usefulness. It is a serious question whether such teachers occupy the best place they can find in society and society can find for them, or whether another place would be a better match and more useful for society at large. The same, of course, applies to students -- as every teacher knows, e.g., students who "haven't got it" or are unsure of themselves or would rather sit it out than learn and learn critically, despite all efforts to improve them: they, too, might be better off elsewhere, and the

---

Here a question may arise: that of the relation between the critical thinking under discussion and the critical thinking advocated and exemplified by the so-called Frankfurt School's "Critical Theory." There is no difference -- except, perhaps, that compared with the former the latter takes a broadly Marxian basis more for granted.

elsewhere might be better off for it than the school is.

But in so far as "thinking hurts," there is a contradiction between the teacher's responsibility not to hurt students and that of trying to make them think. This contradiction is the teacher's perennial occupational burden. The burden is to know how far to push a student; the greater this knowledge, the more accomplished the art of teaching and the more significant the students' learning. The teacher's failure, by contrast -- pushing too little or too hard -- shows in the students' flight from learning into, e.g., political activism or, far worse, cynicism or despair.

Very different kinds of dangers to the freedom of teacher and student come from the outside rather than from themselves: they want to teach and learn critically but are restricted in exercizing this responsibility. I need not elaborate, for the dangers are clear, just as the strategies are clear, whereas the tactics must be developed from case to case, empirically. The danger may come from any and all of the types of individuals, institutions, and agencies that have anything to do with teaching -- from students themselves, other teachers, pressure groups, government at all levels. The required tactics are likely to be frustrating but also are a test of one's capacity of critical thinking in an actual, concrete situation. The fight against infringements, real or threatened, usually is a power struggle which is decided by matters extraneous to the issue at hand rather than by persuasion, that is, rationally.

It may be useful to hear and talk about actual cases of infringements of freedom, of violations of the teachers' exercise of their responsibilities, and we might have a discussion of such cases. My own contribution had better be devoted to a more theoretical problem which, I suspect, will speak to many of you who have listened thus far. You may have resented the abstractness of what I have said. If so, there is justice in such resentment. I have been abstract, I have not talked to concrete situations or suggested concrete policies. This has to do with the extreme gratification I have occasionally experienced -- I referred to it earlier as "marvelous meetings," where "both students and teacher are transformed from the persons they ordinarily are into persons exhaustively identifiable as seekers after what to the best of their consciousness and conscience they cannot help but believe to be true." I added that I called such a situation the ideal of the teaching situation which in reality is rarely approximated. One reason for the impression of abstractness that I may have given is that I don't know whether this ideal is even more remote from reality or is, on the contrary closer to it if the students are younger, in high-school or grade school. I should very much like to hear about this and hope the discussion will make it possible, and we can understand each other better. What I suspect is that my request for critical thinking must be translated so as to be more usable in the teaching of younger students. I think the basic question in this respect is at what age and in what fashion a critical attitude can be taught. One might argue that children have first to learn something before they can be critical of it. No matter how plausible this sounds, I believe it wrong, for what it in fact recommends is that first acceptance and then questioning be learned; and once the matter is thus formulated, the procedure is shown to make for confusion and thus loses all justification.

This becomes clearer when the nature of my recommendation of critical thinking itself gets clearer. Above all, as we well know from our own lives, critical thinking cannot be anybody's only activity, and so it cannot be the only activity even of those whose main endeavor, as I have urged, it should be, that is, teachers' and students'. Even in school, thinking unremittingly is unbearable and would therefore be hated -- it would be self-defeating. As the only food, reality is indigestible; too strong, it must be interspersed with lighter nutrients, which are enjoyed for their own sake. Less metaphorically: thinking must be interspersed with or accompanied by the arousal and satisfaction of three human needs. One is intellectual curiosity -- met by studying science, literature, history, languages. Here the teacher's responsibility is to heighten and refine the curiosity the students bring to class rather than reducing or destroying it. Another is a creative urge, to be satisfied by practicing and learning about the fine arts, and here the teacher's responsibility is to heighten and refine such an urge -- again, rather than diminishing or extinguishing it. Finally, the student's bodies must be nurtured by exercise as well as indirectly, by information.

92

The translation of this idea into practice is fraught with difficulties. Even if a single teacher were competent to undertake all these tasks -- as none can be -- it would be bound to be a matter of doing one's best, given the actual circumstances in which it has to be done. No wonder, therefore, that teaching is referred to as an art, in the same sense in which politics is so referred to -- and this is a second reason mentioned in this paper for calling it an art. But the matter is even more complicated because practically no teacher is in the position just visualized; instead, he or she is one among other teachers and, moreover, lives in necessary relations with additional persons, as well as offices, in the school, the wider educational system, the community. All of them, as we said before, may impinge on teachers' freedom to proceed even to the best of their knowledge.

But there is another reason why my talk, compared with such stubborn concrete questions and problems, may sound abstract or even ignorant of what teaching, schools, teachers, and students really are like. This second reason is that what I have referred to as thinking or critical thinking is by its very nature, necessarily, far removed from everyday life, including the everydayness of school teaching and school learning. For thinking is a solitary process. While I think, I am talking with myself, and this is incompatible with anybody's listening in. Perhaps we can say that what is so marvelous about those classroom situations I have mentioned is that they are occasions of thinking together, of the genuine Socratic dialogue (in contrast to the sense, or rather nonsense, in which this it seems irresistible word is so often misused today). Such thinking-together is a form of love and competes only with physical love , I believe, for the highest kind of human relation possible. In it, we are, as I repeated before, exclusively seekers after what we cannot help but believe to be true -- in short, truth -- just as in physical love we are wholly transformed into lovers. We may also say that in thinking-together we are talking with one another with a purity characteristic of my talking with myself when I think in solitude.

But what is the relation between my emphasis on critical thinking and what I just said about thinking in general? Recall that I suggested that I used the term "critical thinking" as redundant for "thinking" pure and simple -- but that was in the sense of the teacher's foremost responsibility today, given the time in our history in which we live and which I tried to characterize in its unprecedentedness. <u>At this time, in school, from grade to graduate, critical thinking is synonymous with thinking in view of the kind of society in which humankind finds itself.</u> This is to say, we must learn and we must teach to understand and criticize this society because otherwise we lose, at the very least, our capacity to think in solitude, even if we should survive physically. And since it is teachers who have the extraordinary institutionalized responsibility of bringing up the new generation, they more than anybody else also have the responsibility of trying their best in their attempt at inspiring students to think critically. Indeed, I suppose it won't come as a surprise -- but I hope as a small joy, a joy of recognition -- to proclaim, and to urge, that the discharge of this responsibility is the teacher's purest and surest freedom: here, freedom and responsibility are one.

SCHOOL AS COMMUNITY/SCHOOL AS INSTITUTIONS

Of the dilemmas and conflicts that face schools perhaps the least debated has had to do with questions of 'community'. (Interestingly of the three great demands issued by the French revolution and by all revolutions since, Liberty, Equality and Fraternity - the latter has always been given the least attention). Perhaps, our overwhelming concerns for efficiency, productivity and order have seemed to preclude any organizational form other than those that lead to a depersonalized bureaucracy. Yet a great many people continue to express a yearning for human interactions that allow for mutuality and a sharing of responsibility. Such people continue to look for social arrangements that might facilitate dialogue, participation and fellowship while, at the same time, meeting institutional purposes. Within this context the conference considered how we might balance our concern that schools be humane with the concern that schools be efficient, orderly and productive. Is it possible to expect that schools are able to provide a sense of community and at the same time meet the demands of public accountability?

Of crucial importance to Elizabeth and Melvin Keiser is the reconciliation of the 'communal' with the 'institutional'. While they say the latter focuses on the 'pursuit of purposes', the former defines us as 'participants in the fellowship of dialogue'. In their paper they argue that while reconciliation of the two is always a precarious thing that needs to be constantly worked at, it remains a possibility. In educational institutions, as elsewhere, responsiveness to both requires that the acheivement of purpose not violate the mutuality of fellowship. Hierarchy, they say, should not be the means for discovering truth but only for organizing operations: 'Truth should arise in fellowship and be implemented through hierarchy.'

For Gibson Winter schooling in the industrial world inculcates the need of conformity appropriate to the 'impervious system of production'. It is the path to alienation and subordination; a preparation for the techno-economic system which has weakened the personal bonds in local communities reducing every bond to a cash nexus. In such societies, says Winter, an 'organicist communalism' (in the forms of fascism or national chauvinism) becomes a substitute for freedom. In seeking another direction for education in our society he offers the 'liberating metaphor' of the work of art. Through this metaphor we may begin to ask whether the structures of our economic, social and political life disclose or conceal the meaning of humanity; whether they disclose truth, justice, goodness and human community in the way we live, work, play and celebrate. Such an image, he says, provides a helpful context for reflecting on the real tasks of teaching and learning.

95

RECONCILING COMMUNITY AND INSTITUTION:

AN EXPLORATION OF OUR METAPHORIC ROOTS

Elizabeth B. Keiser and R. Melvin Keiser

Community and institution, considered in the context of school practice, are almost invariably experienced as opposites. The communal values of fellowship, where students and teachers can feel at home in learning together and can be mutually responsible, are set over against hierarchical authority and the functional necessities of group life shaped by purposes which take precedence over persons. We know we live in schools as institutions; we do not know whether we can make them communities as well. As teachers and administrators we spend much of our time maintaining institutional operations. Even as we hope for our schools to become communities, we doubt that there is time and energy enough to work on this beyond what school as institution requires of us. More insidiously, we suspect there is an unmitigable recalcitrance in the institutional to the nurturing of the communal. Is there some way in our classrooms and schools in which we can achieve a reconciliation of these apparent opposites? Is there some way in which we can maintain our group existence and yet grow as individuals in a shared life together?

Beyond the nature of institutions as such, we live within a world. Our sense of the total environment in which we teach and administer shapes significantly our institutional work. While this "sense" is largely unconscious, something we live out of rather than reflect upon, it comes to expression in various metaphors. An American philosopher, in an

---

For an illuminating exploration of the nature of community and institution, see the Gifford Lectures for 1953, by the late Scottish philosopher, John Macmurray, THE FORM OF THE PERSONAL (vol. 1, THE SELF AS AGENT, vol. 2, PERSONS IN RELATION [London: Faber and Faber Limited, 1957 & 1961]), especially volume 2, pp. 157-165.

inspired phrase, has called such images, that give us a sense of the whole in which we live, "root metaphors." To obtain that reconciliation of opposites, to establish community in our schools and classrooms, we need to view these apparent opposites within a larger context as it comes to expression in root metaphors. As we explore in them the way we imagine ourselves inhabiting the world, we can discover the place of community in our institutional lives.

Many of our root metaphors, however, obstruct rather than nourish the communal. To reflect on them means to recognize the depersonalizing impact of many of our master images from which we take our cues. We will consider three intrinsic to modern Western consciousness, and therefore very much involved in our academic work. We will then explore another guiding image of our being in the world that founds and fosters the personal.

I. Three Root Metaphors

The three depersonalizing images are the machine, war, and the dichotomy of form and matter. In each of these the given term is joined with self and world so they are seen under its aspect. In the first one, the world is seen as a system of cause and effect, the self as a product of causal determinants. Isaac Newton thought explicitly of the world in these terms but we are usually unaware of its workings in our lives. If we listen to some of our contemporary expressions, we can, however, recognize its presence, in such sayings as: "You turn me on" or "Give me some feedback."

Under the hegemony of this mechanistic metaphor we treat our students as products of a causal system and ourselves as its regulators. What students learn we think of as standardized, interchangeable parts. A good school puts together more parts faster. The aim becomes efficient productivity; every student plays his part in contributing to the functioning of the system. Such a perspective depersonalizes education because students and teachers have no sense of

---

See Stephen Pepper, WORLD HYPOTHESES (Berkeley: The University of California Press, 1961).

participating in a _telos_ more significant than the efficient functioning of the system itself; they learn, we teach, the how but not the why. There is no sense of human agency here, no responsivility for articulating and evaluating one's own aims. Moreover, the group functioning takes precedence over individuals realizing their uniqueness in relation to other individuals. Alienation of students from each other, from their teacher, from their work is accepted as inevitable in this system. Grades substitute for personal satisfaction and shared creativity.

Under the impress of the second root metaphor, war, we experience the world as a battlefield within which we must aggressively assert ourselves in the pursuit of our own self-interests even while defending against similar incursions of others. In the sociopolitical world Thomas Hobbes spoke of this competitive struggle as "the war of all against all." For him in such a perpetual state of warfare only a strong sovereign can molify atomistic self-interest through the imposition of laws. Capitalism is an optimistic variation of Hobbes' image. For Adam Smith there is an "invisible hand" guiding all the individualistic pursuits in a free market toward a harmony good for all.

When we consider our lives as educators in a society shaped partly by this metaphor, we recognize how much we motivate individuals to define themselves by attacking, or defending against, other individuals. The give and take of ideas is here understood in terms of cut and thrust, a polemic debate where an exaggerated emphasis is placed upon the way in which one's point of view differs from and can defeat someone else's ideas. The stress is on the individual, rather than on the self as a part of a larger whole; on conflict, rather than on cooperation; and on success, rather than on opening to others and groping towards new insight. Education is a tournament for heroes. There is no room for the ordinariness of our living and learning, and failure is anathema. As in trench warfare, to survive in the midst of such conflict, we must as students and teachers cultivate the belief that it will always be the other person who is shot down. As teachers either we live in the optimistic expectation that some miraculous bonding will occur through the guidance of an "invisible hand" which will bring good for all our students out of such competition, or we assume the role of Hobbes' strong sovereign imposing order on the unruly mob.

In the third metaphor, the dichotomy of form and matter, we go back behind the Enlightenment period in which these first two metaphors have made their impact and come to the roots of Western sensibility. In Plato, and especially Aristotle, we find an extensive development of the relation between form and matter, which is given modern articulation by Descartes in the distinction between mind and body, and more recently in terms of subject and object. In this metaphor the world is seen as stuff that is meaningless and inert, and in need of shaping and controlling by the form-giving capacity of the human mind or spirit. The world as object is passive; the self as subject is active, imposing order on what fundamentally lacks order. We understand ourselves as craftsmen who can freely choose an end, make a plan to achieve it, and manipulate matter accordingly. Ingredient in this view is the assumption of the superiority of the agent and the inferiority of the patient, that which is acted upon.

Informed by this metaphor we conduct our classes as if students are formless matter and we the teachers and administrators are the formative agency. We assume a resistance in the matter of their lives and minds, but no responsibility or creativity. We place confidence in our own minds, however, to devise and plan and to bring them, even though reluctantly, into conformity with it. There is no recognition of equality but only of our own authority, no nurturing of creative interplay but only the exercise of our own manipulative skills. While there may be cooperation between agent and patient in this form-making endeavor, there is no mutuality of an opening and shared existence together.

Each of these three root metaphors has been extraordinarily fruitful in Western culture. The image of the machine has motivated much of our achievement in scientific understanding; war and competition has underlain much of our socioeconomic, political, and technological success; and form/matter has engendered our creative and rational capacities to reform society, harness the energies of the earth to facilitate living and communicating, and illumine rational and active aspects of ourselves. But each has serious limitations; separately and intertwined

100

together they have been destructive of the personal in our existence. The machine as metaphor has encouraged our denial of freedom and responsibility, war our alienation from the mutuality of fellowship, and form/matter our exploitation of inferior and passive matter, whether exemplified by woman, Black, nonwesterner, or the earth itself. We have already suggested some of the ways each of these metaphors obstructs our efforts reaching toward community in our schools; they are very much a part of the fabric of our lives in the 20th century West, for good or ill. Nevertheless, there is another root metaphor at work in us which, if recognized and allowed to emerge by our living more fully into it, can significantly reorient us toward the personal (while maintaining much that is of value in the other metaphors). To this we now turn.

II. The Root Metaphor of Responsibility

Present in our experience of the last one hundred and fifty years is the image of the world as a process of interaction, what we sometimes now call an eco-system. The great American theologian of our century, H. Richard Niebuhr, speaks of it as a complex network of action and reaction, and sees the self inhabiting such a world as responding constantly within this interaction, as a "responsible self."

To arrive at an understanding of this image of world let us investigate our own being. What is our real community, the environment we live in? Born of two people, is our real community the family? But the family exists within a larger society, within a state, a region, a country. The country exists within a still larger grouping--humanity. We are not only members of a family and citizens of a country, we are members of the human race. But humanity exists within a still larger environment--what some thinkers call the biosphere, life itself. If we move in such a dialectical way in search of our true environment, we

There is an as yet unrealized suggestiveness for educational reflection in the theological work of H. Richard Niebuhr, especially in THE RESPONSIBLE SELF: AN ESSAY IN CHRISTIAN MORAL PHILOSOPHY (New York, Evanston, and London: Harper & Row, 1963), to whom we are richly indebted in these musings.

so often stop here. But we are becoming more aware in
our   day   that   we   also   dwell   within   a   natural
environment of earth and sky and sea.   And beyond
these we inhabit the cosmos of far-flung stars,
galactic dust, and many things we cannot fathom.   Is
not the universe the real community we live in, what
we might call the community of being?

My   real   community   is   not   only   spatially
inclusive; it is temporal as well. My real community
extends backwards to my origins and forwards to my
end.   My origins fit within a past that goes back to
the beginnings of my country's history, the origins of
humanity, of organic life, to the ultimate origins of
the cosmos.   And my future end fits within the future
ends of country,   humanity, life, and the whole
cosmos.   The world is, therefore, the totality within
which we exist as selves, expanding spatially to the
community of all being, and extending backwards and
forwards to the beginning and ending of the cosmos.
In Niebuhr's words the world is "a society whose
boundaries cannot be drawn in space, or time, or
extent of interaction, short of a whole in which we
live and move and have our being."

Entering this world of interaction at birth, the
self, illumined from the perspective of the metaphor
of responsibility, is acted upon and responds to these
actions,   learning more mature ways to do so as time
goes on. Responses occur at many levels: biological,
psychological, economic, cultural, physical. While we
may focus our attention on one level in the moment,
other responses are occurring simultaneously at
different levels, so that most of our responses are
unconscious.   Response   to   action   involves
interpretation. Through largely unconscious metaphors
woven deep into our lives we image the spatial and
temporal   context   of   these   actions.   Only   by
remembering past actions, anticipating future ones,
and answering the broader challenge of the present can
we   understand and respond fittingly to each action.
If, for instance, we image the context as inimical or
beneficient,   or as mechanistic, competitive,   or
rationally formative, we will respond accordingly.
That is to say, this fourth metaphor discloses the
presence of root metaphors in our depths shaping our
thought and action.   The responsible self, therefore,

Niebuhr, THE RESPONSIBLE SELF, p. 88.

holds itself accountable for its responses in terms of their fittingness to the totality imaged in our lived metaphors, and for the adequacy of our metaphoric grasp of the full community of being we dwell within.

In the metaphor of responsibility, the world, in contradistinction to the other three, is more complex. Each of the three reduces reality, either to a monism (there is only one kind of reality and it is mechanistic) or dualism (there are two types of reality: form and matter or friend and foe). Responsibility recognizes, however, a mulitiplicty of realities active on various levels. This is a dynamic world. The self enters a field of interaction already going on. Unlike form/matter, the self is a responder, not an originator. Viewing ourselves as a formative intellect, we begin with inert matter rather than something pressing upon us; after making a plan, we begin to shape materials to conform. There is the assumption of a control and freedom here to arrange and do as one wills, whereas as responsible selves, we are from the first challenged by actions beyond our control, and in responding we must anticipate future reactions to what we do. Our activity and freedom is always a limited one, forever responsive, in more or less fitting ways, to meaning or forms making their impacts upon us. But these impacts are actions and not determinants. While this is a limited freedom, it is freedom. In the mechanistic metaphor things happen as a result of prior causes. In the fourth metaphor an action leaves room for a response, which can be of various sorts depending upon the interpretation of the action in its context. There is then a total activity attributed to the self in the form/matter metaphor and a total passivity in the machine image. In thinking of ourselves as responsible, we exist within the dynamic but limited field of interaction as both receptive and responsive. The war metaphor is closer to responsibility in this regard since it also envisages a field of interaction, but it is exclusively a battlefield. Where the responsible self is receptive the warrior is defensive, where the former is responsive in countless ways, the latter's reaction is always to control and ultimately to defeat the other.

For Niebuhr's explanation of the characteristics of responsibility, see Niebuhr, THE RESPONSIBLE SELF, pp. 61-65.

The unconscious is important in this fourth metaphor as the place where much of the responding goes on. There is no place for it in the image of the machine. The formative process is usually seen as executing a rational plan although it can move towards the recognition of the unconscious in the creative process, but to the extent it does, it moves away from the salient feature of control of chaotic matter. While the war metaphor may acknowledge unconsciousness as a base for self-interest, it focuses our attention upon the conscious strategy of attack and defense. Within the unconscious, the responsibility metaphor illumines the presence of root metaphors shaping our lives. It makes explicit the importance of language in our lives: to be responsible is to respond, is to answer. For this reason Niebuhr speaks of the responsible self as one who is always in dialogue--with others, with the surrounding natural environment, with our history, with ourselves, and we would add, with an encompassing mystery. The dynamism, complexity, and largely unconscious nature of the total interaction means that the whole extends beyond what we do know and what we can know. To discover the existence of this circumambient mystery we have only to ask such questions as: Who am I? Where did I come from? What is death? Why is there something rather than nothing?

Here we have a metaphor of the self acting through dialogue in the world that affirms freedom to think and to act, even though a limited one, unlike the image of the machine which denies it altogether. Freedom redefined within responsibility is not what it is in the competitive metaphor: to be an independent individual, able to pursue self-interest unconstrained, measured often by my difference from others. It similarly is not freedom as control, as in the form/matter image: I am free if I can control the formlessness by decision-making, or some other kind of making, intellectual or technological. In responsible freedom I can never be wholly independent because there are all of these actions impinging on me. Nor can I ever be wholly in control because these actions are occurring most of the time beneath the level of consciousness and I am already responding to them beyond my knowing. Freedom in responsibility always exists in the self being involved. Whatever freedom there is comes in the midst of ongoing challenge and response. Greater or less freedom depends on how I respond within such a world. I am more free if I can

104

open to the entire interactional process, rather than compartmentalizing and defending against it. I am more free as I open to the resources of integration, metaphoric and nonverbal, that exist for me in the world that can carry me towards wholeness. The measure of such freedom is not in how different I appear by standing apart, but in the degree to which I respond to all the actions upon me out of a centered, comprehensive self. Uniqueness, and freedom, lie not in detachment but in the manner of my response--not so much in what I do as how I do it.

Within the master image of responsibility we affirm: a self that, although limited, is free, the mutuality of fellowship in a shared communication, and a nonexploitative and equalitarian way of relating. Through it we can understand the presence of other metaphors at work in our lives and embrace many of their virtues. In the war metaphor we can affirm the invigorating ingredient of challenge and response while understanding this to fit into a context that is not destructive or defensive. The machine we can see as a metaphor wielded by selves in our ongoing dialogue with nature which discloses certain important aspects of our being, while not denying the wielder as a self acting responsively. And in the form/matter image we can affirm our rational, formative capacities but founded on an unconscious base and functioning within a system finally beyond our control and comprehension. In this root metaphor of a responsible self dwelling within an interactional world we now have a larger context through which we can move towards reconciling the communal and institutional in our educational lives.

III. Reconciling the Communal and Institutional

Reconciliation does not mean the elimination of one factor or another, nor does it mean the disappearance of several factors in a merger, but a holding together, a harmony that embraces differences. Through the metaphor of responsibility we can see community and institution as each a pattern of response within the whole world and acknowledge the possibility of carrying on both at once through our capacities to respond to different things and at different levels simultaneously. Dwelling in the mutuality of friendship, we can recognize this is but one set of responses in the larger dialogue within the community of being in which we are challenged by and answer to many phenomena that are not our friends, be they social or natural realities. And in pursuing our organizational goals we can similarly see them within the community of being as a certain set of responses that have emerged out of our ongoing dialogue in which we have articulated these purposes as important and befitting our lives. Our dialogue with being may lack the intimacy of friendship but it nevertheless embodies an equality of response. It will lack hierarchical authority but it, nevertheless, elicits our creativity through which we may choose to organize parts of our lives hierarchically to achieve certain ends.

What is crucial here is to understand that both community and institution are modes of thought and action potential in our interactions within the world, that we move to actualize either or both, and that we can be committed to, responsive to, both simultaneously. Even as we consciously focus on the pursuit of purposes, we can be responding tacitly on another level to each of us as participants in the fellowship of dialogue. But this tacit responsiveness requires that we set up openly such goals and such means to achieve them that do not violate the mutuality of fellowship. This means that we must make as part of our goals the maintenance of fellowship. Productivity, for example, is only acceptable as long as it can be pursued while fellowship is sustained. While efficiency is subordinated, involvement is enhanced, maximizing the quality of the goal achieved. To see hierarchy as part of an ongoing dialogue is to understand that authority finally comes from participation in the dialogue rather than hierarchical postiion, from the perceptiveness of the questions asked and the fruitfulness of the answers given. Those at the top should thus be open to insight coming from any level beneath. Hierarchy should not be the means for discovering truth--that is, what to do and be as a group and why--but for organizing operations. Truth should arise in fellowship and be implemented through hierarchy.

How to get established hierarchical authority in an institution to give up its singular control is a major question. Among the various answers we can think of, the perspective of responsibility directs us towards dialogue: to share with others, including the powers that be, what our needs and desires are, to

106

talk even about the need to talk. As we raise such
questions, make such challenges, we should anticipate
and attend to the responses we receive, expecting to
make further responses which will be responded to.
Moreover, we believe there is a power in metaphors:
they can illumine the unfittingness of our present
lives to the larger situation we inhabit, and elicit
our desires to achieve a greater integration of
ourself in the world. Do not our efforts at teaching
manifest some confidence in the power of language to
persuade, to transform? Fellowship, to whatever
degree we have it, can sustain such hope, and the
requisite patience to persevere in the dialogue.

To reconcile community and institution we not
only need to understand that we can be tacitly
responsive to the former while explicitly laboring in
the latter, but that we need times to focus within the
institutional life on the communal. We should become
for a time tacitly responsive to the institutional
procedures as we turn explicitly to talk about our
life together, sharing our desires, hopes, dreams,
fears, experiences as person to person. Within this
context we can stop, for a time, pursuing the purposes
of the institution and reflect upon them, how they fit
within the context of our and the students' lives.
Where reconciliation is happening--always a precarious
thing that needs constant working at--there will be a
frequent shifting of attention back and forth, to the
institutional process and to the communal life; in
other words, there will be dialogue.

IV. Responsibility in the Classroom

What implications are there in this metaphor of
the responsible self existing in an interactional
world for our work in the classroom, and in the school
at large? From this perspective we can see learning
as a mutual search of both teacher and student.

If we see the student as a responsible self, we
realize he or she is already living in midst of a vast
and complex world that is acting upon them to which
they are already responding with some success. There
is creativity in merely being in the world. This
means that students themselves can discover truth.
They are, after all, already making patterns of meaning
in responding to multiple actions upon them without a
teacher. The teacher can assist, or obstruct, this

process, but it is the student's own doing to make sense out of the world or any particular problem in it.

If we see the teacher as a responsible self, we can admit that we too are trying, and succeeding to some degree, to make fitting responses to multileveled actions. The world exceeds our comprehension, so we can have some humility--and not think, as in the form/latter metaphor, that we control the world. Indeed, our own selves exceed our comprehension, since many of our responses are on the unconscious level; we are neither masters of the world nor of ourselves.

The capacities to discover truth and the past success at already having discovered some truth are givens. Students are not formless matter awaiting our formative activity. They are not tabula rasa for us to write upon. Indwelling the metaphor of responsibility, our job as teachers is to provide a place of hospitality. Henri Nouwen, a contemporary theologian at Yale, speaks of ordinary hospitality as providing a space for the guest to exercise freedom and friendship, to become in this situation whatever seems good. We are not only to allow room for what is present in our guest, but to nurture that which is given. What is ultimately given is the world we inhabit. Our job of nurturing is then one of opening the student to the world, of making them more aware of that in which they already live and to which they already respond. Students will open more easily if we exhibit our own openness, if we embody an attitude of awareness of the mystery and complexity that exceeds our grasp.

It was Aristotle who first said knowledge begins in wonder. Taking it however in a different sense than he meant, the responsible self recognizes the world in which it already exists. Rather than approaching the world with critical standards devised by our own minds, as in the metaphor of form and matter, where the patterns come from the formative

_____

See Henri J. M. Nouwen, REACHING OUT: THE THREE MOVEMENTS OF THE SPIRITUAL LIFE (Garden City, New York: Doubleday & Company, 1975), chap. 4, 5, & 6.

Aristotle, METAPHYSICS, Bk I, ch. 2.

agent and not from the subject matter, to know is to respond initially with an awefilled opening to what is there. We can admit that our standards are but one pattern we have created in response to certain aspects of the world. We can have humility in knowing that our teaching is only a small part in a larger context within which we with our students are learners. The encounter of wonder occurs not only in groups and communication but as well in solitude and silence. Too often we escape into togetherness out of fear of these. If teaching is to open us to the wonder at the world that is given, it is also to make a space--in the words of Virginia Woolf, "a room of one's own" -- where each person can get in touch with his or her total environment.

If we share in the mutuality of learning, what then do we teach? We might take a moment to reflect on what we have retained from our own school experience. We have certainly retained something of the subject matters we were exposed to--math, reading, some history, geography, art and science. Much has however been forgotten or supplanted; more than we realize, we suspect, has been woven into our sense of what it is to be we in this world at this time. Learning these subject matters, and retaining whatever we have been able, has been important to our maturing, but there is something more important we have learned of which we are largely unaware. We have been taught in our schooling, and we subsequently teach our own students, an image of self and world. Whatever the subject matter, we are displaying what it is to be a teacher, what adult authority is, what maturity is, and hence what kind of world it is, and correlatively what it is to be a student, a young person, a self aborning in the world.

We teach what it is to be a self in a world by embodying an image. We manifest, however unwittingly, how to respond to the world--in defense or openness; how to relate to ideas--as alluring or threatening; how to respond to each other--competitively or cooperatively. We show rather than tell (to take a

---

See Virginia Woolf, A ROOM OF ONE'S OWN (New York: Harcourt, Barce & World, 1929).

phrase from Wittgenstein) how to relate to time: what to do with the repetitive, the unexpected, our failures, memories, hopes, and the cycles of year that include low energy and ebullient periods. And we teach, or fail to teach, how to learn to go on learning. Finally we teach how to deal with any formal system, be it mathematical, scientific, historical, literary, or artistic. Is it something to be acquired through "block" learning, where the formal pattern is seen as a series of blocks and the student's job is to receive them from the teacher and pile them in the same pattern as the teacher's or textbook's; or is it to be acquired through creativity or discovery?

In a richly suggestive manner Elizabeth Sewell defines this kind of learning: "Discovery, in science and poetry, is a mythological situation in which the mind unites with a figure of its own devising as a means toward understanding the world." Here is underscored the fact that learning necessarily involves commitment, which the block metaphor does not affirm. All formal systems result from people committing themselves to some sort of figures or patterns. You cannot discover more complicated math without investing yourselves in the patterns of simpler arithmetic. Nor can you make discoveries in science without joining yourself to the technological patterns of instruments and the belief in the intelligibility of nature. To <u>understand</u> truly in any field is to be able to <u>stand under</u> the formal system, which is the knowledge <u>in the field</u>, so as to take up the underlying commitments and to take them up in the way in which knowers in that field do it. Our teaching should not simply deal with the results of the process but should engage us in it so that we can become discovers, learning a formal system by learning how to join ourselves with figures in order to arrive

---

See Ludwig Wittgenstein, TRACTATUS LOGICO-PHILOSOPHICUS (London: Routledge & Kegan Paul, 1969), p. 51.

Elizabeth Sewell, THE ORPHIC VOICE: POETRY AND NATURAL HISTORY (London: Routledge & Kegan Paul, 1960), p. 20

at that pattern, and new patterns.

Does the mutuality of learning fostered by the responsibility metaphor mean, however, a lessening of the level of expectation for the student? If we see students as responsible selves, then we see them as already responding and we can expect them to go on. There is an intrinsic value in developing, in stretching, the capacities we have; we feel more ourselves. But there is also a practical value. If the world is as complex as we have suggested, then they need to develop their capacities of response and pattern-making in order to cope with it. We find the world, as we get older, harder to make sense of, so they had better get on with it.

With compassion we nevertheless embody urgency; be tough on them at the same time as we know from our own experience that it is going to be hard. Our responsiveness calls for us to nurture courage and stamina to reinforce our students' inherent fascination and wonder. We are reminded of a paradigmatic moment of such reinforcement between father and son when we were in graduate school. We were living with the chairman of the department of electrical engineering at a prestigous technological university. While renovations were being made in their kitchen, they were eating with us in our third story apartment. One evening the eight year old son asked about the different base systems in arithmetic. Rather than brushing the question aside or simply giving the answer, the father treated it with seriousness and expressed a confidence, as he asked several leading questions, that his son could figure it out. Responding to the questions, the son arrived in good Socratic fashion at the answer, reinforced in his belief that thinking through to an answer can be fun.

Such ease of learning in the face of unexpectedly complex questions does not always happen, of course. If we encounter obstinacy and closed-offness, we can recognize the same in our own self and deal with them as we would deal with ourselves--hopefully with the

---

For further reflection on this subject principally in scientific knowing, see Michael Polanyi, PERSONAL KNOWLEDGE: TOWARD A POST-CRITICAL PHILOSOPHY (London: Routledge & Kegan Paul, 1958.

same compassionate toughness, that is, with forgiveness, humor, and persistence. We are reminded of yet another paradigmatic moment, this time with our own child. While we were on study leaves in England for a year, our daughter became fascinated with horseback riding. Her instructor, Major Cole, was a no-nonsense, handle-bar mustached, dry-witted, former military officer. He was very strict and all the children, including ours, loved him. On several occasions he would tell a rider to turn his or her horse around in a small circle as the group continued around the riding ring (the "school" as they called it). Frequently the horse would, however, continue on its way. The first time Major Cole ordered someone to turn their horse and the horse merrily went on, we were sure he would give the order once or twice again and then let it go, hoping the horse and rider would do better next time. Much to our amazement he persisted in telling the rider to turn the horse, even as the horse continued around the school, until the rider succeeded. This toughness, I realized, was not an insistence on military authority but was born of a compassion for both horse and rider, and of a recognition of the humor of the situation. Had he not held horse and rider to his expectations, the rider would not have learned basic control over his mount and the horse would have learned it could get away with such behavior only to make it more difficult for the next beginning rider. Do not misunderstand this example. We are not suggesting teaching and learning are like a rider gaining control of his horse, but rather that the teacher must have a persistence, a compassionate toughness, in holding students to his or her expectations, befitting, we would add, the abilities of the student in the given situation. The mutuality of learning of responsible selves does not undermine the challenge in education but intensifies it in knowing more fully why we are called to learn and to go on learning.

V.   Responsibility in the School at Large

If it is possible to nurture the communal in the classroom, is it also possible to find a way in the metaphor of responsibility toward the actualization of fellowship in the school at large?

This is a hard question. We as Americans are anti-ritualistic, and yet it is precisely in the times

112

and places of ritual that community can be experienced in our educational institutions. To be sure, this is not the only locus of the communal but is important and indispensable. Colleges have given up chapel and assembly that up until fifteen years ago were regular ways for the whole school to gather. Now there are no moments when the whole school gathers. In primary and secondary education across the nation, we suspect that this is similarly the case. Thinking over the few instances we know of to the contrary: in Quaker schools we have known there is at least one regular moment in which the communal fellowship is embodied-- the silent meeting for worship. In the British village school our daughter attended for a year, there was a morning ritual of an in unison greeting to the head teacher followed by hymn singing.

What would be appropriate secular versions of such gatherings for public schools? Richard Weller, in his position paper for this conference, "The School as Community and the School as Institution," suggests a common meal. Before such an idea is drowned in laughter, you might reflect: here is a time and place where the whole school is, or can be, together. No doubt some money would have to be spent to create an environment in which such a meal could be a positive common experience--carpets on the floor, sound-proofing on the ceiling, pleasing paint on the walls, ways of dividing up the cavernous spaces that would be conducive to human interchange. And there would have to be among both students and teachers education about and common commitment to such an undertaking, why it would be worth trying, what might result from it. Another possibility might be some sort of morning reading for the whole school, not of the forbidden Bible, but of poetry or a short story. Once again efforts would have to be made to elicit the support of teachers and students, rather than having this imposed on them. It might even be possible to use silence, not as a means of meditation or worship, but as a context for imaging. Students are given to fantasying anyway; why not provide a place and offer some assistance to this process so important to intellectual creativity?

Another area within which the communal can be developed is governance. Is there any area where decision-making can be shared in mutuality? There is a Quaker boarding school called the Meeting School where all decisions are made through the Quaker business procedure of gathering a consensus by the entire community of teachers, students, and staff. This is beyond the reach of most, but there are decisions in every school that could be shared with students, making the school more theirs as well as ours, such as dealing with the spaces we inhabit and have to maintain, the time schedules we live according to, the utilization of even minimal financial resources. There are as well more playful ways of participating in the governance of a school so as to own it as ours: we all remember the special day in school when the students took over the responsibility of running the school for a day. Generating such playful opportunities can be largely meaningless, but if taken in earnest as well as a game, they can elicit communal participation beyond the obstructions of hierarchical seriousness.

We are affirming a communal potential in our school institutions, and have made a few suggestions that will perhaps provoke your own reflections of how to begin to actualize some of that potential in the school at large. But should we seek to develop the possibilities of fellowship within our school institutions? Perhaps it is too difficult and not essential anyway to public education? We are arguing, however, that it is essential because we are essentially communal beings as inhabitants of the community of being and because our learning should go on consciously in this widest of environments within which we in fact exist. But apart from the talk of what is "essential," students in junior high, we all know, are going to create community regardless of what we do. We might as well make room within the institutional structures for community in order to engage more rather than less of the energies and creativity of young people within the academic context. Students learn considerably within their own communities. If we deny the communal room in schools, we set academia in opposition to learning rather than seeing it as the nurturer of educational responsiveness.

VI. Responsible Schooling in Society

If, as we are arguing, we teach within a context larger than the institutional character of our schools, indeed within one which extends to the full community of being, then we should reflect as well as

114

upon the larger environment to which we are responding as we seek to actualize community and institution together in our classroom and schools. How can we be responsive to our society even as we seek the fitting in our academic learning? This is a vast topic; we simply want, in conclusion, to indicate a direction suggested by our metaphor of responsibility.

We might reflect for a moment on the movie "Walkabout." It is an Australian film about an adolescent girl and her younger brother who find themselves lost in the desert and through the friendly assistance of a male adolescent aborigine find their way back to their white culture. A complex and profound movie, it is basically about initiation rites. The aborigine is spending a year by himself as the rite of passage from childhood into the adult world. The white young woman is roughly of the same age and in passage from desert to what we call civilization. Both young man and young woman are faced with initiation into adulthood, and both fail. The young man offers marriage to her; when rejected, he commits suicide. The young woman, while she makes it safely back to her home with her brother, is unaffected by the experience except for a momentary nostalgic idealization of the Edenic existence she might have shared with the aborigine had she not returned and entered a traditional civilized, impoverished marriage.

It is a powerful film, well worth further reflection. We bring it to mind to dramatize the period of life that junior high students are going through. It is the period of initiation from childhood into adulthood. Where primitive tribes perform this rite in short order, even if for a year among Australian aborigines, we in the West string it out over many years, perhaps because we have lost our old ways and not yet found new means of ritualizing this passage. Nevertheless, junior high education is, if you will, one of the ritualizations of this initiation rite. If this is true, we are faced with the question of what should we be doing with this period of education as such a rite. In terms of what we have already said about what we teach--not only a subject matter but an image (or images) of the self in our world--we are called in junior high education to provide images of maturity.

Living within our complex technological society,

we are already confronted with powerful definitions of maturity by the various institutions that influence us. The job market wants somebody who can be productive; the family may image maturity as being able to live in conventional (or unconventional) roles of wife, husband, child; the church may represent the mature as one dedicated to involvement in the religious institution and striving to achieve its ends.

Usually there is conflict between the various images of maturity provided by these institutions. Schools can be dominated by any one of these or torn apart between them; as educators we need to reflect on the appropriate images of maturity coming out of our task. It may be to support one or another of these other social images; it may be yet another one to which it must be loyal. Without foreclosing that search among teachers, staff, and students for fitting educational images of maturity, certain things are suggested by the metaphor of the responsible self. Maturity will involve a responsiveness simultaneously to each of these institutions that it exists in relation to, and it will call for some kind of integration of response. The responsible school sees itself in ongoing dialogue with the various institutions and their diverse demands. They act upon the school and the school does respond. Students are already feeling these pressures; they are already participants in the dialogue. Our job as teachers is to help that dialogue mature, to make them aware of it and of the different voices in it, and to nurture their movement through this period of their lives so they can learn fruitful, fulfilling ways of integrating their responses into a wholeness that will forever go on becoming more complex, richer, and distinctively their own, that embodies both openness and commitment.

This maturity of responsiveness to the larger society we seek to elicit and enhance involves our relating ultimately to the mystery of our total community of being. Our answering to this ongoing challenge is in great measure unconscious, an orienting ourselves toward our ultimate context as inimical towards, indifferent to, or in some way sustaining of personal existence. It is not our job in education to manipulate students toward any particular attitude, on any level; nevertheless, we invariably embody some basic disposition which

permeates all the rest of our responses and is
received on a tacit level by students as a challenge
for their own tacit creativity. While evangelizing is
not our job, it is part of our _metier_ to engender an
awareness of this dimension in our lives, if we are to
be responsible, honest, about the full extent of the
world and the depth of response called forth by it.
Through root metaphors at work in our lives we can
discover such fundamental attitudes, and be sustained
in and transformed by them. It is to such mystery
that the metaphoric roots of responsibility in
education take us; as we learn an openness of response
to the totality of interaction through metaphor, we
can live fruitfully toward reconciling the communal
and institutional in education.

COMMUNITY AND EDUCATION

Gibson Winter

This consultation is an occasion for us to open
our horizon on the educational tasks with which most
of us are engaged. There are many practical questions
which we could explore, but our work here is to
stretch our minds to new possibilities. This will be
the aim of my remarks.

Education is the way a people interprets and
transmits its way of being in the world; thus, our
reflections on school and community turn to the
complex questions of human dwelling. How is it that a
people dwells on the earth? How is it that we dwell
in modern American society? What are the implications
of this way of being for teaching and learning? These
are some of the questions that will concern us.

Human Dwelling

The human species dwells symbolically on the
earth according to the perspective that guides these
remarks. By "symbol" is meant a vehicle of thought
and feeling through which everyday things are fused
with higher order meanings. For example, "land" is a
way of signifiying the earth, usually as cultivated or
developed. In this sense, "land" is a sign with a
perceptible referent. If one wants to purchase a
piece of land, the owner can show it, pointing out
boundaries, woodlot, open areas and scenic views.
However, "land" as symbol also refers to one's
country. This is a truly symbolic mode of signifying
by which a higher order meaning such as homeland or
country is joined with an everyday notion. Symbols
mediate higher order meanings in all realms of human
experience from family to community to cosmos.
Symbols synthesize our experiences in networks of
meaning. We belong within a symbolic world even as we
sustain it by our commitments, actions, and
institutions.

There are different levels of comprehensiveness
of symbols. We have been considering the
symbolizations that order everyday life. On a higher
level, there are encompassing symbols which integrate

the broader horizons of human dwelling. The ordering of the cosmic horizon, sometimes called "world-view" of a people, is synthesized in an encompassing symbolization. In our recent history, this horizon is synthesized in evolutionary notions of growth and development, replacing to a large extent older creation images. Older symbols are not simply displaced, however, for creation thinking is now imaged in evolutionary terms. Needless to say, a network of other symbols and images cluster around a symbol like creation--notions such as original sin, fall, lawfulness and order. Moreover, the symbolization of feelings and values such as peace and justice synthesize the order of everyday life in patterns of rightness and appropriateness. This valuative aspect, sometimes called ethos, synthesizes ways of doing and making, understanding and embodying, celebrating and coping, deciding and working, suffering and overcoming. Ethos and world-view are, in fact, intertwined ways of dwelling that can only be separated in abstraction.

Encompassing symbols are generated over time from originary symbolizations through which processes of dwelling are disclosed as forms of life. These forms such as economic and political order unfold in language even as the symbols undergo transformations and extensions. Thus, originary symbolizations are not static forms but dynamic ways of being-in-the-world for the human species. Mircea Eliade and others have traced certain universal, archetypal patterns in such originary symbolizations across various peoples and cultures. However, such patterns are only accessible through the actual symbolizations of particular peoples. Moreover, particular symbolizations have a style and center which is peculiar to a people's dwelling. Our common humanity is disclosed in the universal patterns. Our particular life as a people is crystallized in the symbolization of our own heritage.

Encompassing symbols may or may not realize the authentic possibilities of dwelling that are disclosed in originary symbolizations. Originary symbols are only partial mediations of rhythms in bios and cosmos, and, to this extent, they are bearers of potential distortions. Consequently, encompassing symbols require critique; moreover, such critical appropriation may also lead to critical revision of originary symbolization. This is clearly the case in the patriarchal bias that has informed images of God in the Western heritage. How long a people can sustain its vitalities when encompassing symbolization has distorted its possibilities is difficult to determine. When asked how Egyptian culture could have collapsed after such vital beginnings, John Wilson once remarked that he believed they had become preoccupied with death. In this sense, the encompassing symbolization had distorted an originary harmony of the vitalities of life with the powers of darkness and death. When this balance was destroyed, the symbolic vitalities were sapped and the energies of the people were dissipated. There is a dialectic of motivational and socio-political patterning in the living out of encompassing symbolization. Either pole may generate change, and either pole may create distortions and decay. For example, our own patterning of technical and productive life has shifted the symbolization of creation and history toward a collective will to domination which threatens to destroy the environment and possibly all life on earth.

We propose here, then, that a people dwells symbolically on earth, not in the sense of an oppressive or dominating order but in the sense that bios and cosmos speak through symbols and disclose rhythms of life and meaning. The forms of life-- familial, communal, economic, political, religious, artistic, philosophical and personal--originate in symbolic disclosures and unfold in a dialectic of symbols and their inscriptions in language and institutional life. The tool, for example, emerges in the struggle for life from hand as tool to throwing and digging stick and on to other tools, each phase of the equipmental emerging as a way of extending the powers of body and mind into the world. An almost infinite number of tools may emerge in a high technology society, but the equipmental itself is a way of understanding and treating the world which is primordial to the emergence of the human species.

The significance of the body in technology illumines another dimension of human dwelling. Symbols require interpretation in myth, ritual, story, modes of working and caring, living and dying. Such interpretations in cultural expressions, ways of treating the world and ways of understanding and feeling are shaped by fundamental images or metaphors. Such images or metaphors furnish clues to the whole of experience. The totality eludes any grasp in concept or idea. Thus, the body may be understood in the image of an organism or of a machine, to take two root metaphors that have dominated Western experience. The organicist imagery of body and nature was dominant until the age of science and industrialism. The interplay of spiritual and mundane powers was imaged and lived within this metaphor, ordering life in a hierarchy of functions, binding life to lineages of blood and soil. The mechanistic metaphor gradually displaced this order of life, challenging the hierarchies which it supported. In the work of Descartes, Galileo, Hobbes, Boyle and others, bios and cosmos were understood and treated in mechanistic terms. Thus the way was prepared for the age of Enlightenment and its dream of a rational, manageable world.

We are experiencing a crisis of root metaphors today. The indicator of such a crisis is the failure of mechanistic thinking to open horizons of creativity in dealing with environmental, economic, international and spiritual tensions. The other side of the crisis is the tendency to regress to organicist forms of life. This is regressive because the spiritual world, the world behind the world, which supported the organicist world has been eclipsed. An organicist imagery without such support becomes a collective will to impose a traditional order on the chaos that is being engendered by an outworn mechanism.

Root metaphors provide networks of imagery through which a people interprets and lives its foundational symbolization. Such metaphors operate at the interface of symbol and society and furnish the interpreter with clues as to directions and priorities in dwelling. If symbols shape the outer horizon of dwelling, then root metaphors organize the inner horizon of priorities.*

Schooling in a Mechanistic Age

Individuals interact like billiard balls on a table in a mechanistic world. Each entity is connected with other entities only by external play of force. Isaac Newton gave classic formulation of this image of the cosmos in his laws of mechanics. However, the groundwork had been laid by his

---

*For a fuller discussion, see the author's Liberating Creation, (New York: Crossroad Publ. Co., 1981).

predecessors who had unfolded this metaphor in various realms of experience. Thomas Hobbes produced the socio-political vision of mechanism in his notion of a war of each against all as a law of nature. Interacting entities could only compose their conflicting interests through submitting to an authoritarian state. John Locke's formulation was much more sanguine about the possibilities of a civil society, yet he understood the human order in a similar imagery. Mechanism gradually triumphed in the economic field through the commercial developments of Europe, the opening of markets and the interpretative work of Adam Smith and Ricardo. With the growth of industrial production and the extension of the market to labor, land and capital as well as goods, mechanism swept the field, relegating organicist thinking to the traditional bastions of church and family. The revolutionary movements of the eighteenth and nineteenth centuries carried mechanism into the political arena, thus wedding the free market with the politics of economic development. The age of Enlightenment cultivated the mechanistic metaphor in terms of a rational world of general laws. This rational world contradicted the relentless pursuit of economic interests which had been unleashed by the mechanistic image of a free market, but the market held sway, assimilating science and technology to its drive for domination. Knowledge of nature became a source of power over the world rather than a clue to the moral order of the cosmos.

Individual autonomy and liberation from traditional authorities were keynotes in the mechanistic world. Individual autonomy was anchored in the paradigm of mechanism, since, as we noted, each entity was conceived to be externally related to every other entity as a unit of force. Hence, power meant power over another entity, or at least power to influence its movement. Freedom meant freedom from external forces and constraints, or the power to do as one chooses. Knowledge meant understanding the coding that governed the interaction of bodies. And moral obligation could only be determined by generalizing the interplay of interests and external accountability. Whether in terms of utilities or according to rule, individual entities are composed in some kind of order in their external relations. Order is an achievement of civil society through the composition of the interests of individual entities by persuasion or constraint.

123

Liberation from traditional authority was corollary to this assertion of individual autonomy. Freedom from authority rested upon understanding of the rational order of the cosmos. It also depended upon an independent economic base in property. Traditional hierarchies of church and state represented alien powers which had to be overcome. In brief the mechanistic age emerged as a struggle for freedom of inquiry, economic development, political innovation, moral relativity and religious liberty. These are values which will continue to further human dwelling, even when the metaphor which informed them has been displaced. However much they are modified and even transformed, the liberating elements of enlightenment have a significant place in the human heritage.

The socio-economic expression of mechanism emerged simultaneously in the market economy and in federalist politics; at least, this was the expression of mechanism in the new world. Industrialization was the scion of this commercial world and its technological dynamic. The drive to mastery of nature and life was at the center of this new age. This drive to mastery forms a fourth component in the symbolization of the mechanistic age. If the cosmos is a complex mechanism with laws which can be decoded, if the human being is a rational individual who can gain freedom through understanding the laws of nature, then the free and rational society will be the industrially advanced society. Hence, individual autonomy, rationality and freedom are fused as the ingredients of the new, industrial age. "Development" means growth in economic power.

The industrial world has proved an inhospitable environment for freedom and individualism, for the techno-scientific project organizes its world through control of resources and labor. Moreover, ownership of the means of production moved rapidly into the hands of an elite group and was later administered by a managerial bureaucracy. Nevertheless, work and economic advancement continue to lure millions into jobs as a promise of freedom and into cities as a hope for a new life. New York City now has a contingent of thousands of teen-age girls and boys who have sought freedom in the city and found peonage to pimps and houses of prostitution. The flight from family and community into the liberated world of industrial work has proved to be a chimera for some and a nightmare for others.

Many explanations have been offered for the emergence of the mechanistic age. Max Weber traced it to the Protestant ethic in the context of Western institutions. Karl Marx traced it to the development of bourgeois capitalism out of the feudal age. Others have argued that science liberated the West for its industrial age. We would locate the dynamic core of this new world in the understanding of being as something knowable and ultimately controllable. This is the heart of the techno-scientific project. In this sense, the displacement of the organicist world of feudalism involved a transformation of being, understanding, feeling and action. It was a fundamental transformation of the encompassing symbols of Western life. The crisis of metaphors in our own time is a crisis of this encompassing symbolization of domination, growth and progress. The resolution of that crisis means the emergence of a new, fundamental metaphor and a gradual transformation of all regions of experience. In this context, some of the tensions in our educational work become somewhat more intelligible.

Education in a Mechanistic World

Education takes the form of schooling in the industrial world of a mechanistic age. Liberation from family and tradition require socialization into the disciplines of work and bureaucratic life. The school gradually becomes a basic step in liberation from home and family. It is also the instrument for developing skills that would be useful in the industrial machine. Schools teach skills, but more importantly they inculcate the mood of conformity to the imperious system of production. Freedom and individual autonomy were the promised goods at the end of the road. And for many immigrant peoples the schools did provide a means of upward mobility. However, for most the dream turned to ashes. Schooling and work became a path to alienation and subordination. Meanwhile, the fabric of human communities was being torn by the mobility and fragmentation which the productive system generated. The techno-economic drive to rational control sundered personal bonds in local communities. This degenerative process eroded the fabric of urban life, reducing every bond to a cash nexus.

The schools were only one aspect of this larger

process of alienation. Schools created the impersonal system of authority which would measure abilities and sort out those who would be acceptable to the system. The educational path to equality and dignity became the vehicle for meting out inequality and failure. The pursuit of freedom became a journey into alienation and subordination. No matter how much teachers and administrators resisted this pressure for conformity, seeking to engender a love of learning and truth, societal pressures from home and community converted education into schooling. Schooling in alienation became the preparatory school for alienated work and conformity to the system.

Two pathologies of contemporary life can be traced to the self-contradiction of the dream of freedom through technological mastery. The exchange of individual autonomy, the dream of freedom, for dependency in school and workplace created a backlash. The form of this backlash is retreat into the private world of consumerism and life-style. This privatization of meaning supports the alienated public structures through a complicity of withdrawal. The middle class traded life-style for alienated work. Life-style became the substitute for freedom and citizenship. The core of the phenomenon is the attempt to salvage a modicum of autonomy from the alienation of school and workplace. One submits to an alienating system in order to maintain one's style of life. The techno-system in turn benefits from this privatization, creating markets for its goods by cultivating these styles of life. Even religious life becomes one more item in the consumer market--a spirituality that has no bearing on the public world.

Another pathology of alienated work is the turn to authoritarian, communal movements. Some of these communal efforts represent serious attempts to overcome the loss of community in the society. Much of it represents a regression to infantile communalism whether in cult or totalitarian political movements. The dream of freedom is displaced by identification with an authoritarian body. The totalitarian body exercises the autonomy on one's behalf. The twentieth century has been plagued by such flights from freedom, as Erich Fromm observed long ago. Whether in fascism or nationl chauvinism, organicist communalism becomes a substitute for the dream of freedom. The familistic communities that have been destroyed are replaced with families that gather around charismatic leaders or

paroxysms of nationalism. Nation is pitted against
nation in perpetual warfare. Organicism without the
spiritual world which sustained it becomes simply the
imposition of a collective will on a mechanistic,
alienated society. The tragedy of Jonestown is
perhaps the most agonizing expression of this
regression to organic community in recent years, but
fascist and collective movements all through the
twentieth century have evinced similar kinds of
pathology. Even now many nations are being assured
that suicide by nuclear warfare is a proper way to
defend themselves from threats to their way of life.
Even in its very pathology, this testimony to the need
for community points the direction beyond mechanism to
a creative search for liberation.

A Liberating Metaphor

For over a century the root metaphor of the work
of art has been gaining power as a way of
understanding and treating our world. The work of
art, like organicism and mechanism, has been a
significant image throughout Western history.
However, the growing awareness of human power to act
upon nature has raised the creative aspect of art to a
new prominence. Even in the natural sciences, which
for so long were discussed in terms of method,
creative imagination is now recognized as a crucial
variable. History has likewise been a realm of
experience in which human initiative and creativity
have gained prominence. It is very difficult today to
relegate human history to a deterministic fate. A
people's history now appears as both given and
created.

The work of art is a more appropriate image than
mechanism for guiding thought and action in this new
age. Art lifts up human creativity without reducing
the work to pure subjectivity. The work of art is
first and last a public event. Through the work, the
public participates in nature and life. Art also
joins thought and action, for in art the way things
come to expression and what is expressed belong
together. In a piece of sculpture, the work
communicates in the way it is. This contrasts sharply
with our techno-society in which medium and message,
tool and purpose, have been sundered, even to the
point where message and purpose drop out of sight. We
seem preoccupied, for example, with maintaining our
economic system and weapons development even when they

no longer serve the purposes which are supposed to justify them. We keep our tools at work even when they threaten the environment and quality of life. The medium is not simply the message, for there is no message--only the medium. Everything becomes a means. The work of art does not dispense with materials, tools and crafts. It merely rearranges our priorities and sets media, materials, tools and crafts in proper perspective. Art uses the linearity of mechanism without surrendering to it. Needless to say, a new fundamental metaphor is not the gift of a new world. However, we drift today from crisis to crisis like a rudderless ship. Our first task is to gain a sense of direction and sort out matters of importance from secondary issues. Here the root metaphor of the work of art promises to liberate us from the mechanical repetition that binds us to a degenerative process.

If we take a people's dwelling as work of art, a people's work, we are asking about the disclosures of truth, justice and goodness in the way we live, work, play and celebrate. We are also asking of economic, social and political life whether those structures disclose the truth of human community and its possibilities for justice and care. Our dwelling is a working art, disclosing or concealing the meaning of humanity. Such an image provides a helpful context for reflecting on our tasks of teaching and learning.

Art and tradition live in tension but not contradiction. Every work of art, unless it is mere imitation, involves a negation of what has gone before in selection, perspective or subject matter. At the same time, the work builds on the heritage of works and craftsmanship. Our educational task is somewhat similar. We are living in a new and different world, one for which we are poorly prepared. Nevertheless, our resources for dealing with this world are to be drawn from our heritage as well as new discoveries. A mechanistic world of future shock merely fragments life unless it is anchored in an authentic cultural tradition. To complicate this picture, we now recognize that ours is the human past reaching across the globe to many cultures and faiths which we have to come to know and understand. No period of "schooling" could embrace such a rich heritage, yet school can be the place where the riches of that heritage are identified and tasted. Some gifted young people will someday enrich that heritage with their own contributions. Others can learn to cherish and preserve it for the next generation. Against such a legacy, young and old can test the proposals of future shock. Without such a legacy, people become the victims of mass persuasion and irrational promises.

Everyone acknowledges that young people have to be equipped, so far as possible, to work and survive in the techno-system. This creates tensions with the appropriation of the heritage, although there can be balance between new and old, innovation and heritage. A similar tension is generated between concern for virtue and human values in contrast to emphasis on manipulative skills and achievements. In the long view, we may recognize that both sides of life are important. Within the pressures of a mechanistic age, virtue and quality of life drop from sight. Perhaps confronting the issue of sexism could open both sides of true education, since skills need to be equally accessible while learning to live with respect and appreciation are essential. Perhaps this is also the context for disclosing and evaluating the debasing image of women that is propagated by the economy and media. In this region of experience, schools could provide a counterpoint to the illusion of freedom as individual autonomy. This is not asking schools to do everything, especially all that families and communities now fail to do. That would be a false expectation. However, in sorting out priorities for the future, we shall have to ask ourselves where and how we begin to cultivate the relationships and skills which create a human community. Many schools and teachers have worked at this for years in the context of their educational process, which is the only appropriate way for education. The work of art would suggest that how we go about our learning, how we treat one another, is inseparable from the final results of our educational work. Such efforts within the micro-system of schooling cannot, of course, be separated from efforts to transform the macro-structures of work and community life. So long as racism, sexism, social class exploitation and disregard for human values are structured into the macro-system, we are asking the impossible in looking to the schools for a new way of life.

A work of art is a special kind of structure in which the play of life, its contrasts and qualities, come into some kind of harmonious working. This interplay generates new sensibilities, insights and possibilities for experience. The public is

transformed so far as it participates in this work
through its own imagination. Our dwelling today, and
much of the schooling which serves it, moves in the
opposite direction. Our consumer style of life
becomes ever more standardized. Preparation for
entrance into the productive system, however
diversified the appearance of the jobs, requires fine
tuning to limited types of skills. The
computerization of our society is now intensifying
this process. A different, fundamental image poses
serious questions about such a style of dwelling. And,
in fact, numbers of younger people, as we noted
earlier, have sought alternative styles of work and
life in order to escape this uniformity. Human
dwelling which attended to the truth and enrichment of
life would develop a much more diverse range of gifts
and competencies. Despite severe institutional
pressures, creative schooling could enrich the styles
of personal development. In the longer view of the
survival of human species life, such diversity may
well prove to be far more functional than our present,
narrow tuning. The specialization of a mechanistic
age is productive over a narrow range, but it may well
prove to be dysfunctional for our survival. It is
clearly inimical to a rich, human dwelling.

Everything we touch in schooling--pedagogy,
sports, administration, teaching, communal life,
balance of skills with quality of life--turns on the
root metaphor that guides our society and its
educational process. The hints of direction in these
remarks are not meant as programmatic, nor are they
meant as utopian. Many of these things are already
happening where creative teaching and authentic
education occur. One of our tasks is to clarify our
priorities and directions so that we can nurture those
things which generate a more humane dwelling. In the
work of art, things can be evaluated by
appropriateness. As we struggle to overcome the
alienation and dependency that is plaguing our common
life, these steps, however small, may commend
themselves to us as more fitting. Freedom in the
image of the work of art is the innovative power to
disclose the human more fully. Freedom is not simply
autonomy. It is openness to truth and goodness, the
possibility to be more fully human. In this sense,
freedom is the capacity to be open to learn through
relations with nature and others.

We may be on the threshold of a post-mechanistic

age.   That will only be determined by what happens in
families,   schools,   neighborhoods   and   the   macro-
structures   of   our   achievement   society.   Metaphors
cannot determine whether we cross that threshold,   but
metaphors are ingredient to the different ways of life
that humans choose in their dwelling.   The metaphor is
the realm of poetic freedom that is of the essence   of
human   life.   This   is   our   freedom   today,   our
possibility to contribute to a fuller human life.

EVALUATION/DIGNITY

The conjunction 'Evaluation/Dignity' in the context of schooling is a provocative one. It suggests, from the outset, the troubled nature of student as well as professional evaluation in terms of their frequently deleterious effects on human dignity, worth and value. Yet education without some form of appraisal of progress seems to be an inconceivable notion. Nor can we discount the public's right to accountability of those employed in the public domain. Around these issues the conference posed two questions: How can we meet the strong public demand for rigorous evaluation with professional and moral integrity? Are there ways to distinguish between legitimate goals of evaluation (e.g. to provide feedback) from the kinds of evaluation that create a sense of unworthiness?

In her paper Maxine Greene notes how education in general, and evaluation in particular is increasingly affected by the language of technology. The 'technicist' mode of thinking, she says, insists that all of the actions having to do with teaching and learning are susceptible to measurement, testing and experimental controls. The results of this, says Greene, are miseducative. They may permit training to take place more efficiently, but they are likely to 'hinder the posing of worthwhile and authentic questions.' Technicians join together with a meritocratic ideology in our schools to assure the legitimacy and universality of hierarchies in our social lives - an acceptance of the notion that failure and humiliation are unavoidably in the nature of things.

For Charity James, too, the evaluations typically undertaken in our schools 'drives out' people's sense of their own personal worth; it provides students a distorted image of who they are and what they are capable of. In place of this James offers the notion of 'appraisal' - a process in which we come to know that we have inner worth regardless of what others, or even we ourselves, think. This knowledge of self is connected to the 'deep search for meaning'. She offers, in this paper, a guide to teachers (and students) on how we may begin to demythologize evaluation in order to enhance individual development and worth.

EVALUATION AND DIGNITY

Maxine Greene

Any viewing of values, teaching, and human
dignity in these times must take into account the
contexts of the post-industrial society. No matter
how separated from the larger world individual
teachers may feel, they cannot but be affected by the
scale and impersonality of institutional structures,
by the unease afflicting the culture, by the sense of
powerlessness that prevails. At once, they cannot but
be aware of the continuing dominance of technicism,
stratification, and what Daniel Bell speaks of as
"functional" rationality.[1] Nor can they be impervious
to the inequities and pressures to which such
phenomena give rise. Not very many years ago, the
taken-for-granted value of progress and modernization
seemed to justify all this; today, both progress and
modernization have begun to appear questionable.
There is little faith in the potency or the promise of
humankind; there is fear that the planet itself will
be destroyed. Nevertheless, and despite their own
nagging questions, teachers feel obligated to
perpetuate the ideology of technocracy and
consumerism. They are expected to inculcate respect
for expertise, to orient themselves to productivity
and efficiency and the expansion of control.

Many teachers try to believe that, if they do
what is expected, they can still promote social
mobility and (to some extent) pursue the ends of
equity as well. They encourage (within bounds)
diverse modes of fulfillment and differential patterns
of personal growth; but they also keep alive the
hunger for commodities, for gadgets, for things.
Whether they intend to or not, they are likely to
communicate the idea that identity is linked to
possession, and that what people are taught to want is
what they actually need.

---

[1] Daniel Bell, The Coming of Post-Industrial
Society (New York: Basic Books, 1973), p. 366.

135

For all their efforts, they and their schools are continually charged with ineffectiveness today. Deficiencies are spelled out in terms of lagging competencies, a particular type of measurable illiteracy, an abandoment of the basic skills presumably plentiful in the not so distant past. Seldom is the ineffectuality ascribed to schools associated with the boredom of their clients, with unhappiness or humiliation in the classroom, with media-induced passivity. Nor is the presumed "incompetence" of students related to deficiencies in the society--the lack of meaningful work, the erosion of family life, the attrition of neighborhoods, the rise in violence and crime.

When test scores are acceptable, no one really cares if a child (like William Blake's "little black thing among the snow") cries "weep in notes of woe." No one thinks very much about the schools' contribution to privatism or to what Christopher Lasch calls "the new narcissism." [2] Nor does anyone think very much about the part played by the schools in the unequal distribution of knowledge,[3] in "tracking" and stratifying. Preoccupied with the discrete and the quantifiable, people may talk vaguely about citizenship; but they evince little interest in educating what John Dewey called an "articulate public"[4] capable of active social concern. And, with few exceptions, they are not inclined to discuss the life of the imagination or the kinds of awareness made possible by encounters with works of art.

Discussions of education are increasingly affected by the language of technology and, indeed, the ethos of technology, or so it seems. This is why terms like "competencies" and "classroom management systems" and "input-output" seem so natural when applied to events in classrooms and to the surrounding

---

[2] Christopher Lasch, The Culture of Narcissism (New York: W. W. Norton and Co., 1978).

[3] See, e.g., Geoff Whitty and Michael Young, ed.s., Explorations in the Politics of School Knowledge (Nafferton, Driffield, England: Nafferton Books, 1976).

[4] John Dewey, The Public and Its Problems (Chicago: The Swallow Press, 1927, 1954), p. 184.

educational world. It may well be that, without
thinking about it, educators have begun engaging in
adaptive behavior: they may be speaking and acting in
precisely the way technicism demands. Technicism is a
mode of thinking that applies empirical and technical
concepts to the interpretation of experience in all
its phases: play, for example; sexual relationships;
the realms of ethics and morality; the activities of
teaching and learning wherever they occur.   To think
of all these as susceptible to measurement, testing,
and experimental controls is to adopt the technicist
approach.   Also, it is to acquiesce in the draining
off of ambiguity and mystery.   It is to distance what
is taken to be "real," to objectify it, to conceive it
as subject to management and control.

     To think this way, to construct reality this way
is to apprehend the world in fragments and in largely
calculative terms.   It becomes, as it were, "only
logical" to apprehend school achievement accordingly
and to treat what is called evaluation as a technique
for measuring visible performances and discrete
skills. Not only does attention center upon product
or output.   The personal reality of the student tends
to be subsumed under his/her test-taking ability.
He/she becomes, in the assessor's eyes, an
abstraction, a cypher. He/she is ranked in accord
with the degree to which he/she has organized his/her
experience (or sorted out some assigned information)
in "acceptable" fashion--the degree to which he/she
has "matched" it to a model prefabricated by some
official Other in the light of external demand.   I
recall Ralph Waldo Emerson, describing the ways in
which "Man" (as he called the person) was
"metamorphosed into a thing, into many things" in the
emerging industrial America:

                    The planter . . . sees his bushel and
                    his cart, and nothing beyond, and
                    sinks into the farmer, instead of Man
                    on the farm . . . The priest becomes a
                    form; the attorney a statute book; the
                    mechanic a machine; the sailor a rope
                    of the ship. In this distribution of
                    functions, the scholar is the
                    delegated intellect. In the right
                    state, he is Man Thinking. In the
                    degenerate state, when the victim of
                    society, he tends to become a mere

137

thinker, or still worse, the parrot of men's thinking.[5]

Emerson might have been describing the reductiveness of our own time. On all sides individuals are being casually demeaned by being reduced to their functions, their roles, their measured "competencies." Too often they are deprived of the sense of personal agency, the sense of being the authors of what they undertake or what they manage to achieve. They are dwarfed by the lack of opportunity to center, to develop themselves from within. This is what Emerson had in mind when he warned against the human being becoming a mere object, a thing.

It is what we see around us in the classrooms when young people are evaluated on the _results_ of prescribed activities (drills, perhaps, memorization, rote-learning) rather than for the conscious pursuit of their own aims or ends-in-view. John Dewey, comparing mere results with aims, said that, in the case of an effect or result, there is nothing in the outcome that completes or fulfills what went before it. An aim, he wrote, "implies an orderly and ordered activity, one in which the order consists in the progressive completing of a process."[6] It cannot be an order that comes from the assignment of lessons or the giving of directions by the teacher. It is a matter, as Gilbert Ryle once said, of the child doing, not the teacher inflicting.[7] The process, the activity, moreover, must be consciously undertaken by the learner who has his/her own end in view: to try to understand why Bartleby the Scrivener "prefers not to"; to make sense of the connection between industrial inventions and particular wars; to identify the reasons why Islamic law requires women to be veiled. The _aim_ must relate to what the learner

---

[5] Ralph Waldo Emerson, "The American Scholar," in _Emerson on Education_, ed. Howard Mumford Jones (New York: Teachers College Press, 1966), pp. 78-79.

[6] John Dewey, _Democracy and Education_ (New York: The Macmillan Company, 1916), p. 119.

[7] Gilbert Ryle, "Teaching and Training," in _The Concept of Education_, ed. R. S. Peters (New York: The Humanities Press, 1967), pp. 105-119.

personally desires to find out; it must give direction
to his/her activity and, at once, allow for choices or
alternatives. "If we can predict," Dewey said, "the
outcome of acting this way or that, we can then
compare the value of the two courses of action; we can
pass judgment on their relative desirability." [8]

To think, instead, of the correctness or the
acceptability of a specific result, to judge in terms
of discrete and presumably testable skills, may be to
prevent students from taking responsibility for their
own learning to learn. It may be to distract them
from the self-initiated quests for meaning that are so
central to the human career. If this is indeed the
case, it follows that the competencies movement, the
testing syndrome, and related phenomena can be
considered miseducative. They may permit training to
take place more efficiently; they may make the
schooling process more predictable. But they are
likely to hinder the posing of worth-while and
authentic questions, as they are likely to prevent
the selection of the kinds of experiences "that live
fruitfully and creatively in subsequent experiences." [9]

New kinds of reflexivity are needed; critical
reflection is needed if teachers are to gain
perspective on what they intend and what they do. By
that I mean a turning back on their own thinking, upon
the simplistic language so easily available today. It
may be necessary deliberately to resist the
bewitchment of intelligence brought about by the
seductiveness of technical talk, because it is as a
consequence of such bewitchment that students may be
injured and demeaned.

There will always be those who (having thought
about it) will take the behaviorist road. They will
choose it because it is the way of efficiency, and
because it enables them to demonstrate what
reinforces, what motivates, what--in the last
analysis--"works." And such teachers may be convinced

---

[8]Dewey, Democracy and Education, p. 119.

[9]Dewey, Experience and Education (New York:
Collier Books, 1963), p. 28.

that an approach going "beyond freedom and dignity" [10]
is by far the most benign. There are others who will
choose (like Soren Kierkegaard long ago[11]) to make
"life more difficult" for themselves and for their
students. "Persistent striving," wrote Kierkegaard,
"is the ethical life view of the existing subject."[12]
And he went on to say that the existing individual is
always a learner, that constant learning is the
expression of his/her consciousness of
himself/herself. Open-ended questioning; tension and
resolution; on-going pursuits of meaning: these are
the hallmarks of such learning. The teachers who
choose to provoke it cannot but try to move students
to seek the kinds of literacy that can never be fully
tested, that open new perspectives one after another,
that exclude both cloture and certainty.

In actual fact, this approach is closer to that
of modern science than is any behaviorist or mechanist
approach. The scientist knows the danger of fixed
categories, as he/she understands the role of human
invention and diverse human orderings. The
objectivism of what is called "scientism" is
meaningless to the scientist; like Werner Heisenberg,
he/she is well aware that science "describes nature as
exposed to our method of questioning."[13]Similarly, the
perspectival approach, the constructivist approach is
the one warranted by a range of modern pscyhologies.
Jerome Bruner has written that "a principal task of
intellect is in the construction of explanatory models

---

[10]B. F. Skinner, Beyond Freedom and Dignity (New
York: Alfred A. Knopf, 1971).

[11]Soren Kierkegaard, "How Johannes Climacus Became
an Author," Concluding Unscientific Postscript to the
"Philosophical Fragments," in A Kierkegaard
Anthropology, ed. Robert Bretall (Princeton:
Princeton University Press, 1947), pp. 193-194.

[12]Kierkegaard, Concluding Unscientific Postscript,
op. cit., p. 204.

[13]Werner Heisenberg, Physics and Philosophy
(London: Allen & Unwin, 1959), p. 5.

for the ordering of experience . . . "[14] Emphasis is placed on going beyond what is given, on fallibility, on the transformation of our models of reality over time. To learn--to be a constant learner--is to engage actively in sense-making, in the patterning of experience; to learn is to move beyond what is taught, to transcend. Of course there are categorial rules; there are schemata and protocols to master; there are the "empowering techniques" made available by the culture. But the crucial point has to do with diverse modes of ordering from particular perspectives. It has to do with self-initiated learning on the part of persons who are participant in a cultural conversation, who can reflect critically on their experience--and know what it is to be free.

Teachers willing to educate in this fashion not only break with current expectations and demands. Whether conscious of it or not, they infuse their classroom work with a critique of existing ideology, as they do with a resistance to technicism and technique. They take, as it were, exposed positions. Moreover, they risk a kind of dreadful failure because they presume their students to be free. Anyone who addresses himself/herself to another person's freedom takes the risk of being thwarted; and there is no guarantee that such a teacher, simply by being there, will move young people to learn how to learn in the way described. Young people, too, after all, have internalized the values of a culture committed to consumption and control. They have experienced the pressures of a school oriented to making them into jobholders and consumers, satisfying market demand. Somehow, their teachers must empower them for critical reflection on their own situations, so that they can perceive whatever deficiencies exist--in the school, the neighborhood, the economic system, the political and social structures that affect lived lives. Possibilities must be discerned, conceptions of what is not yet, of what ought to be. The energies demanded, the capacities required cannot be captured by any list of competencies; and it is difficult to imagine a quantitative measure for what restive students discover, what they finally achieve.

---

[14]Jerome S. Bruner, "The Perfectibility of Intellect," in Modern Philosophies of Education, ed. John Paul Strain (New York: Random House, 1971), p. 200.

It is not the technologizing of things alone that stands in the way of this mode of educating. There is also the tradition of meritocracy, a tradition that carries with it a kind of moral validation. This causes a taken-for-grantedness, not simply with respect to the ranking of people on figurative ladders but with respect to freedom and equity as well. Meritocracy may be conceived as a social arrangement under which status and income are contingent upon talent, intelligence, and certain kinds of technical skills, rather than upon birth, heredity, or (it is claimed) social class. It was and is generally believed that upward mobility and success are functions of intelligence (ordinarily demonstrated by high scores on IQ tests), relatively lengthy periods of education, and a certain type of ambition and commitment. Because, theoretically, persons are judged on the basis of achievement rather than origin, a meritocracy supposedly makes equality of opportunity possible. The "bright kid," no matter who he/she is will "make it." Teachers are likely to cling to a belief in the promise implied. It provides a moral justification for what they do.

But there have been numerous challenges--not only to the fairness and viability of meritocracy, but to what has been assumed about equality and success. Christopher Jencks and his colleagues attracted much public attention when they reported that American public schools were "marginal" when it came to overcome persisting inequalities.[15] Success, they said, was attributable to luck, on-the-job competence, and a variety of manipulative skills more than it was to long years in school and college. The philosopher, John Rawls, wrote a seminal book called A Theory of Justice [16] that pointed out the injustices of meritocracy, for all the claims that it promoted equality and served the interests of society as well. He argued that, although meritocracy used equality of opportunity as a means of releasing human energies in the pursuit of economic prosperity and political dominion, the culture of the poorer strata was

---

[15]Christopher Jencks, et al., Inequality: A Reassessment of the Effect of Family and Schooling in America (New York: Basic Books, 1972).

[16]John Rawls, A Theory of Justice (Cambridge: Harvard University Press, 1971).

impoverished as a result. The culture of the governing and technocratic elite, on the other hand, remained securely based in the service of the national ends of power and wealth. And then: "Equality of opportunity means an equal chance to leave the less fortunate behind in the personal quest for influence and social position."[17] He went on:

> The confident sense of their own worth should be sought for the least favored, and this limits the forms of hierarchy and the degrees of inequality that justice permits. Thus . . . resources for education are not to be allotted solely or . . . mainly according to their returns as estimated in productive trained abilities, but also according to their worth in enriching the personal and social life of citizens, including here the less favored.[18]

It would appear that, according to Rawls, the product orientation and the competencies orientation can be criticized on the grounds of a belief in social justice and a conception of education as a means of enriching human lives. Other criticisms have been raised, as is well known; and certain ones are used to legitimate demands for affirmative action, reverse discrimination in hiring, and the rest. Despite all this, there remains a taken-for-grantedness with regard to the idea of hierarchy, the necessity to rank persons, the inevitability of failure for some.

Robert Nisbet, hostile to the "new equality" and what he thinks of as a levelling tendency, writes about the necessity of hierarchy.[19] Daniel Bell speaks of a "knowledge society" and the need for a "technical intelligentsia."[20] Given the ideological emphases, it remains extraordinarily difficult for

---

[17]Rawls, op. cit., p. 106.

[18]Rawls, op. cit., p. 107.

[19]Robert Nisbet, Twilight of Authority (New York: Oxford University Press, 1975).

[20]Bell, op. cit., pp. 97-99.

teachers to think what they are doing when they structure social reality in terms of ladders, pyramids, hierarchies. They have a habitual tendency to see students in terms of superior and inferior, high up--and lower down--on a scale. The Piagetian literature, with its emphasis on "stages" and its suggestion that development takes place in an upward (more rational, more just) direction, may have given the notion of hierarchies even more legitimation. It is simply assumed that development occurs sequentially, that analytic capacities are "higher" than holistic ones, that the abstract is more worthy than the concrete.

People tend to forget that a hierarchy is a mode of ordering discrepant phenomena, that it is a construct, a kind of metaphor. No hierarchy exists out in the world--like a mountain or a tree. It is a schema, a structuring sometimes arbitrarily imposed. There are precedents, of course; and sometimes it is useful to recall them. Who can entirely forget the great Aristotelian pyramid arising out of inchoateness and formlessness, moving step by step, as matter is increasingly infused with form, from inanimate things to flowers to animals to human beings and, at length, to God, the Unmoved Mover? Who can forget the many images in literature--in The Divine Comedy, for instance--of sullied, fallible people struggling to ascend to where the air is purer, where lusts and drives are left behind, and reason rules? I believe that many educators carry the paradigm with them: they identify the highly cognitive with the formal, the excellent; and (in some half-ashamed way) they identify all of that with human merit, human worth.

Thinking that way, hesitant when it comes to reflecting on it, teachers accept the notion of failure, propagate the idea that some people always have to fail if the order of things (or the hierarchy, or the curve) is to exist. And all this finds frequent expression in the humiliation of individual children--a humiliation that is more likely than any effort at enabling so-called "under-achievers" to perform at what is called a "higher" level. The effects are far-reaching. To be branded a failure is in some respects to be transformed into a deviant, sometimes into a kind of sinner. We talk about self-fulfilling prophecies. Jean-Paul Sartre wrote about an individual (who later became the poet Genet) actually choosing himself to be what he had been

144

accused of being--a thief.[21]

And there are the social effects--the documented effects of stratification and classification on the individual (especially when his/her category is determined by his/her weakness rather than by his/her strength). There is a memorable scene in Herman Melville's _Moby Dick_ that this recalls to mind. Ishmael (former schoolmaster, who has found himself afflicted by depression and decided to go to sea) signs on board the Pequod and tries to find out what share of the whaling ship's profits he is slated to receive. In the whaling industry they paid no wages; but all hands received certain shares, called "lays." These lays, as Ishmael tells us, "were proportioned to the degree of importance pertaining to the respective duties of the ship's company. I was aware that, being a green hand at whaling, my own lay would not be very large, but considering that I was used to the sea, could steer a ship, splice a rope, and all that, I made no doubt that I should be offered at least the 275th lay."[22] He is offered much less than that, because of his "deficiency": the fact that he is a "green hand at whaling," in spite of his many strengths. The shipowners tell him that if they too abundantly reward him they will be taking bread from the widows and orphans who are part-owners of the ship. The real point, however, is that a stratification of diverse individuals (each with a distinguishable range of talents and strengths), a sorting out in terms of shipowner interest, leads to various kinds of alienation and competitiveness on the ship. The crewmen are and remain island men, "isoladoes." Captain Ahab can manipulate and mystify them, can maneuver them into any activity he chooses by offering them cash, "aye, cash," he says. There may well be connections between all this and the fact that the ship eventually sinks in a confrontation with the White Whale--and that Ahab cries, as it disappears, "Its wood could only be American . . ."

Meritocracy, hierarchy, the ranking of people in accord with arbitrarily defined strengths and

---

[21]Jean-Paul Sartre, _Saint Genet: Actor & Martyr_ (New York: George Braziller, 1963), pp. 49-72.

[22]Herman Melville, _Moby Dick_ (New York: Random House, 1930), pp. 110-111.

weaknesses: this is not, of course, confined to
American society.   In A Room of One's Own, Virginia
Woolf rages against the "pitting of sex against sex,
of quality against quality; all this claiming of
superiority and imputing of inferiority . . . " She
speaks mockingly of how important it seems to some
people to walk up to a platform and receive from the
hands of a Headmaster "a highly ornamental pot."   She
goes on: "As people mature, they cease to believe in
sides or in Headmasters or in highly ornamental pots."
And then:

> . . . delightful as the pastime of
> measuring may be, it is the most
> futile of all occupations, and to
> submit to the decrees of the measurers
> the most servile of attitudes.   So
> long as you write what you wish to
> write, that is all that matters . . .
> But to sacrifice a hair of the head of
> your vision, a shade of its color, in
> deference to some Headmasters with a
> silver pot in his and or to some
> professor with a measuring-rod up his
> sleeve, is the most abject treachery,
> and the sacrifice of wealth and
> chastity, which used to be said to be
> the greatest of human disasters, a
> mere flea-bite in comparison.[23]

It would be tonic and, to some degree, comforting
to take Virginia Woolf at her word and dispose of the
problem of evaluation.   But several things must be
said.   One has to do with the freedom to write "what
you wish to write" if you have not mastered the
capacity to write, to translate your feelings and
ideas into words.   Another has to do with the
difficulty, under present conditions, of creating the
kinds of classroom situations that release preferences
and move persons to some degree of mastery.

There is likely to be a great concatenation of
voices, a confusion of demands. Some will continually
remind teachers of the "objectives" they must meet,
the "competencies" that are required.   Others will
express the fears and preoccupations of a public that

---

[23]Virginia Woolf, A Room of One's Own (New York:
Harcourt, Brace & World, 1957), p. 110.

146

depends on "measuring rods" for evidence of children's success. Still others may represent the students and their contesting desires--to conform, to get ahead, to "beat the system," to find an authentic voice. It would do little good to distribute copies of A Room of One's Own.

The point must be made, of course, that evaluation involves more than the production of a measuring rod, that it surely ought to involve more. Actually, evaluation is a process of making value judgments about certain phenomena in educational contexts, judgments that have to do with the worth of papers, say, or recitations, or with the relative desirability of certain curricula. Frequently, evaluation has to do with the teacher's mode of address to students, with determining (say) whether adequate achievement has been gained or whether it has been gained at too high a cost. In the literature of evaluation today, there is considerable feeling about the orientation to output and to measurement.[24] Many critics are insisting that evaluation must be more than that. Then the troubling questions arise. How can value judgments be defensibly made? How can assessments be done without destroying the dignity of persons and their sense of worth?

It seems clear enough that questions like these cannot be dealt with in the absence of a clearly defined context of values and commitments. Teachers themselves have the capacity, ordinarily, consciously to create such a context--to shape what might be called a normative community within their school. This requires them, however, to do what teachers rarely do: to come together for the sake of dialogue with one another. Engaging personally with each other, attending to the norms that govern their lives together, they may well be in a position to identify what each of them believes to be important where teaching and learning are concerned. Many, of course, will turn immediately to management questions, particularly in schools where the children are underprivileged and the test scores low. Others, preoccupied with initiating students into the various

[24]See, e.g., Educational Evaluation: Analysis and Responsibility, ed. Michael W. Apple, Michael J. Subkoviak, Henry S. Lufler, Jr. (Berkeley: McCutchan Publishing Co., 1974).

disciplines, may choose to talk about protocols and principles, about the modes of assessment appropriate where disciplinary learning is concerned. Still others, troubled by the cynicism and indifference of the young, may draw attention to the fact that each living person is "condemned to meaning,"[25] condemned to learn how to interpret experience, to impose order upon it, to make sense. And there are always certain teachers who think in terms of open-ended development and self-actualization, who have no patience with assessment of any kind.

There will be gains if the teachers involved find themselves free to articulate the values they are pursuing, the ends they have in view. Surely, the climate in the school will be healthier if they discover themselves as a plurality and if they are able to speak for themselves. Hannah Arendt describes situations in which persons come together in this way. She talks about an objective reality (in this case, teaching) deriving from the action and speech of the people concerned and constituting an "in-between." But she also talks about another "in-between," created by the group members' disclosures of themselves.

> Since this disclosure of the subject is an integral part of all, even the most "objective" intercourse, the physical, worldly in-between along with its interests is overlaid . . . with an altogether different in-between which consists of deeds and words and owes its origin exclusively to men's acting and speaking directly to one another. The second, subjective in-between is not tangible . . . But, for all its intangibility, this in-between is no less real than the world of things we visibly have in common. We call this reality the "web" of human relationships . . .[26]

It is within and by means of such a "web" that

---

[25]Maurice Merleau-Ponty, _Phenomenology of Perception_ (New York: The Humanities Press, 1967), p. xix.

[26]Hannah Arendt, _The Human Condition_ (Chicago: The University of Chicago Press, 1968), pp. 182-183.

teachers (and young people too, and their parents, and the schools' administrators) ought to be able to disclose themselves and their commitments. If, indeed, it is possible for them to speak directly "to one another," it ought also to be possible for them to refer to the values that sustain the "in-between." There will be differences; but, if the dialogue proceeds and expands, some kind of consensus will come into view. Decisions may be tentatively made about how value judgments should proceed, about what should be assessed and appraised and evaluated--and (just as significantly) to what end.

At the very least, a new process will emerge; something resembling a public space will come into being. This is a space in which autonomous beings come together in the light of some mutual promise or agreement. They contract with one another, as it were, to act in concert in the name of some shared conception of the valuable. In most institutions, including schools, people are thrown together randomly; they perform their functions, play their roles, seldom discover the intangible "in-between" that might draw them together. They are, in many respects, like the "isoladoes" on the whaling ship in Moby Dick: they remain subject to external control they have no power to resist. They are only nominally free, in consequence; since freedom implies the power to choose (and to resist). That power, in turn, is a function of relationship in some public space.

Now my point is that teachers willing to come together in the manner described may discover a new freedom for themselves--a power to decide how they want to conduct themselves and how they want to be judged. Accustomed to viewing their situations as determined, as given, they may be startled to find themselves looking at things as if they could be otherwise. This, too, is one of the dimensions of freedom--the ability to perceive alternative possiblities and find out how to act upon them. To imagine teachers coming together with young people and parents in order to "possibilize" is to imagine new openings when it comes to such phenomena as evaluation. At once, it is to visualize an exemplary educational situation, in which all affected are able to teach themselves. In some sense, they would be transcending themselves (as constant learners tend to do), breaking through limits, moving to what is not yet.

To emphasize what this might mean, I want to turn for a moment to an extraordinary reality: the life and career of the dancer, Mikhail Baryshnikov. As is well known, he was trained by the Kirov Ballet in the Soviet Union, where he was recognized as a great classical dancer when still very young. Clearly, he worked hard for that; he made every effort to realize what he saw as his own possibilities. Then, being self-critical and self-evaluative, he began to question the terms of his existence. He began to envisage the possiblity of dancing diverse roles quite beyond what was offered by the Kirov Ballet. A problem, a deeply felt problem, surged up in him; it must have become a kind of jutting place, an obstacle he had to overcome if he were to become what he hoped to become. It was an obstacle created by the controls imposed upon him, the limitations to his growth. The more he thought that things could be otherwise, the more intolerable found those limitations to be. He began carving out alternative possibilities for himself that had never existed before; among them, was the possiblity of becoming a defector and risking himself in the western world. When he finally jumped over the line, it was in a desperate desire to break through the impasse, to become what he was not yet.

Now it is clear enough that a Baryshnikov could never be satisfied with the actual. Even today, he seems always to be assessing his achievement, evaluating himself, taking new risks. He himself is at stake as he joins diverse dance communities and tries out new dance possibilities: those provided by Balanchine, Robbins, Twyla Tharp, and even by a television program on Broadway musicals. His continual self-evaluating and the dialogues with others that accompany it are aspects of his possibilizing. In many ways, he too is a constant learner, continually in pursuit, never entirely sure.

This mode of being is not only attainable by the extraordinarily talented. I am convinced that situations can still be created in schools that might provoke young people to invent unforeseen projects for themselves, to future, to try to move beyond. We know there are examples in unexpected places; and it seems likely that, if we could ever break with the constraints of meritocratic and technical thinking, we would find ourselves discerning more and more. An instance of this can be found in the work of a remarkable woman named Mina Shaughnessy, who taught

English at the City College in New York and became very interested in the open admissions practices devised by the university and in the whole problem of new populations coming into higher education. She read some 4000 letters of applications from would-be students; and, in her book named Errors and Expectations,[27] she described the problems of the so-called "basic writers" and what she and her colleagues learned to do. The focus in her book is on enabling "basic writers" to correct their errors and reach beyond themselves.

An effort was made to empower the students to do something comparable with what Baryshnikov was able to do on his own initiative. There was a gap between her students' cognitive abilities and their practice that Myna Shaugnessy wanted to close. At once, she wanted to help people define their possibilities, their particular existential goals. She assumed that they had a desire to learn, that many of them had the energies required for learning. But first she had to ask them why. What did they want to do with their lives? Their major problems, she thought, were due to their dislike of exposing themselves to a world that had been destructive of them throughout their lives. They had developed all kinds of writing devices to mask what they really thought and felt--extravagances, exoticisms, flowery rhetoric. All this exacerbated their grammatical and spelling errors; all of it erected screens between the writers and their readers.

Many of Shaughnessy's students learned by making mistakes and correcting their mistakes. The point was that they began feeling a sense of insufficiency in the light of an enhanced awareness of their goals, their purposes. Of course many of them continued to make common errors, some of which were tolerated because of the recognition that standard English was as alien to them as it might be to a foreign speaker.

> If students understand why they are
> being asked to learn something and if
> the reasons given do not conflict with
> deeper needs for self-respect and
> loyalty to their group . . . they are

---

[27]Mina P. Shaughnessy, Errors & Expectations: A Guide for the Teacher of Basic Writing (New York: Oxford University Press, 1977).

disposed to learn it . . .[28]

> The discovery by a student that he can do something he thought he couldn't releases the energy to do it.[29]

The relevance for an approach to evaluation lies in the recognition that the purpose of evaluation, the educational purpose, is to shed light on a particular learning activity--or a range of learning activities--and to make visible what is happening. Moreover, it is to enable both learners and teachers to perceive the lack or the deficiencies in the activity and to act to bring about change.

There must be comparisons, however; and Mina Shaughnessy allows for this, within the experience of individual writers and among the basic writers in a class. Michael Scriven believes that all "useful evaluation is comparative." He writes:

> Is it possible to show that functions or goals are meritorious without any comparative considerations coming in? Suppose one shows that the function is to fulfill a crucial educational need. Wouldn't that prove that something meritorious had been done? That would depend on how the claim about need is defended in this context. If it is defended by showing not only that fulfillment of the need will be beneficial but also that previous efforts have failed, then we can justify our claim of merit--but only because there is an implied superiority to the previous effort.[30]

The point is to show that a given achievement "meets superior goals in a superior way," that it is "worth the cost," and that there are always alternatives (many of them unrealized). He also believes that

---

[28]Shaughnessy, op. cit., p. 125.

[29]Shaughnessy, op. cit., p. 127.

[30]Michael Scriven, "The Concept of Evaluation," in Educational Evaluation, op. cit., pp. 64-65.

decisions should be made contextually, and that the values which are so central in evaluation "come from a context of desires, needs, and performance."

My particular interest is in the kinds of value judgments that lead into "possibilizing" on the part of teachers and learners both. Also, I am far more interested in what Scriven calls "formative evaluation," meaning the judgment of a work in progress, than in "summative evaluation" or the judgment of a final product. There are, of course, institutional evaluators and various kinds of measurement experts who will continue to do "summative evaluation." But the voices of students and teachers must continue to be heard, so that the ethical questions remain audible, so that less will be taken for granted as the time goes on, so that fewer doors will close.

There remains the problem of the parents, however, and the demands they make. There are middle class parents worried about SATs, insisting on high achievement, whatever the cost. There are poor parents frightened by persisting illiteracy, people who want an exclusive emphasis on the three Rs for the sake of job training and survival in the mainstream. There are academic parents who purport to know more about education than do the teachers; there are zealots who want human relations "experiences" and non-cognitive play; there are fundamentalist parents afraid of certain novels, or of evolutionary theory, or of sex education. It becomes increasingly clear that students, parents, teachers, and the general public have different and competing ideas about how schools should be judged. Their assumptions differ; their values differ with regard to what good schools ought to be. Obviously, in a time of limited resources, not all the possible valued outcomes can receive adequate attention, and there will always be people who believe their concerns are being ignored.

Premises change as the climate changes; and concepts of what represents effective schooling compete. We have undoubtedly thought too little about the need to respond to diverse publics and to discover what their interests are. We have thought too little about what it might mean to talk with them about alternative possibilities. They, too, may feel oppressed by traditional notions of success, by the assessments that demean them in a society at odds with

itself. Certain ones of them might even be enlisted
in efforts to renew the schools.   Certain ones might
be attracted by the notion of a learning community
that in some manner includes neighborhood people,
children, teachers, administrators as well.

There is no question but these are difficult
times for those of us concerned about releasing human
beings, empowering them to think what their lives
might be, provoking them to move towards what is not
yet.   I have been trying to find a way of talking
about evaluation as liberating. I have been trying to
find a way of making "possibilizing" meaningful again.
It is a matter of taking new initiatives,   of
reaffirming what we stand for in this society, where
dignity is concerned--and human freedom.   The task
will be hard; the way will be long; but evaluation may
some day serve the cause of growth and constant
learning.

EVALUATION AND HUMAN DIGNITY

Charity James

Perhaps you are familiar with the concept of ley lines, lines of great power and energy that are said to crisscross our planet. It has been suggested to me that ley lines may well meet in this area of North Carolina, the site of an upsurge of intellect and imagination and of a serious concern for human life.

Certainly some of the words we are dealing with in this conference bear with them startling power and energy: equality, excellence, community, institution, human, dignity -- and evaluation. I confess to having some discomfort with the word evaluation. Excellent when it is used, as it originally was in France, to reflect a high culture's estimate of the monetary value of its works of art. But the etymology reminds me that it brings not only power but danger. Even at its most favourable interpretation the evaluator is working out value, a quite quantitative notion. If with some justification one takes a less optimistic approach one can say that in evaluating someone one is driving out the value of that person, just as in excommunicating him we drive him out of a community. Much evaluation does just that: it drives out people's sense of their own personal value. On this interpretation my title could be rephrased as "Human dignity (or worthship) and how to drive it away".

Dignity is a good word. I like also to use the word worth because of its evocative connection with worship. In the '70s I spent a year living around a great saint. Every evening he would start his teaching by saying, "I welcome you all with love. That is my great worship." He would often go on to explain that loving one another, seeing god in one another, is man's highest duty and privilege. If I love you aright I recognise your true worth as extraordinary, incomparable, indispensable beings. In fact if any one of us had no existence (in life or after life) then there would be no world; we are as much a part of the essence of things as that.

When I wrote <u>Young Lives at Stake</u> I didn't have quite the same understanding as I have now, but already I refused to use the word evaluation when thinking of students. I would be happy to evaluate the curriculum (using the word in its more positive sense), but for students I used the word appraisal, since implicit in it is the notion of approaching praise, drawing toward a being's true price. And we are pearls of great price.

So I suggest to you that if we are to put a letter to appraise the worth of ourselves, our colleagues and our students the only appropriate one is N, infinite. And the only numeral value is an eight on its side: ∞ . Not A, B, C, D, E, not 75% either, nor 10/10. If as student or teacher I can always remember this truth then no one can drive out my sense of value, for I am a being beyond the power of the human mind to value. If we were living in a society in which each person knew that, we would have nothing to discuss today. If all our students knew that they were N the attribution of As and Bs and even Es and Fs would be no assault on their dignity. It might be stupid and in that sense beneath our dignity, but the problem would be more one of tools than of ultimate morality.

When I was first asked to prepare this talk I was reminded of the story of the Lords' Club. (Of course it is also a Ladies' Club, but our material is complex enough without getting into alternate pronouns). The members of the Club all know that they are Lords. They want to run this club together, so they arrange to take turns with the various chores involved. For a time a member may be President, and might then become janitor or barperson or could have a stint on the accounts or on cleaning the swimming pool. There is no dissension because the system is fair -- and no loss of dignity because what could affect the inner dignity of a Lord? And they all know that the same is true of their fellow members. Everyone is beyond caring about ascribed status because their internal sense of worth is so strong. That is the Lords' Club.

Imagine now at the other end of the town a very different place, a place people do not join as members but go to (some gladly, some sadly) because they must. This place is called the Mirror Acquisition Department, and its function is to fit people out with distorting mirrors. Each entrant, starting at the earliest age and moving through every stage, often into middle age, is provided with a mirror which is

fixed to the head in such a way that it reflects them
back to themselves. Wherever they look they see
themselves, or rather a distortion of their true
appearance for the function is to distort. Once
affixed, the mirror cannot be avoided. In the rooms
there is writing on the walls, letters and numbers.
Sometimes the mirrors pick these up -- an A or a C or
a 10/10 or a 60%, and when that happens the tendency
to distortion is even more greatly accentuated. If
one is very good at something that someone in
authority finds important one may find oneself
reflected as a being of astonishing beauty. Others
are permitted to see themselves fitted for a time with
an alternative mirror which shows them in a series of
heroic or sexually inviting stances, but these usually
wear out rather soon, leaving a great disappointment.
Others try to mist their mirrors by taking drugs. But
the distortive mirrors are part of our social
equipment and stay with most of us throughout our
lives. The only ways of losing them that I know are
to become so indifferent to them that there is no ego
there for them to hang on to -- or to become so sure
of our worthship that one breaks through their bonds.
Friends or family or teachers who offer insights into
that worthship early in life are a great gift of
providence, but for most of us the work of
conscientization in an even deeper sense of the word
than Freire's takes a life-time. A good sign is when
one can say with a Joyce Carol Oates character, I am
no one's idea but one's own. Beyond this comes the
place where one can say, in Sanskrit terminology,
So'ham, I am That. The Hindus say that we spend the
early months in the womb in blissful contemplation of
our Thatness, unceasingly hearing the mantra So'ham.
Shortly before birth it changes to Ko'ham, Who am I?
So we come into the world very vulnerable to the
culture, which is only too willing to demonstrate, in-
formally through the family and later on through
M.A.D., exactly what it thinks we are.

One answer to Ko'ham is Amen; so-be-it;

What is your name?
My name is Amen.
What are you like?
I am like a butterfly only bigger.
Where are you going?
I am going into the long grasses.
What are you hoping to find?
I am hoping to find a common:place

I believe that most of us in this room have some
sense of that flow of being. It has been a hard haul
for us, part of a deep search for meaning, to know
that we have inner worth regardless of whether others
like what we do, and regardless even of whether we
particularly like it either. Perhaps the lack of that
knowledge is what T. S. Eliot referred to in The
Hollow Men

> This is the way the world ends
> This is the way the world ends
> This is the way the world ends
> Not with a bang but a whimper.

Today it looks as if it might be a bang, but that
would still be a whimper if we remember who Man is.

I have introduced these two communities (or
institutions), the Lords' Club and M.A.D., because I
want to underline the point that we are dealing with
the moral problem, and actual moral behavior is of
necessity contextual. Kant spoke of treating all
beings as a Kingdom of Ends -- what for today I would
like to call a Kingdom of Ns. This generalised
instruction is a universal teaching of great minds:
Love your neighbor as yourself, Tattvam Asi ('thou art
That'), See God in one another. In practice, when we
try to follow the great imperative we need to exercise
what the Buddhists call "skill in means". One aspect
of that skill is that our actions be appropriate to
our context.

It is our hope and will to obey Kant's great
imperative in our work with children. Yet the context
in which we work does not make our task easy:

--- Most of our superiors and certainly
    many of our colleagues have no concept
    of the difficulties this conference
    finds in taking part in the
    conventional evaluation of children.
    The State of North Carolina likewise
    enforces evaluation by letter code,
    and your legislators also would
    therefore probably find it hard to
    comprehend why you wince at the task
    they lay on you.

--- We live in a meritocracy in which it
    is felt to be an advance in social

justice that at last caste and class, wealth and hidden privilege, are supposed to have given way to merit, "I.Q. + effort" as the basis for advancement in the world. Hence over the last century or so the school and university have become the recording angels who destine young people for the heaven of success or the hell of failure. Teachers are seen as reneging on our social functions as the organ for selection if we ask only to teach our students and our subject matter with skill and respect.

--- Most of the parents who take an interest in school and therefore influence our procedures are themselves in the meritocratic marketplace. They love their children and interpret this love to mean that they should help them to have the success they have not enjoyed -- or have enjoyed. Parents invest much emotional capital in their children and some of them watch the numbers and letters we give them with much the same hope or dread that investors have about Dow Jones.

--- Most children have not experienced membership of a Lords' Club. They have not learned from Wordsworth that they come into the world "trailing clouds of glory" and they rapidly accept the values of "the prison house". A developmental point abets this acceptance: when they start school they are likely to be in the good boy and good girl phase of Kohlberg's inventory of moral development: they want to be good and they want to be seen to be good. Moreover to young children teachers and parents have an august quality bordering on the divine. (Few children have the sturdy independence of a young friend of mine. At age 4 he had this conversation with his sister, aged 7. "Serena, is God looking at me?" Serena, with empressement, "Yes, Richard". Five minutes later, same question, same reply. Finally once more, "Serena, is God still looking at me? Well, what's he following me around for?" Now it is a ticklish adventure in discrimination to discover that good-ness and good-at-ness are not one and the same. If teacher is pleased when I am well behaved and pleased when I get my sums right, how am I to distinguish the two? So the habit of equating success with virtue roots early, and deep.

Since we have to act within this context our skill in means is very important. I suggest we consider our options under three headings:

I.   Inherent Difficulties about Evaluation.
We need ourselves to be very clear about the inherent difficulties of what we are asked to do; otherwise we may too easily get caught up in the unrealities of conventional procedure. Using the imagery of the distorted mirror I have suggested that what we are asked to do is damaging to the human psyche. Now I want to go on to suggest that it is also basically absurd. We should not practice evaluation as it is prescribed and what we do will not make sense when we have done it.

II. Some Positive Alternative Proposals.
If we deal with this problem in a spirit of an enquiry, searching for alternatives and trying them out on a small scale (or at least making them known) we have some hope of encouraging colleagues and parents to enter on a programme of reforms. Emotional withdrawal will not help but practical suggestions may.

III. The Aim: Partnership.
We should find ways to draw our students into partnership with us so that they too can witness the problems of evaluation, and can learn positive habits of self-appraisal.

In sum, we need to demythologise evaluation. This is where skillful means will lead us.

I. Some Inherent Difficulties in Evaluation

1. Standards of Expectation.
Dr. James Macdonald has written with acumen about the problems of evaluating against a supposed standard of excellence, so I will leave this aside. I want to turn to another form of appraisal, record-keeping, superior both in principle and in practice, although still open to this is some dangers. I have suggested elsewhere that we can properly think of appraisal in terms of the individual's personal growth, of helping people to move toward becoming who they really are. For this, record-keeping is essential; it is also one of the strengths of good elementary teachers who maintain a running selection of each students' work ranging from sums to paintings. These form a substantial body of evidence for a longitudinal study and for analysis of recurring behaviors. Many of us keep records of what marks we gave to children but we do not maintain evidence of what work they gave to us. Good record-keeping alone enables us to recognise the continuing ebb and flow of an individual's learning.

The only danger comes if, once again, there are fixed expectations of the line that growth should take, rather as a nation or a business predicts a required angle of growth on a graph. It is all too easy to extrapolate from one period to another, to suppose that because a student did such and such work in September there should be a fixed increment by December, easier still to suppose that the line maintained will continue through June. We all know about growth spurts and plateaux of learning -- it is the stuff of the most elementary courses in education -- but still it is easy to be disappointed, easy to fall into guilt and anxiety, and easy too to be complaisant and ignore possibilities for sudden improvements. The purpose of record-keeping is to diagnose strengths and difficulties

161

and to find ways of creating appropriate
opportunities. It focuses our attention on
individuals and it should not be polluted by
fixed ideas of excellence in growth.

2. Subjectivity.
There is a more fundamental difficulty about
appraising a student's work in our classes.
Modern physics for half a century has
recognised that the presence of the observer
affects what is observed: observer and
observed are one total event. We cannot
stand outside physical reality in its most
intimate and secret flow of movement and
suppose that we arrive at objective
judgment. We necessarily contribute to the
event. How much more obviously do we
contribute to the teaching-learning event.
We set up its requirements, its limitations,
its time-frame, and in ways of which we are
not conscious we influence its outcomes by
body language or by subtle (or not so
subtle) inflection of the voice. We are
most surely part of the event of our
teaching. That is what we are paid for.
But we are also required to look at the
other side of that event, the student's
learning, as if we had nothing to do with
it, as if we were just God following him
about. The trouble is that we are not yet
in a state of infinite wisdom and even if we
were we would not have been able to provide
equal opportunity to our extraordinarily
diverse students. It is true that a quite
open climate and curriculum which gives
opportunities to students to work in
different ways and at different rates of
involvement and withdrawal can provide the
best data for appraisal (so long as plenty
of overt structure is provided for those who
need it, and the happy isolate is allowed
for as well as the group enjoyer). But not
all teachers can work well in this way, or
wish to, and if they work against their
natures that message comes through also.
And then if one does provide the most
admirable opportunity to a whole range of
different children to learn in the way most
appropriate to each one, the true absurdity
of the usual standard evaluation procedures

162

becomes obvious; how can all that be translated into letters or numbers?

So there are two aspects to our subjectivity. First we inevitably contaminate the purity of our data by our presence and by our actions. Secondly we are inevitably partial beings in a double sense: only partial knowledge is available to us and we are partial in our attitudes. The claim to impartiality is only a sign that we do not understand how partial we are.

3. Teachers' Partiality
In looking for a matrix to order our understanding of human partiality I have found Jung's Psychological Typology has given me more insight than any other system, and I want therefore to refer to it in some detail. I have some reservations about some of the uses to which it is being adapted in this country, where it has been simplified and operationalised for the purpose of classification and placement. Jung's intentions were quite otherwise: as a therapist he had a totally dynamic approach to human nature. Early in his work he found in dealing with great numbers of patients that he could recognise some ways in which human beings are trapped in opposites: they have a strength in one way of engaging with inner and outer reality but are deficient in its opposite function. He taught that this is inevitable: some behaviors come into prominence early in our lives, they become part of our persona and we and others recognise ourselves through them: they work well for us and so they are reinforced. The opposite or "inferior" function remains in the shadow. The inferior function is rather like an under-study waiting in the wings for a chance to make her or his contribution to the drama. Jung taught that the process of becoming whole or "individuated" comes through welcoming this inferior function, bringing it to consciousness. In doing this we will find our true wholeness and will be able at any time to act freely, drawing on all that we intrinsically are. This is part

of the individuation process, which is the work of a life-time.

I am told that in his later years Jung expressed concern about contemporary tendencies to use his typology otherwise and himself ceased to refer to it. But I believe that if we follow his own guidance in Psychological Types and the more recent work of his close associate Marie-Louise Von Franz we can find it an invaluable tool for recognition of ourselves, our colleagues and our students, a true guide to empathy and hope. I would like particularly to recommend Von Franz's long essay on the inferior function. This is a good deal more airy and spacious in tone than Jung's earlier Psychological Types of which she writes, "Psychological Types is one of Jung's earlier books. When he wrote it he was in many respects struggling in the dark". More important still she concentrates attention on the inferior function, and thereby her work is particularly significant for teachers, whose need is to understand the possibilities of personal growth and the obstacles that we all face.

In Psychological Types Jung posited four main functions, comprising two pairs of opposites. Two are rational: thinking (T) and feeling (F). Two are irrational: intuition (N) and sensation function (S). It will be clear at once that he is not using these terms in a usual way. Thinking is recognisably thinking in that it refers to orderly conceptual argument and analysis. But for Jung feeling is also a way to know: one might describe it as a recognition of the issues, personalities and values involved in a situation. Again the word intuition should not be confused with some kind of hunch bordering on ESP; it is the power to make connections and above all to see possibilities. Sensation function, although based in sound focusing in sensed perceptions goes beyond this to the ability to deal with daily reality in an accurate way.

We have to remember that Jung teaches that we all have access to these four functions. Nevertheless, within each of these pairs of functions, thinking-feeling and intuition-sensation, one will inevitably be more available for an individual's use than the other. Take the four functions together and you will find that the strongest function of all (the so-called superior function) will always most obviously overshadow its opposite, the two other functions being as a rule more evenly balanced. Thus if you look at the ordering of any individual's functions you might find, for instance, that A's functions run N1, S4 (strongest vs. weakest) T2, F3, whereas B's might be T1, F4, S2, N3.

To these four functions add two basic attitudes, extraversion (E) and introversion (I). The extraverted person "so lives as to correspond directly with objective conditions. The objective factor determines his consciousness". (p. 3) The intraverted person makes his or her decisions on a subjective basis. All of us of course are extraverted at times and introverted at times but the extravert usually likes to arrive at decisions in concert with others whereas the introvert is more readily a solo performer.

To Jung's basic hypothesis Isabel Myers-Briggs, leader of a very energetic program of research and application of her own typology, has made an addition which I find convincing. She has separated off another pair of opposites which in Jung's work are placed elsewhere: perceiving and judging. The perceiver (P) is one who finds closure uncomfortable, who observes and partakes in the drama of life rather than coming to judgment about it -- and in my experience is apt to be untidy both with objects and in work habits. The judger (J) prefers closure, knows pretty well what he or she thinks about pretty well everything, and knows very well that there is a right place for everything and it had better be in it. (And not as a P friend of mine once declared, "Everything is in its place and its place is the floor").

With these four sets of opposites we can show a diagram:

Clockwise:

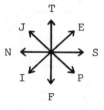

T = thinking
E = extraversion
S = sensation
P = perception
F = feeling
I = introversion
N = intuition
J = judgment

The diagram may remind us that wherever our most active and favoured functions or attitudes may lie the opposite will be primitive, relatively unconscious and probably a source of discomfort. I shall discuss later on some of the ways in which we may use the typology to benefit ourselves and our colleagues and students. For the present I want simply to make a point of principle. Our personal type must skew our assessment of students.

Some useful research from the Myers-Briggs group makes the scale of the problem clear. David Keirsey and Marilyn Bates quote California research on the proportions of students and teachers of different types.

	School Personnel	Pupils & General Population	Difference
SJ. . .	56%	38%	+16%
NF. . .	36%	12%	+24%
NT. . .	6%	12%	- 6%
SP. . .	2%	38%	-36%

Using intuition and sensation function as initial binary dividers, they show that one of the two largest groups of students, those with a high sensation function and high perception -- and hence with inferior intuition and judgment -- have to meet a faculty with only 2% of the same

166

disposition; these are mostly art teachers. Here are perfectly valid young people, with a gift for life and immediate enjoyment, who will find it hard to meet the requirements of faculty whose basic ways of being are quite different.

The figures of faculties are likewise interesting, indicating why so many schools are rent with disagreement, and incidentally why so many of your colleagues have no conception of your discomfort about evaluation: of these figures 56% are SJs, 36% NFs. In dealing with such a rift it is also wise to remember about the universal tendency of human beings to projection: interpreting other people's actions according to what they would mean if they were done by us and disliking those aspects of others with which we have most difficulty in our inner personal lives. Of course where colleagues have grown in self-awareness and mutual appreciation this very difference can be a source of great effectiveness.

II. Some Practical Proposals

Those of us who recognise the inherent problems of evaluation and yet are forced by convention and even by legislation to engage in it are clearly trapped in an ungainly position which we cannot find congruent with our own human dignity or anyone else's. The question now is what to do about it. Wringing of hands, passing the buck or calling out _tua culpa_ -- these are not very dignified behaviors either. It is all too easy to get into the way of "If only . . ." or "What a pity that . . .", negative mantras with great power to reduce energy and hope. I prefer anger to sorrow and laughter to either, for laughter energises, and the human situation really is absurd:

Prometheus, you're not very dignified
straddled and pinioned there
your body all awry
your rump your backbone
clamped in a stinging agony
on the corroding rock

167

as you hurl castrato ripostes at your Maker.
you're a comic figure
really you are
a fall guy for the intrusive vulture.

But when your moment comes
in ire and humour
to laugh a belly laugh
your heart your spleen your gizzard
will erupt and spatter with glowing scarlet
    particles
a dying sky

and we shall call it

Fire.

Laughter is significant not only because it has a
fiery energy within it but because it is a form
of witnessing, it aids us to observe our
situation rather than being overwhelmed by pain.
I know it is easy for me as an outside person to
say this kind of thing, easy too to make
recommendations. But since I am invited to speak
to you I will suggest three main ways of handling
the situation. These are to demythologise the
process by breaking routine, to approach the
problems in a spirit of enquiry and to work
collaboratively. All these approaches apply
equally to our relations with parents, colleagues
and students: I shall put partnership with
students in a special category at the end of this
paper because of its supreme importance for our
daily classroom life. But parents and
colleagues, when victims of the evaluation myth,
are emotionally involved to their own cost and
are separated from one another -- and often from
their children -- by these customary procedures
of evaluation. They too are Ns (infinite, not
merely intuitive). So in a spirit of scepticism,
enquiry and partnership we need to move towards
them. Here are some suggestions:

1.   We might pay more attention to students'
     behaviors (intellectual, practical, social,
     emotional) than to their success and failure
     at imposed tasks, (which as we have seen are
     products of our own partiality). If we
     concentrate on behaviors, strategies,
     chosen ways of working, this demands that we

168

provide a curriculum and classroom procedure which make it possible for students to manifest them. For instance, to be able to ask good questions is a valuable behavior which can be manifested in most classrooms. But in life it is not much use asking questions unless we or someone around us can suggest ways of answering them and possibly set out on a soundly conceived plan of enquiry or research. Such opportunities for answering our own questions are much less frequently offered to students. So thinking about behaviors broadens our concepts of what might go on in class and soon leads to record-keeping of a diagnostic style. It thereby enables us to individualise programmes effectively. "What a pity that" a useful term, individualisation, has been used for programmes of a very narrow and ill-conceived kind. We can do something about that in our own work.

2.   If possible, we should collaborate with colleagues in formulating an index of behaviors to be noted, preferably working with a team, but failing that seeking the input of people who have different priorities from one's own. Since we are all partial it is good to make use of our diversity of insight. The Jungian typology could make a useful basis for an index, or at least a starting point. Some teachers are likely to note with approval (and give opportunity for) the high intuitive characteristics, asking many questions, fluency of ideas, seeing connections; others will be well grounded in the sensation function and will pay more attention to good work habits, accuracy, attention to detail. A third group will argue strongly for the importance of thinking behaviors, such as insightful analysis and the readiness to be comfortable with large scale conceptual argument that is more concerned with logic than with the individual case. These will be balanced by teachers who reward students able to make sound and emotionally cogent appraisals of a situation though their grasp of underlying theory may be rather unsure. Intraverted and extraverted behaviors,

fluidity of perception and the readiness for closure would also be welcomed by a diverse group of teachers.

3.   Looking for relative strengths
        When I wrote <u>Young Lives at Stake</u> (which deals with some of this material and more) I was so conscious of what I have today called the distorting mirrors provided by M.A.D. and of the hollowness and lack of sense of worth that they engender that I asked teachers to exercise a self-denying ordinance and for a time to look together only at the relative strengths of each student, ignoring weaknesses. We are used to looking for weaknesses: It is habit that we learned from our own education, and it stems from teachers' anxiety and sometimes guilt under the pressure of external demands and constraints. So to concentrate on the positive can create a breakthough from our mind sets which leads to a new chance to observe children in their complexity. I therefore proposed an index of behaviors, mostly shared, some perhaps arising from the special concerns of a discipline -- refined motor skills, for instance, would affect shop more than social science. And I suggested a simple form with the names of students in vertical sequence down the side and behaviors horizontal across the top. All that each teacher does is to make a single check when a child evinces one of the behaviors, e.g. works well on her own, collaborates well, argues his point soundly, and the rest. They keep these records and at the end of a chosen period, perhaps 3 to 6 weeks, share them with others teaching the same student. Teachers working in this way find there are two groups of students who call for special attention, those who have check marks only with one teacher (what does that signify? a special talent or a compatibility that others could learn from?) and those who have no checks at all, the children who with conventional evaluation pass through the school almost unnoticed.

        Today, after working with Jung's typology for nearly a decade of in-service

170

and community classes I would further recommend that teachers look out for manifestations of students' inferior functions, training ourselves to see them not with exasperation or deep concern but as inevitable shadow companions to their relative strengths, companions who need to be treated with the greatest possible caution and sympathy since they can carry so much hurt within them. (I return to this point when considering our partnership with students.

4.   "No marks without remarks" is a good watchword if marks are absolutely required. Marks give a false appearance of mathematical correctness and they do not give any opportunity to students to understand their own work. Cliches that provide neither diagnosis nor evidence for the judgment made such as "excellent work", "very poor" or "could do better" could themselves do better. Today, attentive parents receive some oral remarks because they come to meet their children's teachers. Explanatory written remarks which diagnose and explain the basis for the student's future programs can help disaffected, ignorant or uncaring parents to have greater understanding. They also give all parents an opportunity for shared discussion of the teacher's assessment: "Well, how do you feel that you did? Did you discuss these points with your teacher? Do you understand the basis for the teacher's comments about future work plans?" and so on. There can be a good deal of tension between parents, teachers and students and it would be unrealistic to suggest that it will always be relieved by the provision of information. But in some cases this will happen and will help parents to help children to become informed participants in the appraisal of their progress and to learn how they are seen by others to operate in the school world.

5.   De-ritualising appraisal procedures
       The prevailing system is for the school oracle to pronounce its mysteriously coded

171

message at fixed seasons of the year and for all the students at once. The postman knocks at the same time for every family on the street. Such ritual breeds anxiety and often rivalry; the distorting mirror is affixed more firmly than ever. And from the standpoint of faculty it is a nightmare. In fact some of us who teach 150 children or more find it difficult even to recall much about some of the low-profile students. So in Young Lives at Stake I suggest creating a more flexible system whereby throughout the school year different groups, which can be chosen by birthday or initial or randomly, are under special observation. The effect is that there can be a steady but gentle flow of faculty case conferences and of meetings with parents, and the teacher's task is reduced to manageable proportions. Thus the myth of the great infallible evaluation event is laid to rest and a closer partnership can be formed between the human beings involved.

III. Developing a partnership with students.

The most important partnership is that between teachers and their students, and it is our students who will most profit by learning to witness their own progress and partake in decisions about it. Many teachers can achieve that partnership. The students know they have the teacher's basic human respect. They sense that in this situation both are members of the Lords' Club even though one plays the part of teacher and the other of student. They can recognise that the teacher's comments, even when most severe, are consonant with their personal dignity, and are made because the teacher has a better image of them than they have themselves.

However, there are few teachers who do not have some students with whom that rapport is hard to come by; it is there for a moment and then fades or it can't be reached at all. Every comment, favorable or unfavorable, seems to add to the emotional distance. In some instances, of course, this is due to some emotional disturbance, in others children inherit family or group mistrust of teachers as a breed or have

172

been made wary by painful past experience with uncaring or incompatible teachers. Where none of this applies, I believe that an understanding of the Jungian typology will give quite specific help.

It is proverbially true that like likes like: birds of a feather fly together. What is less commonly understood is how great are the psychological distances between people who are unlike. They are divided by a No Man's Land, the territory of the primitive inferior function, which is heavily mined, ready to explode in pain or anger if some stranger intrudes. It is like Matthew Arnold's "darkling plain . . . Where ignorant armies clash by night". We hit and we hurt and we don't know what we have done. To avoid that clash we need to have some means of recognition of the workings of the inferior functions, our own (which are hidden to us, of course, and always likely to cause us trouble) and those of our colleagues and students, which we may recognise more readily and yet still be oblivious to the pain we cause.

In introducing this material so briefly I have to be simplistic. I can give examples of the shadow aspects of the four functions and the attitudes, but each personality is a complex interweaving of different aspects. So the actions and reactions, for instance, of the extraverted intuitive (with inferior introverted sensation) are different from those of an introverted intuitive (whose extraverted sensation function is weak) -- and so on all through the possible interconnections.

First for a look at the different responses of introverts and extraverts. I would like to quote Van Franz on the behavior of a highly introverted young child:

> Jung once told of the case of a child who would not enter a room before it had been told the names of the pieces of furniture in the room -- table, chair, etc. That is typical of a definitely introverted attitude, where the object is terrifying and has to be banished or put in its place by a word. . . In such little details . . . you can observe the tendency towards introversion or extraversion in a very small child.

I have chosen this extreme example because we may have such a personality in our class five or fifteen years later, and be unable to credit how much effort it takes for survival in an outside world that is experienced as bizarre or threatening. Since 75% of people are said to be extraverted in this country, it is probably the introvert who most needs our understanding. Some research undertaken about 25 years ago (which I cannot now place) described the different responses of extraverts and introverts to praise and blame. Extraverts were shown to respond much better to criticism than introverts, who deeply required the reassurance of praise, presumably since their relationship with the outside world is not highly conscious or differentiated. Not long ago in an in-service group which had taken a simple typological inventory, I set the Is on one side of the room, the Es on the other. The task happened to be to replay a painful episode in one's life and try to give it a more positive ending. The Is sat quietly, were fairly soon finished and then exchanged a few words. The Es promptly formed into small groups, talked with animation -- and would not stop. Finally I shouted at them. Oh no, they called out, we must go on, we are just solving X's problems with her retarded son, and so on for each cluster. With the introverts I could not possibly have been so fierce, even though I was humorous about it. The extraverts didn't mind at all.

Extraverts have their own difficulties. Since their introverted attitudes are relatively primitive the trauma comes for them if they are left alone too much. Again, Es find it much harder to get deeply into a pice of work: they are often seen as lacking perseverance, but a teacher who is comfortable with their extraverted attitude will see that they need more breaks and more changes of activity, as well as profiting by more criticising than an introvert can usually handle.

Hence each group appreciates a matching teaching style. The I teacher, delivering a well-planned, coherent lecture-type lesson, is a source of comfort to the I student, who is much confused by the give-and-take, the apparent loss of thread and the intermingling of activities that are the stock-in-trade of the E teacher. It is really hard for the I student to process all that and come to a solo estimate of its meaning. A more extraverted student may find the I's teaching almost intolerable, since it requires a privacy of response rather than shared open discussion, and an orderly acceptance of another person's thought sequence which the E may find hard to grasp and recall, and which may feel to him or her like a steam-roller. Such differences of attitude must surely cast doubt on our ability to provide objective evaluation of our students' learning.

Von Franz's study of the typology is particularly helpful in explaining the sensitivity of the shadow or inferior functions, which have some of the same fears of coming out into the world that the introverted child had of entering an unknown room. It is really hard to credit the degree of sensitivity many of us endure. Take the example of the student with a high feeling and low thinking function. Von Franz describes a fellow student who had shown her a paper:

> She was a feeling type. The paper was very good, but in a minor passage where she switched from one theme to another it seemed to me there was a hiatus in connection of thought . . . So I said to her that I thought it an excellent paper but that on one page she might make a better transition. At that she got absolutely emotional and said: "Oh, well, then it's all ruined. I shall just burn it."

This scene lasted some time and one may suspect it was particularly awkward for Von Franz, a thinking type, to handle; she may have found it hard to produce the simple gesture of affection which would come easily to a feeling extravert.

The effective thinker can find it hard to behave appropriately in specific situations, being so apt to act on the basis of general laws. "Of course I had to take in Mrs. X's child even though I hardly know her and it is hard on my husband and our son. But we are supposed to do that kind of thing for one another" (where it was clear to her hearers at one of my classes that the neighbor was exploitative). Or it may work the other way, as in an example I heard at a class I attended: Husband (F), "I feel awful today." Wife (T), "What am I supposed to do about it? I'm not a doctor." I suspect that one of the strongest arguments against tracking in schools is that it is likely to isolate the high thinker and the high intuitive, both of whom have some difficulties in dealing with reality, from readier and more realistic peers.

175

After describing her contretemps with her fellow students, Van Franz comments on the inferior function that "it tyrannises its surroundings by being touchy". People with a low intuitive function, are individually touchy if they do not get a point quickly. They are apt to be thought dull by intuitives but they often have good managerial skills. So in order to defend their territory against the invasions of the intuitive mind they become accomplished in making sensible down-to-earth comments which puncture the balloon of possibilities that the intuitive likes to play with. This is a form of tyranny. Ideas which other people find interesting are threatening to them, almost to the point (as one S friend said to me about me) of vertigo. Any reference to progressive or alternate ideas in education may be turned aside with as much contempt as if one had spoken of astrology , or ESP, which are seen as absurd.

At a divorce workshop I gave, one S woman well on in her process of individuation described how she had been working toward greater wholeness. First she had fought her tendency to compulsive tidiness by use of her sensation powers: enjoying the forms and colours made by piles of mess in other poeple's houses. She was not so free she didn't feel compelled to make her bed. (Naturally her high intuitive hearers were amazed at her delight in something which could cause them no difficulty). Then she had felt drawn to study dreams,"but thank goodness" she added in her realistic way, "it was a pretty down to earth course". This was extraverted sensation. An introverted S person may have great difficulty in your classes. They often stare at the teacher glassy eyed. Within, all is well: "-- the impression falls deeper and deeper and sinks in", but "outwardly the IS type looks utterly stupid". One such student said to me "Now you mention it, I've noticed other lecturers look at me and look away very rapidly". By next term she had developed, under the guidance of an EF friend, a charming smile, a little glassy but approving, and we did not have to look away.

With a majority of teachers as SJs a high S student who can produce good written work in the form of efficient answers to questions and well organised statements of what has been taught, is likely to have satisfactory grades from teachers who themselves are content with the grading system. The high SPs, who cannot easily manage such closure and whose intuitive grasp is not a strength either, may well need to look for help and understanding to the intuitives on a faculty, particularly those who are more inclined to perception than to judgment.

As an example of a low sensation function, I may use myself, because owing to my interest in the typology I have begun to see how it has applied me. A few years ago I felt a need to work with clay -- a wise decision according to Jung, since ceramics and sculpture are the best means of helping intuitives to steady the flow of ideas. In fact he says that all the arts are important for the various inferior functions. My first course was on coiling. It was rather too much for me and I had to escape into Greek drama from time to time. One afternoon when I came back I was told that Bernard Leach, a very great potter, had been in our studio, had looked at my coiled jug and had asked whose was that splendid mediaeval pot. "Mediaeval?", I asked. "Yes, well it means roughly made". I never looked at it again. Mediaeval meant clumsy, and the most hurtful remarks my touchy and tyrannical inferior function had experienced from my teens onwards were all comments on my clumsiness. I could not even hear the praise.

As we learn to be more affectionate towards our own inferior functions we may threaten other people's even more, even if they are the same. I greatly pained a young teacher only a few months ago. Her inferior function like mine was sensation, so she had trouble filling in her Jungian typological inventory. I am well used to that sort of thing, so I teased her in a companionable and I thought sympathetic way. Six weeks later, at the end of the course, she stayed late to tell me how cruelly hurt she had been. This is the real stuff we are talking about, the stuff of people's pain, resentment and low self esteem.

So in appraising students' work in their shadow aspects we need to be supremely cautious if we are to arrive at any partnership. For the best summary I know I turned to Von Franz once again:

In Van Gennep's Les Rites de Passage one finds examples of how explorers approach a primitive village. They have to stop several miles away, and then three messengers from the village come; the villagers have to be assured that the explorers have no evil designs and especially

177

that they do not intend to use black magic against the inhabitants. The messengers then go back and when they return gifts are exchanged.

She goes on to describe this as "bush politeness", and contrasts it with personal politeness. "It is rather a matter of having real feeling and understanding for the other person's weakness and not daring to touch that weakness."

We have to be very careful. Indeed, we must remind ourselves that it is through making good connections with our inferior functions that we move slowly into wholeness, but this is a life-time's work. With young students we may help best by reinforcing their relative strengths and by quite simply explaining that the cost of being strong in one aspect of life is that one has relative weaknesses also, and that this is quite understood. We may, that is to say, try to demythologise the notion of the perfect student and allow that life would be very boring if we came into the world ready made and had no inner work to do. Certainly we shall do well to follow another piece of practical advice from Van Franz. She suggests that it is wise not to confront the weakest function of all (which I have described as no. 4, the opposite of our main strength) but to try gently to deal with no. 3 which is shadow twin to our secondary function and therefore not so emotionally charged. We might work on this with many students.

I would like to end by paying tribute to two mentors whom I have been blessed by knowing in recent years. Both are artists and are important to me because of the pain I have suffered in that field. Other people will recall teachers who have helped or are helping them in their most sensitive areas of being. One mentor taught a course in Cambridge, Mass., called "Drawing for people who can't draw a straight line". All of us who came had suffered in art classes ("my first death" as a student said to me not long ago, and indeed failure in the arts is very deeply felt because they are so much an expression of our inner being). But she swept us all along on a tide of adventure. In the third class we did life drawing, in the sixth (our first with paint) we did life painting. It was like being in a hurricane, but we knew, each one of us, that no harm could come to us. She understood our weakness and would protect us from it. Our teacher was totally fearless on our

178

behalf. She never said, yes, yes, how nice: she simply saw what we had done, made judicious technical comments, loved it, loved us. She once said that people who came to these classes had more promise than those who studied intermediate drawing. Of courses we had. There was so much pain in there for all of us, and we were now prepared to face it.

The second mentor is a distinguished potter and writer, a good friend in whose studio I sometimes work. Years ago, not long after my episode with the mediaeval pot, I was trying again. I made some little mud pie happening and scrunched it up in disgust. "Why did you throw that away, she asked, and I explained. "A pity. It was the beginning of an emerging form". And it was indeed the first stirring of a little series of pinch pots that always lacked their beginning. I find this a splendid metaphor for our work in partnership with the young. If we can only help them not to be thrown off balance by success or failure, not to look outside for praise or blame, but with some inner confidence to watch themselves as emerging forms, then we shall be doing our work very well indeed. Our dignity and theirs is ensured by our fearless faith in witnessing the first stirring of an emerging being who will take a life-time to complete. And the longer that we can protect them from M.A.D. and quantitative grading the freer they will be to move unhindered on their way. Even if one can hold off only until the early teens young people learn to see through the mystique of marks, and to be able to make very good sense indeed of our constructive remarks.

POSTSCRIPT

May I please have an appraisal of this paper? Do you feel a need to evaluate it with an A, B, C, D, E, F, or an excellent, fair or poor, a "could do better" or a "has done worse"? Or may I persuade you not to evaluate but to observe the behaviours I have evinced?

Of course there is internal evidence of a high intuitive, low sensation function person -- that is stated in so many words. But you might also discover it from other hints. The liking for connective imagery, such as M.A.D., or quotations from poems, reveal the high intuitive and there is a typical optimism about creating new forms. The low S function is somewhat obscured (I hope), but a high S person would surely have provided much more detail about a possible index of behaviours, and would probably have done more research on the schools which have been working in line with the proposals in Young Lives at Stake: definitely more data all round. The second strongest function (F) is pretty much in evidence. The writer obviously cares more for cases than for theories, and the delight in anecdotal examples (which must be quite tiresome to high thinkers) suggests that she cannot really believe that anyone can manage many pages of sequential thought or down to earth proposals without some "human interest". The corresponding weakness in T functioning has been fairly well overcome through arduous rewriting, but there are still places, no doubt, where the connective links are muzzy. Also the way the material is argued indicates a somewhat obsessional attitude which is typical of a weaker function: it is doubtful if a genuine T person would need quite so many Latin and Arabic numerals to prove that he or she was in control of the subheadings. The paper is obviously the work of a Perceiver rather than a Judger, since it requested all options be kept open at all costs, and one senses that any negative judgment made on anyone at all would cause a good deal of pain. As to extraversion or introversion it may be difficult to judge by the outcome, but anyone watching the process of composition would recognise an E. An introvert would certainly not have welcomed interruptions by her friends with such alacrity, and would not have felt it necessary to dead-head the gardenias with quite such minute particularity nor to make so many spontaneous trips to the beach.

The next step would be for you to begin to conceive a program of study for me, but this would require a closer partnership than is possible between writer and reader. It may be useful to say this. I plan to teach more philosophy and to write more often (T and J respectively), and to take a course on gardening which should be helpful to that ever struggling S. And of course to continue on my spiritual journey toward discovering that I am truly That.

I hope that this postscript will not seem to be an ego trip. It is intended as a manifestation of certain principles which recur in the main paper: the principle that watching behaviours is more

180

constructive and more seemly than evaluating, that
such diagnosis is necessary for the planning of
programs that are appropriate to the individual, that
although we are all members of the Lords' Club or the
Kingdom of Ns our personalities are inevitably
complete and partial, and that ultimately our dignity
is best served by our being allowed to do our work,
which is to move towards wholeness in the best ways we
can discover.

CRITIQUE

The final section of this book is intended as a commentary and a critical companion to the preceeding papers and to the context in which they were presented. They include critical reflections on some of the ideas found in the papers, consideration of the meanings of community, moral development and human enpowerment, and discussion of the phenomenology of the conference as a context for a liberating pedagogy.

ETHICS, PEACOCKS, AND A CHANGE OF SEASON:
A REPOSITIONING OF ISSUES

John G. Sullivan

In Carolina, the month of March marks the turning
of season. Winter is receding and spring is
tentatively moving in. One can sense it in the air,
in the smell of the earth, in the sounds of birds and
insects still too new to form the unnoticed background
of our thoughts.

It was March, and I was to spend two weekends at
Quail Roost, attending a conference devoted to values
in the secondary schools. Quail Roost, once a private
residence, now a conference center, stands in the
midst of 90 acres. The drive to the main house is
through heavy woodlands. But the other side of the
house fronts onto a lawn sloping down a rolling
hillside. In the valley is a working farm devoted to
the breeding of cattle. The vista from the front steps
of the house is quite worthy of a country squire. The
setting is pastoral and pleasant -- quite conducive to
the thinking of solid, sensible, prudent thoughts.
Then one catches sight of something most extraordinary
-- peacocks on the lawn -- three of them. Throughout
the conference, I remained fascinated by the peacocks.

Like others, I have come to expect things of
retreats. By changing place, I expect a certain shift
in consciousness. I expect to move from the space of
ordinary thoughts to a more reflective space, a
different landscape of the mind. I also expect a
change in my sense of time. I anticipate a break from
ordinary routine, a slower rhythm, with time
stretching out as on a long beach or across an expanse
of ocean. With this stretching of time, it is easy to
review one's life.

Since retreats promise a different sense of
place and time, I felt I had a right to expect these
things. But I had no right to expect the presence of
the peacocks. That was truly extraordinary, a matter
not of right but grace. Retreats are supposed to take
us from the ordinary to something a bit out of the
ordinary. But peacocks are so extraordinary that they
suggest a very great distance from familiar life.

185

Peacocks are birds of immortality. They suggest a contrast between time and the timeless, between the familiar and the mysterious. They evoke a deeper rhythm. Call it a move from the ordinary to extraordinary, or from the surface to the depth, or from the profane to the sacred. It is an experience our ancestors also knew. The peacocks are birds of immortality. The seasons are markers in the passage of time.

To Quail Roost came several groups of parents, teachers, principals. Missing were the students -- those in junior high -- at that most awkward season of change of adolescence. The adolescent change of season was present as background at our conference. Perhaps it was also sensed in the weather of those March days as the ground felt muddy beneath the feet, as the first flowers were testing themselves, and the first robins inspecting the terrain. Every now and then, there was a glimpse of the peacocks.

The First Weekend: Text and Context -- Ways of Conceiving Persons and Community

On the first weekend, William Arrowsmith spoke of excellence and Gibson Winter discussed community. I should like to reflect on our ways of thinking and talking about persons and community. Ethics arises, it seems to me, when we consider self and others and the shared standards which bind us together. The tension between the individual and society is an old theme in philosophy.

To put the point paradoxically, there _is_ conflict, and yet, at some ultimate level, there cannot be conflict. What it means to be a person and what it means to be in community must, we deeply feel, converge. I am both a whole and a part. Perhaps better, we can draw on a formulation most recently revived by Ernest Becker.[1] Becker sees the human suspended between everything and nothing, trying to be something. I cannot be everything. I fear being nothing. I desperately seek to be something, to be somebody. It seems clear to me that if I am something then I exist with other things. If I am a somebody, then I live in a world where there are others who also

---

[1]Ernest Becker, The Denial of Death (New York: Free Press, 1973).

186

are and seek to be somebody. I am not the whole mosaic nor the empty wall. My wholeness is the wholeness of a part and my meaning and value depend on where I am as much as what I am.

We know the shape of the solution -- person and community must co-define each other. Our problem is that we mistake our present formulation for the final one. We mistake the sketch for the portrait. We mistake individualism for true personhood. We mistake collectivism for true community. We mistake compromises among pressure groups for the common good. We believe we have a way to harmonize self-interest and group-interest only to find that we have drawn our group too narrowly and produced a new ethnocentrism.

Person and community are intertwined. At a certain level of abstractness, we can talk of the human community, the community of moral agents, the kingdom of persons who deserve to be treated as ends, not means. L. T. Hobhouse put the point well: "The double meaning of 'humanity' as an expression for a certain quality that is in each man, and as an expression for the whole race of men, is not a mere ambiguity. The two meanings are intimately related, for 'humanity' as a whole is the society to which by virtue of the 'humanity' within each of us, we really belong, and these two meanings are the poles between which modern ethical conceptions move." [2]

Such is the shape of the solution. But a common jibe uncovers the tension: "I love humanity. It's people I can't stand." If we seek to expand the human circle, we purchase breadth of concern at the price of abstracting from specific faces. If we focus on the specific faces of relatives and friends, we purchase concreteness at the price of narrowing the human circle.

Besides the tension connected with space and the human circle, there is also a tension connected with time and development. Pindar sounds the note in The Pythian Ode: "Become what you are." We are persons-in-community. We are trying to become persons-in-community. To develop an ethical consciousness is to

---

[2] L. T. Hobhouse, Morals in Evolution: A Study in Comparative Ethics, 3rd ed. (London: Chapman and Hall, 1951), pp. 357-358.

realize these fundamental truths more deeply. From
ancient times, ethics for the individual has been seen
as a process of transcending a narrow notion of self-
and-others toward a fuller notion of self-and-others.
At times, this is talked about as a movement from a
self-centered to an other-centered perspective. Such
a formulation has all the limits we have come to
discover in the ambiguities of self-sacrifice and
altruism. Modern theories of moral development, such
as that of Lawrence Kholberg, try to flesh out the
process. The details are in dispute, but the basic
movements seem solid enough.

We start in a pre-conventional stage. We
understand social practices to be right and wrong
insofar as they affect our ego-self. Gradually, we
come to appreciate the good of order, the value of
maintaining those group structures which promote the
good of the unit. We appreciate and do our part to
maintain the conditions for group living. We
appropriate to differing degrees the values embodied
in our conventional standards. We measure right and
wrong practices in terms of how they affect the good
of the group. We see ourselves as deeply involved in
institutional structures larger than the ego-self. We
begin to think of our "self" as a center of
relationships, as a knot in the web of roles and
responsibilities. We come to feel allegiance to the
continuance of group life.

There are limits here too. Though it may be true
that all morality is group morality and that we are
social beings to the core, still there are blindspots
in group morality which are all too well-known.
Further growth can be thought of as widening the human
circle and reflectively evaluating the conventional
rules and roles. At our best moments, we see our
"self" as, in a way, universal, connected with the

See Lawrence Kohlberg, The Philosophy of Moral
Development: Moral Stages and the Idea of Justice
(San Francisco: Harper and Row, 1981). The aspect of
Kohlberg used here -- his three levels -- is
integrated rather than rejected by Kohlberg's most
recent constructive critics such as Carol Gilligan,
Robert Kegan and Jurgen Habermas. For a full study of
Kohlberg and his critics, see my "Kohlberg's Progress
Toward Understanding the Moral Life," Diss. University
of North Carolina at Chapel Hill, 1982.

human story and perhaps the cosmic drama. There are moments when we glimpse a profound connectedness, when we identify our journey with the journey of everyman, everywoman, when we experience our kinship with deeper, wider, and higher realities.

These are the themes which lately have occupied my thinking. With these issues in mind, we may approach Arrowsmith on excellence and Winter on community.

1) Excellence: Antigone to Philoctetes

In Frederico Fellini's film Amacord, there is a scene in which snow begins falling on the village. Suddenly, for a brief moment, we catch a glimpse of a peacock flying through the falling snow. The image is exotic -- wondrous and rare. It evokes something within us. The blue of the peacock's breast shines like lapis lazuli. And, at our best moments, we think there is something in each of us precious like the lapis lazuli, something in us waiting to take flight, like the peacock, through the snow-filled world.

Such is the quality of excellence. It is the god-like within us. And it is fitting that we see this excellence shine forth with exceptional clarity in the springtime of our history -- in the clear air of Athens. The peacock is, after all, the bird of Hera.

William Arrowsmith, the classicist, came before the group as a teacher with a text. His excellence was to bring that text to life. He was servant and custodian to the text. The text requires transmission. Both the teacher and the learner stand before the text. When the text is a classic, the text is normative in a special way. Calling it a classic is a way of saying that, again and again, it speaks truly and deeply to those with ears to hear. It has stood the test of time. It stands in a sequence of texts which define a tradition. To recover the meaning of the text is to make that tradition live again. And the sequence of texts provides its own norms. In reaching up to the text, our understanding is refined, or developed, or even radically changed. [4] As Arrowsmith would put it, we read the text and the text reads us. Though the process is circular, the circle is not vicious but virtuous. Coming to recover the meaning of a great text enables us. It gives us a touchstone of excellence. It gives us an image of the heroic. In the presence of the classics, we reaffirm excellence achieved.

Arrowsmith selected a play as his text. In the Greek, the word for teacher, "didaskalos," is also the word for playwright. So the true teacher is Sophocles. Arrowsmith chose to bring to life Sophocles' play Philoctetes. He also mentioned a better known play of Sophocles, Antigone. I want to set these two plays in contrast. But where Arrowsmith chose to speak of excellence, I want to think of excellence against the theme of individual and community. We will first look at Sophocles' Antigone and then at the Philoctetes, which was written some forty years later.

In the first play, the heroine, Antigone, is a young girl on the threshold of womanhood. She is the daughter of the ill-fated Oedipus and is under the care of her uncle, Creon, who is King of Thebes as well as head of Antigone's family. Antigone's brother, Polynices, is a traitor to his own city. He dies in battle and Creon refuses him burial. Antigone believes that she has a duty to the gods to bury her brother even in defiance of human authority in the person of her uncle, the King.

Antigone is a fascinating figure. People of modern times tend to see her as a teenage rebel, as the archetype of the person who stands up to authority, who appeals to a higher standard, who refuses to compromise even if the refusal leads to death. To modern eyes, she becomes a modern heroine and her excellence is honored as if it were a modern autonomy. The portrait is as tempting as it is misleading. To this, I will return.

Against the Antigone, consider a play from Sophocles' old age, the Philoctetes. Here we find

---

[4]On this sense of the classics, see Bernard J. F. Lonergan, Method in Theology (New York: Herder and Herder, 1972), pp. 161-162.

Philoctetes, an old man stricken with a wound in the foot which will not heal, exiled to the island Lemnos, isolated in the most literal sense. He possesses the bow of Heracles, his former master, now a god. To the island come crafty Odysseus and young Neoptolemus, son of the fallen hero, Achilles.

An oracle has prophesied that Troy will not be taken until Philoctetes comes to Troy of his own free will bringing with him his wondrous bow. At the center of the play is the relation between the old man Philoctetes and the young Neoptolemus. As Arrowsmith notes, it is the story of their friendship, a friendship that brings out the best of Neoptolemus, a friendship sealed by Heracles, a friendship which restores Philoctetes to the human circle. The excellence of these two friends is an excellence of complementarity. We can imagine the two figures, as Arrowsmith suggests, exiting yoked in friendship, carrying together on their shoulders the god-like bow. Perhaps two are needed for heroism, for deep change. Perhaps there are forms of excellence in which two people -- the smallest of communitites -- surpass themselves in serving purposes higher than their own. Such excellence is community-building. It is at the heart of teaching.

On a first reading, the two plays of Sophocles present a striking contrast. On the one side, the young Antigone stands in opposition to the dictates of Creon. On the other side, the young Neoptolemus becomes better by aiding the wounded Philoctetes to complete his destiny. But look again, and the contrast blurs.

Antigone is hardly modern, hardly a law unto herself. She stands her ground out of loyalty to the laws of the gods. She is hardly living out the modern "doctrine of sincerity and self-realization." [5] Her deed is done out of a deep love for her brother and a still deeper sense of the bonds of kinship.

Philoctetes and Neoptolemus likewise live in a

---

[5] The phrase is that of W. B. Yeats, Per Amica Silentia Lunae (London: Macmillan, 1918), p. 26. As a form of the lifestory, the notion is developed by John S. Dunne in A Search for God in Time and Memory (New York: Macmillan, 1969).

god-bathed world where respect is due to the aged, the infirm, and the suppliant, a world where appeal could still be made to heroism, to "noblesse oblige."

What conclusions emerge about moral development? About the theme of person and community?

First, there is the text and the teacher. Behind the text is Sophocles, a great teacher. The text itself is a classic, a work of acknowledged excellence, rich in its imagery and detail. Models live for us in the richness of their human story. Presenting the text is William Arrowsmith, a master teacher who is in love with the legacy he, again and again, seeks to articulate. It is the living word, the embodied drama, which awakens the glimpse of the peacock.

Secondly, we were seeking a way to evoke excellence and to understand this excellence not as the excellence of the solitary individual but of the person-in-relationship. At first, we thought superficially that Antigone exhibited individual excellence and Neoptolemus and Philoctetes a communal excellence. On closer inspection, we found that this was not a helpful way to think of things. Both heroes inhabited a world where ties of earthly kinship and signs of transcendence formed a part of the world view. The world view forms a context behind the text. Perhaps this is a lead to follow.

2) Community: Root Metaphors and the Recovery of Meaning

"It was the best of times, it was the worst of times . . . " Thus did Charles Dickens introduce A Tale of Two Cities. The times were the years of the French Revolution. Rousseau had prepared the way with his ideals of autonomy and participatory democracy.[6] Kant had reinforced the theme of autonomy in his treatment of ethics.[7] But the French Revolution

---

[6]See Jean Jacques Rousseau, The Social Contract and Discourses, trans. G. D. H. Cole (New York: E. P. Dutton and Co., 1950).

[7]See Immanuel Kant, Groundwork of the Metaphysic of Morals, trans. H. J. Patton (New York: Harper and Row, 1964).

raised the cry far louder than philosophers. Liberty, equality, fraternity! Death to kings!

In the Protestant revolution, we saw an end to the ideal of spiritual mediation. In the French revolution, we saw an end to the ideal of temporal or political mediation. Henceforth we were on our own, to stand on our own feet, to make our own decisions, to stand unshielded before sun and storms.[8]

We in the West like to think in terms of threes, trinities, triads. Hegel took the triad and set it in time and motion with his "thesis -- antithesis -- synthesis," but the tendency to see opposites reconciled into a third-stage synthesis was hardly Hegel's own invention. We may think of our times as the best of times or the worst of times, but if we think in threes and add a sense of history, we will doubtless think of our time as the central present, arising out of the past and unfolding into the future. Take a long enough view and the scheme makes sense. However dissimilar the primitive world, the Greek world and the medieval world, they seem alike in viewing life within a hierarchical order and a cosmic context.[9] Take a long enough view and our period seems to stretch from Reformation and the age of exploration to the twentieth century and the global village. The future is already here in seed; it is not yet here in full flowering.

Does it do any good to think of time in such an oversimplified scheme?   Gibson Winter seems to think that it does. He spoke of three root metaphors, three networks of images, three quite different ways of conceiving self, others, and our common world. The first root metaphor is to see reality in terms appropriate to the organic and hierarchical. The second root metaphor is to see reality in terms appropriate to inanimate matter in motion, in terms that are, at base, mechanistic. The third root metaphor is to see reality in terms appropriate to

---

[8]On the modern period as one marked by the breakdown of mediation, see John S. Dunne, op. cit.

[9]See Sam Keen, Apology for Wonder (New York: Harper and Row, 1969), chapter three, and Ernest Becker, The Birth and Death of Meaning, 2nd. ed. (New York: Free Press, 1971), chapter thirteen.

poetic language and artistic expression. The third metaphor is the most self-reflexive. With the third metaphor comes the capacity to "see through" metaphors in a double sense. It is to see what is revealed by the metaphor's power and it is to see what is concealed by the metaphor's partialness.

In speaking of three root metaphors, Winter is speaking of three world views, three language systems in which to think and talk. I want to take these three world views and map them to three seasons and three colors. [10]

First, consider the season of early autumn. Its color is the yellow of earth and harvest. Secondly, consider the season of winter. Its color is the wintry blue of oceans and of sky. Thirdly, consider the season of spring. Its color is the green of living things.

Let us suppose that the history of the race has its seasons and let us focus on these three. To each of Winter's three world views, let us assign a season and a color. The use of color language will, I believe, be helpful not only in reflecting on Winter's talk but in applying it to our concern, namely, the ways of conceiving person and community.

If we think of three seasons in world time, Winter's first season stretches from the primitive through the medieval periods. In all seasons, Winter sees human beings as dwelling within their symbol system, as talking and thinking in terms of characteristic images. In the first season, the language within which people dwelled and thought was shot through with metaphors and images of organic life, hierarchically ordered. We might think of Aristotle's biological world, a world where every ecological niche was filled but all was eternally

---

[10] In this mapping, I take liberties with an older and richer series of associations found in the Nei Ching. See The Yellow Emperor's Classic of Internal Medicine, 2nd ed., trans. Ilza Veith (Berkeley, Calif.: University of California Press, 1972).

ordered. There was fullness but no real evolution.[11]
Suppose we color this hierarchical, mediated, organic
world earth-yellow. In this world, every key concept
and every key image will be more or less yellow. The
notion of freedom will be a yellow kind of freedom.
The notion of excellence will be a yellow kind of
excellence. The notion of community will be a yellow
kind of community, and so forth.

The next season will be like winter and it will
be colored the blue of ocean and sky. Where people in
the first age dwelled in earth-linked, female imagery
of receptivity, people in the second age think in
height or depth metaphors which are predominantly
masculine in tone, stressing independence and self-
assertion. Winter sees this, our own age, in terms of
a mechanistic metaphor. We too dwell within a
characteristic language and we tend to think and talk
of "the real world" in terms appropriate to
factories, to bureaucracies, machines, and computers.
This is a world where each individual is seen as an
isolated autonomous atom, and where each atomistic
individual is on its own trajectory. This is a world
where freedom is seen as space to fulfill one's wants
and desires without hindrance. It is a world where
society is seen as an aggregate of individuals and the
common good is seen as the result of compromises
between interest groups. It is a world where the
language is that of the market place, the language of
efficiency and the accountant's "bottom line," where
utility is king.

Suppose that we color this mechanistic,
individualistic, masculine world blue. It is the cold
blue of the space-age, the blue of cool efficiency,
the blue, also, of loneliness. In this world, every
key concept and every key image will be more or less
blue. The notion of freedom will be a blue kind of
freedom. The notion of excellence will be a blue kind
of excellence. The notion of community will be a blue
kind of community, and so forth.

After the thesis and antithesis (earth and sky,
female and male), one expects the synthesis. Winter's
third season is the most reflexively conceived. Here

---

11 For a look at Aristotle the biologist, see
Marjorie Grene, Portrait of Aristotle (Chicago:
University of Chicago Press, 1963).

195

the metaphor is metaphor itself, the notions of symbol
and image, the language of art and poetry. Here we
not only live symbolically and poetically, but we are
aware of this fact. We are aware that we dwell within
a language whose symbols both reveal and conceal.
Consider the making of poetry or the making of
pottery. In part, we invent; in part, we discover.
In the poem, there are the personal associations we
bring. But there are also the archetypal
associations, those universal themes and images which
are older than we are, which cling to our words
whether we consciously intend them or not. In any
significant artistic creation, the work embodies more
than the artist knows. Again, if we are potters, we
work in dialogue with the clay. There are forces,
patterns, "lines of directionality," as Gibson Winter
would say, which are inherent in the material,
suggested by the artistic tradition, linked to
archetypal realities. Yet we also contribute. Within
the constraints, within the givens, more than one work
of art can find expression. So the poet loves the
words, the carver respects the grain of the wood, the
potter feels the tendencies of the clay.[12] A sense
of mystery and cosmic connectedness is present but the
meaning must be recovered.

Suppose we color this symbolic, mysterious,
multi-dimensional world green. Green is the color of
life which is never quite dominated or domesticated.
Green is the color of spring, the season of hope. And
hope is a mark of a living future. If we combine the
yellow of earth and the blue of sky, we get the color
green. In this world which is already foreshadowed,
every key concept and every key image will be more or
less green. The notion of excellence will be a green
kind of excellence. The notion of community will be a
green kind of community, and so forth.

What conclusions does this exercise in seasons
and colors suggest?

---

[12]On poetry and pottery, see Mary C. Richards,
Centering in Pottery, Poetry, and the Person
(Middletown, Conn.: Wesleyan University Press,
1962). On the woodcarver, see Thomas Merton, The Way
of Chuang Tzu (New York: New Directions, 1965), p.
110, or Chuang Tzu, XIX, 10, in The Texts of Taoism,
trans. by James Legge.

First, we come to see that the culture, like the playwright, is a powerful teacher. Indeed, world views and cultures may be seen as dramas into which we are born. Within the language and imagery of the culture, we dwell.

Secondly, for ethics as for everything else, there are no uncolored terms. The very words used in ethics have the color of their time.

Thirdly, in a blue period where an individualistic way of thinking dominates, it will be difficult to think of person, community, freedom, excellence, etc. in anything but blue terms. Since root metaphors are a network of images, our critiques will most likely be partial. We will succeed in changing the color of one term but fail to alter the color of the network.

Fourthly, each color has its beauty. We do not want a monochrome world. Nor is it quite enough to switch from one monochrome to another. Our own image both reveals and conceals. We want to be bilingual or trilingual, and not just speak one language however marvelous.

Fifthly, we must attend very consciously to the language in which we dwell. Women and blacks have discovered that a change in people's thinking can be effected by pushing for a change in people's language. I suspect that, in an individualistic age, we need consciously to seek a more communal langauge. To do so might be a part of the changing of the season, a first appearance of the green of spring.

The Second Weekend: The Actual and the Possible Tensions Within Ethics.

On the second weekend, Kurt Baier spoke of responsibility and freedom. Maxine Greene spoke of evaluation and dignity. I should like to reflect on their presentations with special concern for the theme of the actual and the possible. Such a tension runs as deeply through the history of philosophy as does the tension between person and community. For Aristotle, the actual has priority over the possible. For existentialists such as Sartre and Heidegger, the possible has priority over the actual. My concern, here as earlier, will be with time and the social. The closer we come to our own age, the more we tend to

197

pay attention to a concrete sense of time, history, and development, which was absent from the ancients. To see the actual and possible in a concrete context is to see them in the light of time. It is to think of what is already and what is not yet.[13]

There is another theme in ethics which reaches its classic formulation in David Hume. That is the tension between the "is" and the "ought." [14] First, we separate with an abyss what is from what ought to be. Then, we attempt to build bridges. Perhaps we might think of this dispute in conjunction with the theme of the actual and possible. When we try to do this, it appears that the "is" and the "ought" are on a circle or perhaps a moving wheel. What is has coloration. It is not color-neutral nor value-neutral. The ethical consensus, though changing, is present, as part of the drama, in the positive law, the conventional morality, and the stage of religious understanding. What is now was what somebody thought ought to be at an earlier time. And what is now can be continually criticized in terms of an evolving notion of what ought to be. So perhaps some reflection on the actual and the possible may shed light. All dichotomies are unjust, but I want to consider Baier's comments on the side of the actual, the suitably colored "is." And I want to consider Greene's comments on the side of the possible, the suitably colored reminders of what could be and ought to be.

1) Responsibility: The Actual and the Language of Law

To speak of law and order evokes the image of the army. I want to begin this section with that image. I take the image from the ancient Chinese text, the I Ching. Hexagram 7 of that book of wisdom bears the name "shih" -- the army. By way of comment, we find the following:

---

[13] On the formulation of the "already" and "not yet", see Oscar Cullmann, Christ and Time (Philadelphia: Westminster Press, 1950).

[14] See David Hume, An Inquiry Concerning the Principles of Morals, ed. Charles W. Hendel (Indianapolis: Bobbs-Merrill co., 1957).

"An army is a mass that needs organization
in order to become a fighting force.
Without strict discipline, nothing can be
accomplished, but this discipline must not
be achieved by force. It requires a strong
man who captures the hearts of the people
and awakens their enthusiasm."[15]

There is a particular tension embodied in the
image of an army. Like all primitive realities, it is
fearful and fascinating. In the army, there is a
clearly marked chain of command, a highly organized
specification of duties, a sharply outlined ethos of
paternal authority and well-disciplined obedience.
Traditionally, armies support law and order, stand in
defense of the status quo, and revere efficiency and
effectiveness. For many, army life is the antithesis
of freedom.

Kurt Baier spoke with the precision of one
trained in law. As he outlined his distinctions, I
thought quite often of military images. I want simply
to recall some of those distinctions. There is task
responsibility, the failure to discharge it, the
liability for the failure, and answerability to the
one who assigned the task and can penalize for
failure. In the school system, teachers have one kind
of responsibility to the students whom they benefit
and another kind of responsibility to their superiors
to whom they are answerable. In general,
responsibilities can be assumed or incurred. At least
for children and the inexperienced, paternalism has
much reasonably to recommend it.

Such distinctions are careful and useful. They
give us, in a phrase of Maxine Greene, "the grammar of
the status quo." Since the status quo is the most
pervasive, if not the only, game in town, one is well
advised to learn the rules and perhaps even to
appreciate the wisdom they contain. We do live in the
status quo and there is more hierarchy around than we
care to admit. Bureaucracy may be THE institution of
our time and the parallels between bureaucracy and
army regulations are well known. In truth, we dislike
talking about such things. We do not like to be

---

[15]The I Ching or Book of Changes, trans. Wilhelm
and Baynes, 3rd. ed., Bollingen Series XIX (Princeton:
Princeton University Press, 1967), p. 32.

reminded how hierarchical, even medieval, our structures are. To face such features flies in the face of our myth of autonomy, of being our own person, of not having anyone tell us what to do. It goes against the grain.

When Baier spoke, there was a resistance from some in the room, and nods of agreement from others. The resistance came, in part, from facing hard sayings. Many dislike hearing about authority and legality. It is difficult to acknowledge that we can be assigned responsibilities (told what to do) and that we are answerable to others for our failures. It is more difficult still to be told that we can incur responsibilities even though we are unwilling to assume them (though, of course, we can ratify what we did not contract). Perhaps most difficult of all is to be told that sometimes we don't know or can't be persuaded that something is really good for us, and, in such cases, there may be justification for paternalistic force.

Such reaction tells us much of the color of our age. But I want to focus on the language which Baier used and to suggest how such a partial language fits into a total view of ethics.

Notice first that Baier's distinctions arise from, and are at home in, the context of law. The law is a strong part of the actual circumstances of our lives. That is why it is quite appropriate to speak of "the grammar of the status quo." Secondly, Baier stressed one segment of the language of law, namely the language of responsibilities, of duties, of obligations. Generally, we are happier talking and thinking in the langauge of rights than talking and thinking in the language of responsibilities. Somehow responsibilities suggest answerability and constraint more directly than rights do (although in thinking thus, we think superficially).

But what, one wants to say, of freedom, of choices, of autonomy? The web is tangled, but it may help if we call to mind an old distinction within ethics. One legal philosopher, Lon Fuller, suggests that we should distinguish two ends of a vertical moral continuum. He calls the bottom end "the morality of duty" and he refers to the top end as "the morality of aspiration."[16] Perhaps the whole continuum is in motion. What is seen in one age as minimum requirements for civilized living or for attaining certain ends seems all-too-minimal for another age. Again, what seems above and beyond the call of duty in one age may seem a commonplace in another. Nonetheless, we draw lines and we do speak more than one moral language. I think it is helpful to think not of two moralities but of two languages. With this modification, we can rephrase Fuller. The language of duty is closely akin to the language of law. The language of aspiration is closely akin to the language of aesthetics. To speak of duty is to be concerned, at one end of the continuum, with minimum standards of group living. Fuller likens duty to grammar, which gives the minimum standards of communication. At the other end of the continuum, to speak of aspiration and excellence involves a vocabulary akin to that of literary criticism where the highest standards of art come into play.

I should like to map these two areas or languages onto our theme of the actual and the possible. We are born into the conventions, customs, rules, and rituals which make civilization possible. They are actualities. To conform to them wins no praise but to violate them brings blame. We are also discovering and rediscovering human possibilities. To strive to emulate the great masters and heroes and saints is a noble quest. To seek such excellence wins praise; but if we fall short, there is, as the Chinese put it, "no blame."

I believe that we experience the moral life under both aspects - as constraint and as attraction. An adequate picture of the moral life must have place for both. To speak adequately of the moral life one must be bilingual. But both languages - both sets of images - will be colored by the root metaphors of our age.

What conclusions can be drawn from this for our theme?

First of all, we should be attentive to our language. At certain times, we must be reminded of

---

[16] See Lon L. Fuller, The Morality of Law, 2nd ed. (New Haven: Yale University Press, 1969), chapter one.

the demands of existing institutions and agreements. Here the language of duty is appropriate. At other times, we must be urged on to reform practices or recover meanings, to seek what is almost more than possible. Here, the language of aspiration is appropriate.

Secondly, to speak either language exclusively will distort the real which comprises both the actual and possible. To respect what is and what is not yet seems to require bilingual capability. Speaking only one language tends to distort the real.

Thirdly, we must recall that both at the base line and at the upper reaches, the terms of ethics take on the coloration of the age. Hence, it is well to look to our avoidances and to our preferences. In any age, langauge conceals and reveals. So it is likely that there is much we do not understand about the language of duty and much we do not understand about the language of aspiration. There may be deeper senses of responsibility than captured by legal language and there may be deeper senses of excellence than are mirrored in our present language of approbation.

Fourthly, in teaching and in learning, we again need to consider task responsibility. We need to recover the values of the actual, the resonances which the term has in an older tradition. Our initial quote from the I Ching spoke not only of discipline and organization but also of the superior person "who captures the hearts of the people and awakens their enthusiasm."

2) Evaluation: The Possible and the Language of Art.

Maxine Greene seems most at home with the existential and the arts. In her view, the arts are radical; they reveal the roots of life. They release us from the actual to the "as if," to the "possibly otherwise." They open possibilities.

It is true, I think. The arts, like a glimpse of the peacock, take us out of ourselves or bring us back to ourselves, to our roots in the human. The arts, like a mirror, can shatter our carefully constructed image and show us how we are in the general messiness of things. As Plato knew, artists can be dangerous.

These dream weavers can incite and lull. Artists, like preachers, are set to comfort the afflicted and afflict the comfortable. In revealing to us how it could be otherwise, artists dwell with ambiguity, possibility, and the multi-dimensional layers of the real.

In speaking of evaluation, Greene told the story of the great Russian dancer, Mikhail Baryshnikov. As a youth, he became enchanted by the excellence of the dance, and became a member of the Kirov Ballet. But possibilities stretched out before him, and he chose to break from his homeland in 1974 to pursue the dream. Beyond the classical ballet were the possibilities of modern ballet in the West. Most recently, in 1978, he defected a second time, leaving the American Ballet Theatre, where the star system and high pay reign. He defected to the New York City Ballet, where pay is poorer, and where the ballet, not the dancer, is star. But here he could work with master choreographer, George Balanchine.

What does this story have to do with evaluation? It shows us a most unusual case, a world renowed figure, one who is pushing toward the possibilities of his profession, one who is seeking an excellence of the highest sort - what Baier called in the discussion, "an eternal excellence." Evaluation here is intrinsic in a double sense. First of all, Baryshnikov is inwardly motivated. His strongest evaluation is self-evaluation. Secondly, the parameters of excellence - the criteria of evaluation - seem themselves intrinsic to the task. There is the text (the tradition of dance), and the context (what is going forward in dance). There is the actual as restraining (the state of the dance in Russia) and there is the possible as liberating (to work with the best choreographer in the world). Here we are indeed at the very limits of excellence, at the very limits of evaluation. We speak naturally here in the language of aspiration.

Let us return again to the continuum of the moral. Let us think of it as a vertical continuum. Let us contrast the actual world (the world of duty and its minimum demands) with the possible world (the world of aspiration and of excellences not yet achieved). We can now sketch the contrast with images. There is the soldier and the lawyer, with a masculine, detached sense of abstract order. They are

the maintainers of <u>where</u> <u>we</u> <u>are</u>, the guardians against
a drop toward barbarism. In contrast, there is the
dancer and the teller of stories, with a feminine,
involved sense of the concrete. They are the doubters
of theories, the dreamers of <u>where</u> <u>we</u> <u>might</u> <u>be</u>, the
lovers of unpredictable, intractable life. The
soldier and the dancer may seem opposites, even
enemies. The problem, as always, is to turn what
appears as "the enemy without" into the friend who
shows us new potentials within ourselves.

How can these two opposite standpoints be seen as
complementary? At base, life, in its personal or
social forms, is a conjunction of the actual and the
possible. Kierkegaard thought about this in similar
terms. He considered <u>the</u> <u>necessary</u> (which is
actuality most hardened) and <u>the</u> <u>possible</u>. In a
brilliant book, Ernest Becker recovers Kierkegaard's
meaning by translating his insights into more modern
terms.[17]

Against the vertical continuum of duty and
aspiration, consider a horizontal continuum of mental
health which, like Aristotle, stresses excess and
defect. Consider the ends of this horizontal line,
the extremes of mental imbalance. One can have <u>too</u>
<u>much</u> <u>necessity</u> (too much boundedness to the actual)
and <u>not</u> <u>enough</u> <u>possibility</u>. At this extreme is
<u>depressive</u> <u>psychosis</u>, seen most graphically in the
catatonic. Here, one becomes "bogged down in the
demands of others." One experiences too much
limitation, too great a weight of the bodily and the
finite; one is paralyzed by the fixity of the actual.
At the other end of the seesaw, one can have <u>too</u> <u>much</u>
<u>possibility</u> and <u>not</u> <u>enough</u> <u>necessity</u> or actuality. At
this extreme is <u>schizophrenic</u> <u>psychosis</u>, seen most
graphically in the schizophrenic. Here, one becomes
overwhelmed by symbolic possibility. One experiences
too much of the unlimited, the infinite, the manifold
faces of what could be. One is unanchored in the
actual, ordinary world. Most of us are simply <u>normal</u>
<u>neurotics</u> struggling to balance stability and risk-

---

[17]See Ernest Becker, <u>The</u> <u>Denial</u> <u>of</u> <u>Death</u>, chapter
five. The key references are to Kierkegaard, <u>The</u>
<u>Concept</u> <u>of</u> <u>Dread</u>, trans. Walter Lowrie (Princeton:
Princeton University Press, 1957) and <u>The</u> <u>Sickness</u>
<u>Unto</u> <u>Death</u>, trans. Walter Lowrie (New York:
Doubleday Anchor Books, 1954).

taking, struggling to decide how much to play the social game and how much to oppose it, struggling, like a tightrope walker, to maintain our balance and momentum.

In a classroom, one feels the tension between accrediting people for tasks which society demands and nurturing in each student a sense of his or her own voice and the dignity that transcends this or that task.

In discussion, Baier mentioned that assessment is unavoidable. He also noted, below or beside the eternal excellences such as ballet, that there are the temporary excellences that society at a given time rewards. Interestingly, he chose an example from the army to illustrate the latter. The cavalry soldier who fought on horseback had excellences once rewarded, now no longer needed. Some students, he went on to say, have few or none of the temporary or eternal excellences. One must then find a way to communicate to them that to be human is to have worth "independently of the excellence that society at a given time rewards."

This I take to be the hard case. But it illumines the experience of most of us who have not the genius nor grace to leap so high as Baryshnikov. This links the problem of evaluation with the problem of ordinariness.

In a pluralistic world, there are many yardsticks. We do well to measure up tolerably well on one or two. It is impossible to measure up on every yardstick. Add to this the fact that society now touches this, now that, yardstick and makes it socially the most important. So if making money is a measure of worth, then, on that yardstick, teaching may not rate highly. But, on another yardstick, it can measure highly. This is true, but it neglects the power of the culture to award the crown. When the culture awards the crown to one yardstick, we need both courage and a support group to make real to ourselves the value of other yardsticks.

This is the deeper problem. How can we sustain a sense of dignity when we do not measure very highly on many or any yardsticks? How can we sustain a sense of dignity when we do not measure up on the culturally preferred yardstick? This case is what Baier had in

205

mind when speaking of a worth deeper than this or that task, or, in our present imagery, a worth independent of any and all culturally set yardsticks. In our best moments, we affirm this. We hold that all of us, as persons, as members of the human family, have such worth. We are multi-dimensional, or, in older language, we are mysteries, too rich to be reduced to a function or set of functions. I believe with Ernest Becker and Otto Rank that the ultimate solution to ordinariness is a religious one.[18] Only when we feel that we matter in a cosmic way can we achieve a heroism which transcends culture and its yardsticks and rewards. No finite reward system will be enough to give worth to the wretched of the earth, ourselves among them. I realize that to mention a religious solution is to invoke something as potentially dangerous and demonic as it is wondrous and fine. Yet East and West seem in agreement. Without some sort of cosmic drama, we remain all too earth-bound. Perhaps Baryshnikov's leaps are an image of something more.

Postscript: Going Home

The spring returns us to where we are, knowing both the mud and the peacocks, the ordinary and extraordinary. One cannot live always near a glimpse of peacocks. But leaving them, I had a new respect for what might be found around the bend. I drove home along the back roads.

---

[18]See Becker, _ibid._, chapters eight and eleven, and Becker, _The Birth and Death of Meaning_, chapters ten and thirteen. See also Otto Rank, _Beyond Psychology_ (New York: Dover Press, 1958).

EDUCATION AND THE LIMITS

OF LIBERAL IDEOLOGY

H. Svi Shapiro

Introduction

In the bourgeoning attempt of the last ten years
to explicate how education in western industrial
societies corresponds with the imperatives of
capitalist development the very real struggles and
conflicts in education have frequently been submerged
in a Marcusean view of totalitarian domination.
Education has come to be seen as little more than an
epiphenomenon of more important economic structures
and social relations. There has been a widespread
acceptance of a 'vulgar' Marxist schema in which the
ideological 'superstructure' is no more than a
reflection of the economic 'base'. While such a
perspective has significantly deepened our
understanding of the purposes and process of education
in contemporary society it has paid insufficient
attention to the disjunctures and conflicts that
pervade educational practice. It has produced, what
may be described as, a radical-functionalist account
of education.

In attempting to resist such a view the work of
the French philosopher Louis Althusser and the English
cultural scholar Raymond Williams are especially
important. Each (in quite different ways) has made
clear the extent to which contradictory tendencies
pervade, not only economic practices in capitalist
society, but also those that are political, cultural
and ideological. From this perspective education is
best understood, not as a uniform functional response
to societal 'needs' (or the needs of the dominant
interests in society), but the product of competing
ideologies and alternative constellations of values,
beliefs, moral and aesthetic judgements. The most
significant of these are, I believe, educational ideas
rooted in liberal-democratic ideology, and those
reflecting capitalist economic values. While the
latter emphasize utilitarian, bureaucratic, and
technicist values, the former reflect a concern (at
least in principle) with, among other things, human

development and cultural 'literacy'. The structure of liberal-democratic and capitalist ideology that prevails in our society forms no smoothly-integrated or harmonious set of values, beliefs and attitudes. As a consequence, we must reject the view proposed by a number of revisionist educational historians that all attempts at liberal or progressive reform be seen as simply attempts at ensuring a more thorough adaptation of schooling to capitalist social and economic forms. Such a view ignores the extent to which 'progressive' tendencies in education have often failed or remained marginal to the dominant features of the school system. It overlooks the degree to which education in liberal-capitalism contains the juxtaposition of incongruent, incompatible, and contradictory ideas and practices.

The papers included in this volume and reviewed here are, I believe, in the mainstream of attempts to provide an education characterized by its concern with genuinely human values and needs. And in this they make a distinguished contribution to such concerns. At the same time, as has commonly been the case for those proposing progressive educational change, there is sometimes a failure to recognize how capitalism limits or thwarts such change. There is a failure to recognize how the goals of meeting 'individual needs', ensuring an 'all-round development' or 'democratizing culture' are fundamentally incompatible with an economic system responsible for specialization, hierarchical social relations, and the fragmentation of human experience. Only in a radically transformed society can the liberal ideas from which such educational notions spring -- self-determination and self-realization, freedom and autonomy, community, etc. -- become reality. Even among the authors where such a recognition exists, the political implications of attempts to secure educational change are not clearly stated. Most insidiously, while the human concerns of these writers is never in doubt, the practices advocated are frequently pervaded by distortions arising from the 'taken-for-granted' assumption of capitalist values and judgements. They become examples of the power of a hegemonic culture to restrict or mediate the articulation of alternatives to what presently exists. It is just such a power that ensures the inability to transform liberal-democratic ideal into radical possibility.

Hierarchy, Institutions, and the Illusion of Community

Nowhere are the contradictions between liberal ideals and present reality more clearly demonstrated than in the paper by Elizabeth and Melvin Keiser ("Reconciling Community and Institution"). For them there appears to be no fundamental incompatibility between the development of community or fellowship within the context of a hierarchical insitutional structure. Their work reveals a remarkably non-ideological approach to the pervasiveness of hierarchy in our institutional life. Its basic assumption lies in the seemingly clear-cut, apparently common-sensical determination, which associates the 'achievement of ends' with the presence of hierarchical social relations. Given such a determination we may understand why the pursuit of 'community' is limited to the interstices of our social existence -- the spatial and temporal 'in-between' where the fullness of our personalities does not need to be suppressed in the name of goals, ends, purposes, etc.. And in the overall ordering of our lives it is clear in what way the expression and experience of such fullness is restricted. It is, at best, a community that is limited to the margins of our social and personal lives. There is, in our belief, a direct line connecting such arguments and assumptions with the ideology which underpins the 'weekend' search for fellowship in American society. In accepting as logical and necessary the hierarchical and bureaucratic arrangements that dominate and pervade our lives for so much of the time we are compelled to search for those alternatives, where the fullness of selves interact with one another, in the interstices of our social lives; 'encounter sessions', 'consciousness raising groups', voluntary associations, religious followings, or the neighborhood bar. Just as the authoritarian, competitive and atomistic experience of schooling in the United States will not be mitigated by lunch-room conviviality or the fellowship of a morning assembly, nor will the fragmentation and coerciveness of occupational life be ameliorated by company newspapers, or bowling teams.

Awareness of the fundamental rupture in human fellowship or community caused by hierarchical social relations is not limited to the advocates of radical social and institutional change. Indeed, the attempt to locate community within the very context of a divisive, competitive, and fragmented social structure lies at the heart of liberal-capitalism. It has been at the center of attempts to make the inhumanity of our organizations and institutions bearable to those who must endure them. While the authors of such attempts have differed as to the degree of naivete, malevolence, or paternalism with which they approached their project, all have been united in their acceptance of the coexistence of human fellowship with domination. It is clear that the Keisers' paper is not alone in its attempt to juxtapose mutuality and subordination. Indeed it may be argued that such a project has been central in all attempts at maintaining some sense of human connectedness and rootedness in a culture whose overriding concern with extrinsic ends ensures the alienation of human activity. As Bertell Ollman notes,[1] it was Marx who clearly explicated the use of the political state in liberal-capitalism to create, in the midst of an egoistic and divisive society, an 'illusory community.' While man in his role as bourgeois was required to fight for his own self-interest -- compelled to see his fellows as actual or potential competition for the scarcity of goods, jobs, recognition, etc., as a citizen of the political state he is a member of a community which is governed (in principle) by universal obligations, equal considerations and mutual expectations. The two domains juxtaposed hierarchy with equality, egoism with mutuality, and fragmentation with organic social relations.

Nor did such contradictions only characterize the macro-structures of liberal society. They are reflected also at the institutional level. Factory owners have frequently seen the benefits of facilitating among their employees an illusory kind of fellowship. Such ties operate so as to obscure or mystify the real human relations of coercion, domination, and hierarchy, and help to ensure an uninterrupted production line and the steady accumulation of profit. The company's social clubs, newspapers, athletic teams, outings, pension funds, and the like, obfuscate man's real significance in such an environment. He is, first and foremost, a commodity whose value is determined by the quantity of

---

[1]Bertell Ollman, Alienation: Marx's Conception of Man in Capitalist Society (New York: Cambridge University Press, 1976).

labor that may be squeezed from him in a given time. In such circumstances the Christmas Party and the gold watch are the hollow rituals of an attempt to affirm an identity in which the individual represents an end, not simply a means to some owner's profit-making concerns. And yet, as is well known, on the day after the final goodbyes are said, along with the gold watch, what remains is not so much the sense of a fellowship lost but the gnawing doubts of a life lived according to some kind of Faustian bargain. Such community as is found in many of the institutions of our society exist in the interstices of a world ordered irrespective of the needs of its constituents; a world in which human beings are expected to become appendages to tasks that must remain for them unquestioned. It is a 'community' in which appeals to the notion of 'team spirit' and 'family' are slogans propagated by management anxious to channel workers' frustrations, grievances, and militancy away from activities that might upturn the overriding goals of the organziation (or, more accurately, the goals of those who control such organizations).

Nor is the attempt to ameliorate the institutional consequences of schooling in America with the rituals of fellowship a new one. Such tendencies are well described by Joel Spring in his history of American education during the progressive era.[2] He points to the 'organizational technique of creating social solidarity' which became popularly known in the 1920's as extra-curricular activities. Such activities included the use of student newspapers, clubs, athletics, and assemblies. The school newspaper, for example, was viewed as a means of teaching teamwork and creating a spirit of unity in the school. Through it the student would be able to gain a sense of the unity of school life and a feeling of loyalty to the educational institution. Likewise, the spirit generated by athletics was generally viewed as another means (certainly still the case) of unifying the school body. Of course it is a unity founded in the generation of a community-focused hostility against another collectivity. Such parochial fellowships create a fertile ground for the nourishment of other aggressive and xenophobic forms of togetherness such as militarism and racism (not for

---

[2]Joel Spring, Education and the Rise of the Corporate State (Boston: Beacon, 1977).

211

nothing was it said that the Battle of Waterloo, or for the empire, was fought on the playing fields of Eton). Nor is the suggestion of a school assembly more than a resurrection of an already tried vehicle for promoting or imposing a sense of school unity. As Spring notes, by the 1920's it was hailed as the great unifier of the comprehensive junior and senior high school. As early as the 1880's the noted progressive educator Francis W. Parker would begin each day at the Cook County Normal School by reading to the entire faculty and staff a short passage from the Bible or a book of poetry. The practice was believed to be the best means of providing the basis for ensuring life as a corporate body.

The centerpiece of all such rituals for developing the school as a community was the concept of student government. Never conceived as being concerned with anything more than the mechanical details of democracy, all such activities rarely had any contact with real issues of power. Its actual goal was to assure the formation of a corporate identity. The important Cardinal Principles of Secondary Education report issued by a special committee of the National Education Association in 1918 in urging that the school must become a democracy stated that "the comprehensive school is the prototype of a democracy in which various groups must have a degree of self-consciousness as groups and yet be federated into a larger whole through the recognition of common interests and ideals."

Like the factory welfare program of clubs, outings, assemblies, magazines, etc., used to combat the fragmentation of life on the assembly line, such school activities developed as a response to the changing organization of school which emphasized the increasing differentiation and specialization of educational programs. Given the seeming immutability of institutional bureaucratization, and the separation and fragmentation of human experience in them, the 'ritual of fellowship' provided (and continues to provide) means, not to confront the fundamental inhumanity of organizations and social forms in the era of liberal-capitalism, but rather to soften their blows to the human psyche. While the underlying

---

Quoted in Spring, Education and the Rise of the Corporate State, p. 113.

reality of such structures may be characterized by egoism and domination, they appear submerged under the thin veil of a moral form that claims mutuality, fellowship, and equality as its foundation. Such a contradiction, I believe, is the true essence of all those parallel rituals that have emerged in 20th century corporate industrial society - the camaraderie of the jackboot, the aggressive zeitgeist of the sports arena, the unquestioning loyalty to the party, firm or other corporate entity. They are the distorted and mystified forms of human community that are rooted in the soil of social arrangements that are, by their nature, dehumanizing.

The underlying premise then, concerning the nature of institutions, is that the tasks or goals of such organizations make hierarchy, impersonality, and instrumentalism, their necessary consequence. There is, of course, something that appears as intuitively logical and sensible about this view. It is, indeed, a firmly rooted part of our 'world-taken-for-granted.' The ubiquity of hierarchy in all of our social arrangements lies, it appears, only in its instrumental value. It is, in other words, 'the best way to get things done.' In such thinking, ends and means, following sound posivitist logic, can be neatly separated.

Despite the confidence in such delineations our accelerating understanding of the real purposes of schools in capitalist society (and, of course, of other institutions) makes it increasingly difficult to accept such logic. The work of Habermas, Marcuse, and others make clear that means as well as ends, technique as well as purpose, must be considered ideological. The medium is indeed the message. The proliferating literature on the 'hidden curriculum' of schools makes painfully clear that not only are the ostensible purposes and goals of such institutions related to issues of ethical judgements and social interests, but the methods themselves carry the same imprint. Hierarchy as a mode of social organization is not the necessary, logical or, indeed, the only means of achieving ends. It becomes so only when certain values and judgements are accepted as preeminent. Such judgements might include a preference for control instead of participation, acceptance of expertise and specialized knowledge in place of a democratized culture, and a belief in the co-terminality of authority and power. In penetrating

213

the assumed rationality of hierarchy we need to go beyond many of the assumptions that surround it as a social form. Steve Marglin, a Harvard economist, has, for example, suggested that the development of hierarchical and bureaucratic forms of industrial organization is not clearly related to real gains in efficiency of output over other methods.[4] He argues that the real purpose of such organizations are related to questions of control and domination. On the opinion that there is no known organizational technique superior to hierarchical control, Herbert Gintis and Samuel Bowles[5] argue that such a view is controverted by the extensive evidence of the efficiency of worker participation in decision-making. They note that even moderate worker participation in decisions and goal setting increases productivity; that the average quality of work by a group is greater than the average quality of individual decisions. The best results are obtained when individuals think up solutions individually, then evaluate and choose among these solutions as a team.

Such a view begins to suggest that the real purpose of hierarchy, whether in school or work, lies less in the external consequences (the achievement of tasks) than in the nature of the social relations themselves and the ontology that springs from it. Hierarchy, in the institutions of modern society, ensures that few individuals are exposed to more than a fragmented and an incomplete view of the activities engaged in. Such an effect ensures the reification of social and organization structures - they assume a facticity and an imperviousness to human control. Hierarchy ensures for those who stand in subordinate positions a sense of their own appendage- like role. They become the objects rather than the subjects of human activity. Hierarchy, in short, ensures alienation. Meritocratic ideology which posits greater degrees of control with parallel increases in intelligence is, of course, validated by such arrangements. So is the division of labor which separates those who appear capable of planning and

---

[4]S. A. Marglin, 'What Do Bosses Do?' in Andre Gorz (ed.), The Division of Labour (N.J.: The Humanities Press, 1976).

[5]S. Bowles and H. Gintis, Schooling in Capitalist America (N.Y.: Basic, 1976)

conceptualization from those who appear able only to execute. Of course in schools such a separation includes not only students from teachers, but teachers from administrators. In short, hierarchy in school or elsewhere is its own goal. The ostensible purpose of school life - educational activity around the curriculum - is in fact the means through which the 'deep code' of the experience is transmitted. Hierarchy is not so much the instrument for fulfilling educational tasks, rather the latter facilitates acceptance of, and familiarity with, hierarchical social relations. The basic message of school life is the learning of social relations apposite to a hierarchical, class divided, and bureaucratic social structure. The differentiation of students by 'intelligence' or 'ability' or 'motivation', the unequal allocation of experience and knowledge, the distinctions in the character of pedagogy or learning milieux - all of these are but aspects of the same concern. This is the need to prepare and inure individuals to positions of domination and subordination in the social and institutional structure.

The ability to view hierarchy in the organization of our institutional life as no more than an instrumentality rests on a positivist world-view. Like science or technology it is identified as residing outside of the conflicts of ideology or interests which are generally understood as belonging to the domain of 'ends.' Science claims its legitimation as a matter of technical logic - a neutral intervention into our environment, not in itself predisposed towards particular values. These claims reach their most dubious end-point in the 'science' of organizational or administrative theory. Such theory often does no more than rationalize managerial ideology with its concern for profits, employee acquiescence (or, at least, internalization of management goals), and system predictability and control. Needless to say rarely is it suggested in such theory that the fundamental locus of control and decision-making be moved to subordinate groups in the institutions of the society. Democratic control by actors in an institution is rarely advocated. Where some notion of democracy is involved it is usually less a concern with the transfer of substantive power than a means to win the support or the cooperation of employees for the goals of management (the often argued need for 'participation,' 'consultation' or 'sharing' in decision-making). Such 'progressive' management techniques create the illusion of control or ownership by those in subordinate positions. The ideology of liberal-capitalism, implicit in most forms of organization theory, legitimates the dichotomy in social relations into those spheres where man is treated as an end, from those where he is a means. Such a separation underpins the distinction between community and institution, conflating the latter with domination and hierarchy, and excluding, for the most part, any real concern with democratic participation or human fellowship.

Social Transformation and the Limits of a Radical Phenomenology

In her essay "Evaluation and Dignity," Maxine Greene clearly expresses why the pursuit of community in the American School can, within the present context, only be a chimera. Fellowship and mutuality can only be the ritualistic flourishes of a society permeated to its marrow with values and concerns antithetical to such characteristics and dominated, instead, by the effects of "technicism, stratification and . . . 'functional' rationality." Correctly she identifies how such ideology ensures that we construct reality and apprehend the world in fragmentary and largely calculative terms. The individual is not so much regarded in the fullness of his or her personality but is subsumed under their test-taking ability; not treated as a unique 'end' but " 'matched to a model prefabricated by some official or other in the light of external demand." In the classroom, as Greene notes, individuals are evaluated on the results of prescribed activity, not the conscious pursuit of their own aims. Such anti-individual and anti-communal notions pervade the present preoccupation with competencies and tests. Nor, as she points out, is it only this 'technicist' perspective that undermines our quest for community. It is also the pervasive effects of ranking and hierarchy which invade all of our educational categories - separating and organizing individuals into opposing strata of success and failure, valued and valueless; fermenting the egoistic struggle for apparently scarce resources; and perpetuating a 'war of all against all.' It is not fellowship and mutuality that are ensured by such social arrangements so much as isolation, human conflict, humiliation, arrogance and distrust of

216

others.

To begin to deal with the questions posed by this
inhumane environment Greene believes that it requires
the establishment by teachers of a "clearly defined
context of values and commitments . . . a normative
community within their school." Such a normative
community would respect a 'public space' where
teachers (as well as young people, parents and school
administrators) would be able to disclose themselves
and their commitments. While she acknowledges that
out of such disclosures might arise differences of
values and procedures "some kind of consensus will
come into view." At a deeper level she claims that
teachers willing to come together in this manner might
discover a new freedom for themselves - "a power to
decide how they want to be judged." Accustomed to
viewing their situation as determined and as given,
she says, they may be startled to find themselves
looking at things as if they could be otherwise.

We have moved from the argument in which
'community' is used to complement or offset the
negative effects of institutional life, to one where
community opens the way to the undermining of
institutional life as it is currently constituted.
Maxine Greene's community does not represent normative
coexistence so much as radical strategy. It is not a
limited ritual for reminding ourselves of the
humanistic dimensions (or residues) of our social
existence, but a matrix for transcending such
existence by the empowering of autonomous beings. And
yet, no less than with the authors already discussed,
it is not clear whether the development of such a
community is really only a strategy, or whether it
represents, in itself, some kind of ultimate
fulfillment. It seems that the ability to <u>look</u> at
things as if they might be different - to
'possibilize' is one of the dimensions of her notion
of freedom. (In fairness it is claimed that
'possibilizing' also includes finding out how to act
upon situations). There is no word here of the
effects of such mental activity when connected to
practice - no word on the institutional and political
consequences of attempting to change the way things
are done; no word on the confrontations, conflicts or
struggle that are surely connected to such activities;
and no word on teacher suspensions, firings, or
administrative harassment that would undoubtedly
follow from any such institutional interventions. Let

us be clear, the process of 'possibilizing' or dreaming about the way things might be, in school or out, has rarely been treated as a crime of subversion. Indeed, it may be that such fantasizing has played an important role in the stabilizing of the social system. It is only when such dreams begin to inform social and institutional practice that heads begin to roll. It becomes increasingly clear that Maxine Greene's solution echoes the circumscribed radicalism of the phenomenological perspective. It empowers itself through an inflated idealism in which consciousness precedes existence, and the dereification of the world implies its disintegration.

Nevertheless the attempt to effect educational change by invoking a phenomenological account of the world is by no means entirely ineffective. Such a perspective is of undoubted potency in the effort to undo the 'taken-for-granted' nature of things. It is an important means to de-objectify the apparent facticity of the social world. At the same time (and here I do not wish to recount the structuralist vs interpretative argument), it does leave out those aspects of our social existence which have a reality that endures despite our loss of belief or refusal to affirm them. It is not simply our common understanding or belief in the social world that 'makes it go round.' The roles generated by our social structure, institutions, etc., only require that we act or behave appropriately to ensure that the process is maintained. Such behavior, or normative compliance, is, of course, most effective when it is underpinned by sincere belief - this however, is not imperative. Indeed, it may well be that much of what we do in our social roles represents no more than a 'performance' - the decision to act appropriately for a given situation despite what may be our distaste or downright hostility to the nature of the act. The issue, in other words, may not be one of reducing or undermining individuals' identification with, or belief in, dominant norms or values, but of offering concrete opportunities or means for instituting alternatives. Nor can we assume that merely reinterpreting our social understanding will facilitate a change in our social practice. The social structure has a life of its own and persists not as a simple consequence of belief. Social structures, and the roles that they imply, represent a particular crystallization of power and resources. Those who see their advantaged positions threatened by

218

a 'reinterpretation' of social relations and practices can be counted on to resist with all the means at their disposal. 'Possibilizing' alternative institutional and systemic arrangements, reducing the 'givenness of our worlds, may be useful steps towards social change, but they are not a substitute for struggle or confrontation - only a prelude to it.

One other weakness of the phenomenological strategy is that it inadequately accounts for the persuasiveness or hold of ideological hegemony. In bringing together, for example, a group of teachers to reevaluate grading procedures, curriculum etc., it cannot be assumed that the conclusions they reach will be any less reactionary or more humanistic than those practices currently in vogue. It is as likely that the gathering will demand greater discipline, compulsion, etc., than they will suggest a less authoritarian learning environment. We know enough now about ideology in contemporary society to see that at some level it provides a set of meanings that do indeed make sense of the world. And that such meanings are not entirely unrelated to the needs of individuals in that society. In other words, ideology is not merely a _false_ understanding of the world that can be stripped away to reveal the alternative possibilities. Even rebellions against the 'old' ideology will be couched in its meanings and terms. Only transformations that are predicated on the notion of praxis - the dialectic of subjective reinterpretation and actual or objective challenge - provides the means to transcend the present ideological terrain.

In using the notion of community to affect educational change all of the authors we have looked at have been trapped (though in quite different ways) by liberal ideology. The earlier writers, in attempting to 'balance' the apparently necessary inhumanity of hierarchical institutional structures with communal 'experiences', have accepted the categories of liberal-capitalist society (and its characteristic polarization of 'society' vs. 'community'). Greene, however, makes no such compromise. Her argument does, nevertheless, suggest a reliance on subjective reinterpretation as a way of overcoming the undesirable in our social lives. It is a strain of thought that has had a particular appeal in American life with its emphasis on individual salvation and personal accountability, and its scorn

219

for social movements, class conflict and collective change. Out of such soil springs the Horatio Alger myth, notions of 'positive thinking', the resort to personal transcendence by social 'dropouts' or followers of mystical cults, and the psychologism of 'consciousness-raising' and 'self-improvement' activities. All such thinking suggest the possibility of overcoming or transcending oppressive social conditions through an act of mental will and a personal reinterpretation of our social reality.

Despite this, there is, at least in some degree, a tension in Greene's strategy for moving beyond the 'givenness' of the present oppressive situation. While it seems to skirt the issue of confrontation, politics and the struggle for power, it does certainly suggest awareness of the hegemonic character of ideology. Her strategy acknowledges the inseparability of the development of critical awareness from the conditions in which such awareness may develop. The goals of radical pedagogy are inextricable from the pedagogy itself.

Individualizing Education and the Affirmation of the Bourgeois Perspective

While such an awareness is present in Greene's pedagogy it is clearly absent in that of Kurt Wolff ("Responsibility and Freedom in the School"). Certainly his emphasis on the need for critical learning is harmonious with our concern for an education that will have an instrumental role in the genesis of a just and humane society. It arises from the need to meet the demands of the human condition. A condition in which the "uncontrollable development of technology" is not sufficiently contained and accompanied by a corresponding development in intelligence or morality. As a result, our global society has the capacity to obliterate itself. By becoming aware critically, Wolff says, we may understand that in comparison with what we may visualize all human societies have fallen short of being good societies.

Despite the nobility and the implicitly radical nature of such goals there is a curiously bourgeois (or is it aristocratic) character to Wolff's pedagogy. There seems to be no notion of praxis in his development of critical understanding. He argues, for

instance, that "critical thinking is by its very
nature, necessarily, far removed from everyday life."
This hardly suggests the understanding that emerges in
the moment of struggle, or the awareness that arises
from confrontation with the elements of coercion and
power in our social and institutional order. Wolff's
'critical learning' seems to be of a kind that
develops best in the most traditional of academic
settings.

At the same time, while a <u>collective</u> seeking
after truth may offer an aesthetically 'sublime'
experience for Wolff, it is not seen to be
fundamentally linked to the development of a critical
consciousness - not an inseparable part of a radical
pedagogy. Thinking, he suggests, is a solitary
process, and while one thinks it is "incompatible with
anybody's listening in." Where in such a formulation
is the important element of a collective setting which
offers the social-psychological support necessary to
sustain those grappling with, and confronting,
existing reality. Or the realization that social
settings augment, dialectically, individual
contributions to an alternative ideology. It is
precisely for such reasons that social groups or
social movements offer the most powerful matrices for
the formation of a critical consciousness. It appears
as if the author's notion of critical thinking is
still rooted in bourgeois images of heroic
individualism, or a Hegelian unfolding of pure
consciousness.

Nor is Wolff alone in his emphasis on a pedagagy
whose mode is preeminently an individualistic one. In
both Charity James' "Evaluation and Dignity" and
Maxine Greene's "Equality and Excellence," the
solution to the problem of educational evaluation and
inequality is sought in a radically extended
individualism. In James' profoundly humanist
statement on education, educational practice must
never be severed from that "deep search for meaning,
to know that we have inner worth regardless of whether
others like what we do, and regardless even if whether
we particularly like it either." Her search for
alternatives is predicated on the need to refute the
meritocratic selection process in which "over the last
half century or so the school and university have
become the recording angels who destine young people
for the heaven of success or the hell of failure." In
its place she suggests that we can properly think of

appraisal "in terms of the individual's personal growth, of helping people to move towards becoming who they really are." The preferred educational environment is one in which there is an open climate and a curriculum which gives opportunity to students to work in different ways and at different rates of involvement and withdrawal. In her advocacy of a Jungian psychological typology she concentrates her attention on a means by which teachers may understand the possibilities of personal growth - a tool by which a student is encouraged to "become 'individuated'." Practically, it is a means by which we may be enabled to "individualize programs effectively."

Maxine Greene's statement on the historical role of schools in American society goes to the heart of its functions in that society. She makes clear how the categories of educational differentiation have been linked to the structures of a racist, sexist, and class-divided society. In seeking to ensure an equalitarian educational structure she juxtaposes what appears to her to be the programmatic alternatives. Either a brave new world in which all members of a given group or community are treated in exactly the same way or an individualized concept of educational practice which begins with an "acknowledgement that human beings differ in countless ways: in capacity, in strength," etc.. Underlying this is a philosophy in which the equality of men and women is transposed to signify the right to equality of consideration: "This means that every living individual is entitled to the kind of treatment and attention that express regard for his/her integrity and permit him/her . . . to act upon his/her freedom."

Despite the deeply humanistic impulses embedded in these authors suggestions for educational reform, they represent no more than the outer limits of a pedagogy rooted, once again, in the values and judgements of liberal ideology. In such a pedagogy the focus of educational performance, activity, and appraisal remains at the level of the individual. It is the quintessential bourgeois perspective. It emphasizes individual activity at the expense of group work and support. Success or failure at the task is seen primarily as the responsibility of the individual. Indeed the problem itself is seen as principally the concern of the individual. Such a pedagogy reflects an epistemology in which knowledge is not so much the collective historical product of humankind, but the incremental accumulation of men acting in their individual capacities. At best the liberal approach acknowledges the co-existence of others (as Green argues, "any class ought to be seen as members of a plurality") but not in the radically different sense of a 'collectivity.' The latter would seek to reflect in the classroom what is in fact the reality of human scientific and cultural endeavor - the socialized and entirely interdependent nature of such activity. The liberal (even in its most radical form) commitment to an individualized notion of education reflects an ideology which mystifies the social nature of human creativity, understanding, production, etc.. In its place it stresses the isolation of the individual ego and the fragmented nature of human experience. In all fields of scientific, cultural or aesthetic endeavor our bourgeois mentality avoids the collective or social context which is the indispensable matrix for new insights, products, etc.. Nor does it recognize what is in fact the great contribution of the bourgeois form of human organization, the scientific division of labor which requires not so much a competence measured in individual terms, but a generalized social competence. In such organization it is precisely the integrated linking of specific individual abilities that makes possible accelerated technological development. (Though, of course, for reasons of control, specialization and narrowly defined preoccupations ensure that this interdependence is not subjectively realized). In short, it is the collective or group that needs to form the locus of educational activity, problem-solving, appraisal and development. It is through the solidarity and mutuality of such an environment (not through the pursuit of personal autonomy or individual 'excellence') that the isolation, alienation, and fragmentation of contemporary human existence may be resisted.

As Charity James notes it is indeed sad that individualization has been used for programs of a very narrow and ill-conceived kind. It may be, however, that such tendencies are rooted in the notion itself. It is clear, for example, that an individualized mode of instruction, oriented to the student's particular aptitudes, interests, abilities and styles of learning take place only rarely. Nor can it be presumed that it is a product of only teachers' inflexibility or tradition-bound instructional methods. It is a result, instead, of what might be termed the overall culture of the high school. Such a culture, it has been argued by many critics, motivates creativity, originality and interdependence only rarely; for the majority of students passivity, obedience and conformity are the required traits. According to the 'correspondence principle' of Gintis and Bowles, the degree of passivity and obedience required increases as one 'descends' through the levels of academic standing. The classroom environment closely articulates with the anticipated roles of its students. Among those students, for example, who may expect professional or managerial positions, school facilitates (to an extent) independent or self-managing behavior. Such behavior is congruent with job roles which demand the internalization of professional organization norms, and their fulfillment in a self-initiated manner. At the other end of the spectrum, obedience, docility and passivity are the major characteristics of the classroom environment. Such characteristics are congruent with job roles that demand acceptance of rules, dependability, and the willingness to perform monotonous, repetitious and stupefying tasks.

Unifying Means and Purposes: Educating for Liberation

Perhaps the most helpful insight to emerge from the papers considered in this brief review is that suggested by Gibson Winter ("Community and Education"). Concerned with the process of human liberation he offers the 'root metaphor' of the work of art as a means to transcend the mechanical image of human activity that dominates Western society. The radical thrust of this image is that unlike in the prevailing ideology where purpose and means are sundered, in art action and thought are joined: "for in art the way things come to expression and what is expressed belong together." Indeed, Winter argues that in our "techno-society" tool and purpose have been so separated that the message and purpose "drop out of sight." Thus he claims that we maintain our economic system and weapons development even when they no longer serve the purposes which were supposed to justify them, or that we keep employing our tools even when they threaten the environment and the quality of life: "The medium is not simply the message, for there is no message - only the medium." In one sense, however, it may be that this formulation is not entirely correct. There are, I believe, messages, albeit ones that rest on the stimulation of false needs, or an understanding of reality that is distorted by the imposition of class, gender, racial or other sectional interests. (The latter might include the need to be continuously mobilized to fight the 'communist menace', the goal of endless consumption, the need for 'law and order' - all part of the familiar litany of American 'purposes'). It may, in fact, be more accurate to see the separation of means and ends as one in which the latter remain only too apparent, while the former has a shadowy, unquestioned character. It is clear, for example, that our instrumental view of human activity ensures that the notion of means remains, at best, a secondary consideration. Work, for example, for the mass of people is an affair of little joy, satisfaction, intellect, or creativity. It is undertaken as an alienated activity through which human beings exchange their labor for the ability to sustain their existence. Political activity is, for the majority, less an on-going process through which individuals are affirmed as potent members of the polity, than a set of occasional and perfunctory experiences concerned with the selection of leaders. The pervasiveness of this mentality with its disregard for process and expression has resulted in a neurotic compulsive sensibility: play becomes subsumed by winning and 'great feats' (note the obsession with the statistics of performance by sports commentators); sexual expression is increasingly associated with orgasmic performance; and education defined through the measurement of certifiable 'competence.'

In other ways, however, it is clear that Winter's formulation is accurately constructed. Nowhere is it more illuminating, for example, than in the attempt to understand the nature of present-day pedagogy. In the current obsession with 'basic skills', techniques or methods become everything, ends or purposes nothing. It is the quintessential application of the technicist perspective to education. Absent is the attempt to focus on the goals for which communication skills are developed - an isolated, de-contextualized notion of communications 'competence' fills the pedagogic void. By emphasizing techniques and eliminating the question of ends, we are able to avoid or obscure the structure of values underpinning the existing organization of purposes. And such purposes, of course, generate the characteristic social, political, and economic order of our time.

Winter's, metaphor which joins purpose and means, thought and action, is the renewal of a struggle to reunite man as both subject and object of his world. It is the attempt to ensure that man is not only the author of his world but that he knows himself to be that. To the extent that schools are characterized by activity that is removed from conscious human purpose (beyond that of a technical proficiency) so they reproduce a world in which man is alienated and dominated by his own acts of creation; a world in which meaning is replaced by, or conflated with, skill, purpose with "competence", and consciousness with information. The struggle in schools, and in the other areas of human practice, to conjoin the question of 'why' to that of 'how' is the renewal of the struggle for critical awareness or consciousness. The struggle for such consciousness implies the elimination of the separation between questions that are purely 'educational' from those that are 'political'. It is the radical unification of domains historically sundered by liberal ideology. It is, indeed, the true meaning of the distinction between liberal and radical pedagogy.

CALLING TO MIND AND TAKING TO HEART

Some Reflections on Adult Moral Development

John Sullivan

Andre Gide: Everything has already been said, but no
             one was listening, so we have to say it
             again.

A teacher: I know these things, but I forget them.

In the spring of 1979 and 1980, two conferences
were held in North Carolina. The conferences explored
human values in the context of school practice.   By
all accounts, both conferences were an extraordinary
success. The components of that success are the focus
of this paper and the cause of some reflections on
moral development.

Three general approaches to moral development can
be illustrated by three stories: one of ascent, one
of descent, and one of awakening.   The first two are
stories of quests.   The third points to   an
enlightenment that dawns when the quests are forsaken.
These stories will provide a background for discussing
the conferences.

The first story is the most famous parable in all
of philosophy. It is Plato's analogy of the cave.[1]

One must imagine prisoners chained to their seats
in a theatre-like cave, their faces fixed so that all
they see is the wall of the cave.   One must imagine,
above and behind the prisoners, some hidden
puppeteers.   A fire in the rear of the cave casts
shadows of the puppets on the front cave wall.   We
understand that the prisoners are simply seeing the
images of puppets and artifacts projected on the wall.
For the prisoners, however, what they are watching is
the only reality they know.

---

[1] The story is told in the Republic, 514 ff.

There comes a time when one of the prisoners is released and taken from the depth of the cave to the light of the world we know. Slowly, as his eyes adjust to the light, he makes out the people, trees, and houses of our world; he comes to see a new reality, the result of his ascent. Finally, he is able even to look upon the sun.

Such is Plato's image of the ascent--an ascent, to quote John Henry Newman's motto, "from shadows and images into the light." But for Plato, the story is itself an image and an analogy. The point of the analogy still strikes us with its ancient power. We are the prisoners. We are in the cave. This world which we take to be the real world is only a shadow of a higher world, the world of the Forms, of the Eternal Pattern which life here only approximates. Suddenly, the beautiful story becomes an indictment. We are ignorant and deluded, imprisoned in a false reality. We are shocked at the seeming arrogance of being told that what we take to be real is acutally maya, a theatrical delusion. We are witnesses to a play, we are participants in a play, and we take the play to be reality. We think we know what life is about. We have taken our culture's standards of meaning and value as our own. Now we are told that our sense of reality is a fiction. It is not so much that the physical world is less substantial than we thought. What wounds our deeper sense is the value reversal regarding social reality. We are told that what we take to be meaningful, what we take to be valuable, what provides for us our motivation to reach success-- all these things are mistaken assumptions. We believe we are tough-minded inhabitants of "the real world." We are still in the cave.

How do we escape from our false values and ideals to taste the truly real? Plato's metaphor is that of an ascent.[2] Drawn by beauty, we ascend from beautiful bodies to the beauty of personality, from the beauty of the natural world to the beauty of the good of order, thence to the universal perspectives of the sciences, and, finally, we catch a glimpse of

---

[2]The ascent by way of beautiful things to Beauty Itself can be found in Socrates' speech in the Symposium, esp. 210-212. The education program for the guardians is sketched in the Republic, VII, 521 ff.

Beauty Itself. We need not dwell on the program of education which this entails, nor how the guardians are to be drawn upward from a life of pleasure, through a life of service, to a life in which wisdom reigns and the quest for the good, the true, and the beautiful informs all of life. We need only retain the image of an ascent in which concrete living becomes more and more dissolved into an abstract, impersonal vision. And we would do well to call to mind another theme of the early Plato--the curious notion that coming to know what is real is a process of remembering.

I set before you this image of an ascent because the metaphor is a pervasive one. In our time, Lawrence Kohlberg has sketched progress in the moral life as an ascent to the ever more general.[3] At the first level, we understand right and wrong, good and bad, in terms of rewards and punishments, in terms of prudential self-interest. At the next level, we come to see ourselves as members of groups to which we owe our loyalty and our support in maintaining the good of order which transcends and makes possible individual striving. At the highest level, we come to grasp a more universal vision of what persons are and what life in community might be. We grasp ourselves, in Kant's phrase, as members of the Kingdom of Ends. We critically valuate family roles, political rules, cultural meanings and values in the light of a wider, more universal vision of what is meant to be. For Kohlberg, there is indeed the ascent from the concrete world of ego-centric interest to the more abstract world of social order and finally to the universalistic values which ground all social orders and call them to account. In Kohlberg, we have the ascent but without the theme of recollection.

---

[3]Kohlberg's work continues to be work-in-progress. See Lawrence Kohlberg, The Philosophy of Moral Development: Moral Stages and the Idea of Justice (San Francisco: Harper and Row, 1981) which is the first volume of a planned trilogy of Kohlberg's essays on moral development. These volumes will increasingly reflect Kohlberg's own recent revisions in his thinking. For a discussion of Kohlberg's difficulties with adult moral development, see my "Kohlberg's Progress Toward Understanding the Moral Life," Diss. University of North Carolina at Chapel Hill, 1982, especially chapters 3, 7, 8, and 9.

My second story is a journey to the depth. This
is one of Rilke's Stories of God.[4] The story is
titled "A Tale of Death and a Strange Postscript
Thereto." Since Rilke intends us to be part of the
story, we can begin by imagining ourselves taking an
evening walk near a churchyard and gazing into the
evening sky. We are startled by a voice, the voice of
a gravedigger whose interest is not in the sky, but
centered on digging into the rich earth. And we hear
a story which comes not so much from our mouths as
from our memory. It matters little who tells the
story. The story goes like this.

Once, in olden times, when people prayed with
arms outstretched, God would come and cast himself
into the dark abyss of the human heart. Then came a
new faith and a new way of praying with folded hands.
When God looked down, he was frightened by the folded
hands and the Gothic cathedrals with sharp points
facing him like the weapons of an enemy. God withdrew
into the deeper darkness of space which reminded him
of men's hearts. And he longed for the warm darkness
of men's hearts, for though the heads of men are
lucid, their hearts remain in the shadows of mystery.
"There is nothing wiser than the circle," says Rilke.[5]
And the God who fled to the sky may someday come to us
again out of the earth. Perhaps the gravedigger one
day will "dig free the door."

I set before you this image of the gravedigger
digging for God because the metaphor of depth is a
pervasive one. In our time, Carl Jung has guided us
into the dark depth of our unconscious. Past the
surface self and its shadow, past animus or anima,
into the world of the archetypes, Jung takes us on a
journey toward wholeness or individuation. The
wholeness is imaged in the ancient symbol of the
mandala. Jung, like Rilke, understood the wisdom of
the circle and carved a stone mandala for his garden.
"The spiritual adventure of our time," Jung tells us,
"is the exposure of human consciousness to the

---

[4]See Rainer Maria Rilke, Stories of God, tr. by
M. D. Herter Norton (New York: W. W. Norton, 1963),
pp. 87-96.

[5]Ibid., p. 89.

undefined and the indefinable."[6] The Journey is into the dark dream world within. And with Jung, as with Plato, there is also the theme of a kind of collective remembering.

The third story comes from the East. As I recall, the story is this.

There was a prince, a youth of noble spirit, who had himself heard stories, stories about the pearl of great price. So he set himself to find the pearl and indeed his life was a single-minded quest for this one object.

We need not recount his travels, the lengths to which he went, the years consumed in searching. It is enough to report that he failed to find the pearl in any of the places he visited. At last, he returned home, weary of heart and darkened by the dust of his latest pilgrimage. Thinking to wash himself, he went to a clear pool not far distant. As he bent over the pool, he noticed the reflection of his face. And there, embedded in his forehead, in the place where some speak of the third eye, he saw the pearl. It had been there all along, but he had not noticed or perhaps he had simply forgotten.

So we have three stories--one of an ascent, one of a descent, one of a reality which breaks forth when the quests are forsaken. I want to apply these three stories to the issue of moral development, especially moral development in adults.

Sometimes I think, with Plato and Kohlberg, that moral development is an ascent to an ever wider vision, abstract and universal. Sometimes I think, with Rilke and Jung, that moral development is a process of deepening, a journey to the depth of ourselves to rediscover what is ancient and archetypal, concrete and personal. Sometimes I think, with the masters of the East, that moral development is not to be had by striving, that what is most human is there all along and we need only awaken the human by calling to mind what we know and taking to heart what we realize. These three modes of approach may

_____

[6]C. G. Jung, Psychology and Religion: West and East, tr. by R. F. C. Hull (New York: Pantheon, 1958), p. 105.

help us to understand the case in point, the two conferences where moral development did seem to occur among adults. Since I started by telling stories, I shall present the case in point as if it too were a story, one which we are seeking to understand.

The conferences were set up as residential experiences with two weekends for each conference. The weekends were separated by a space of nearly two weeks. Area junior high schools were invited to apply, and those selected sent a team composed of teachers, administrators, and parents. A set of four topics was provided, with the topics structured in the form of value pairs. In addition, there were group leaders for discussion; there were films; and there were four speakers of high caliber. The speakers, group leaders, and conference planners spent the weekends with the participants. All came together to explore anew some fundamental issues which lay close at hand in teaching and learning.

The first conference was successful beyond all expectation. Some marvelous things happened, and the planners, with some trepidation, agreed to present a second conference the following year. At the second conference, a majority of the participants were different. All but one of the speakers were different, and even the one speaker who returned addressed a different topic. The four value pairs were retained, but position papers were substituted for a case study, and all but one of the films were different. Circumstances even forced a change of place. Despite the changes, the second conference also succeeded. And again, some remarkable things happened.

This, in short compass, is the story. It is a very sketchy story, a success story, and a rather ordinary one at that. But I am convinced that what this success story tells us may shed some light on the wider question of moral development in adults. Perhaps we shall find that the story is about more than moral development. Kierkegaard may be right in believing that the aesthetic stage is transformed into the moral stage, and that the moral stage pushes on, in a new reversal, into the religious stage. [7] Perhaps the conferences succeeded in briefly awakening the human with all its dimensions--aesthetic, moral, and religious.

I have chosen to present the conferences by recounting them as a story. This suggests that we might analyze what went on in the manner that we analyze a narrative. But any story or narrative can be analyzed in terms of four elements: <u>setting</u> <u>or</u> <u>atmosphere</u>, <u>plot</u>, <u>character</u>, and <u>tone</u>.[8] My observations will be placed in this framework, though admittedly I shall stretch the framework here and there for present purposes. The ideas I will set forth are not new. What is new is the way they are recovered and recombined. You will, I trust, remember having stumbled across these ideas before. I will simply call them again to mind. "I know these things," one of the teachers at the conference said, "but I forget them."

Setting: A Place Apart and Atmosphere which Empowers

Literary critics speak of the setting or atmosphere of a narrative. As Wesley Kort notes: "The atmosphere of a narrative suggests those conditions which the characters or narrator cannot change; it includes the time, place, and circumstances in which characters or narrators find themselves and with or within which they have to live or work." [9] The conditions may be limiting or enabling. Most often they will be a little of both.

The conferences were residential experiences. The participants, planners, and speakers all spent

---

[7]See Soren Kierkegaard, <u>Either/Or</u>, tr. by David and Lillian Swenson (Garden City: Doubleday Anchor Books, 1959) and <u>Fear and Trembling</u> and <u>The Sickness Unto Death</u>, tr. by W. Lowrie (Garden City: Doubleday Anchor Books, n.d.).

[8]For consistency, I utilize these notions as understood by one critic, Wesley Kort, in his book <u>Narrative Elements and Religious Meaning</u> (Philadelphia: Fortress Press, 1975).

[9]<u>Ibid</u>., p. 20.

some days together. They stayed both times in a
retreat setting, away from the public place of work
and the private space of home. The settings were
rural with gentle woodland hills opening onto farm
country. In coming to the conferences, all entered
another space and another time frame.

There is something nourishing in moving to a
natural setting. Periodically, we all feel a tug to
get away--to withdraw into woods or wilderness, into
mountain retreats or cottages by the sea. This theme
of withdrawal for reflection is echoed by all the
great spiritual traditions. I am tempted to say that
we exchange profane space for sacred space. Not that
every place is not sacred, but we forget that, and we
seem to need a physical change to remind us.
Deepening takes place according to some rhythm and we
remember the rhythm when we experience more directly
nature's time unmeasured.

Such was the physical setting, but more important
was the human setting and how people felt themselves
received. The atmosphere of the conferences was set
so as to empower people. It is this theme of dignity
and empowering that I wish to take up now.

During the second conference, Charity James spoke
of her guru, Muktananda. "He is a saint," she said,
"and around saints, good things happen."[10]

We need gurus, in Charity James' view, because we
find it hard to believe that we are of infinite worth
just as we are. So we project the worth onto
another, and if the other is expert in skillful
strategems (upaya), then, more and more, we come to
reclaim what initially we projected.

"I welcome you in love," Muktananda is accustomed
to say. "That is my worship," or as Charity
translated, "That is my worth-ship."

A short film was shown which contrasted two

-----

[10]This remark and James' view of the function of
gurus were made in private conversation during the
conference. The quote from Muktananda and the
distinction between "evaluating" and "appraising"
which I allude to in this section come from James'
presentation.

ballgames--one a pickup game organized by grade school youngsters, the other a Little League game with emphasis on success, performance, and, of course, failure to measure up.

In schools and in later life, we play performance games. We "evaluate" where we might better "appraise." The game is arbitrary, and yet we are players, like it or not--players and evaluators of performance. Still, we know that the play and performance are one thing, and our worth quite another.

A parent says to a child: "I love you--you are of great worth--and that is quite independent of what you do or don't do." In that moment, the parent is saying that a person's being is the measure of his or her doing, and not the reverse. This insight is also present in the great spiritual traditions. When Krishna tells us to act without seeking the fruits of action, he stresses this primacy of the quality of the act or person over the results.[11]

And yet, do we not create ourselves in our doing--our choosing and acting? Are not some things more worthy of doing than others? Are there not some skills which are so central that not to learn to do them is an impoverishment? One wants to say, "Yes-- this too is true."

The issue here concerns being and doing, but this is still too abstract. A more concrete approach is to examine what I call "the empowering of people." A significant feature of the conferences had to do with this empowering of people. But there are questions: Why is this empowering important and in what does it consist?

People find it hard to believe that who they are and what they do matter. In a world of many culturally established yardsticks, it is impossible to measure up on all of them. In a world where success (on most yardsticks) is a scarce commodity, many will feel the pain of failure. However much one succeeds, there are always bigger and better, older or newer standards which relativize the success itself. There is also the cost of success. Oscar Wilde once

---

[11]See The Bhagavad-Gita, II ff.

quipped: "There are two tragedies in life: not to get what you want, and to get what you want." In the face of such complexity, people lose faith in themselves and their endeavors. The teachers at the conference felt this, as did the parents and administrators. Since we all at times administer and parent and teach, this conference sample speaks to all of us. Hence, the importance of empowering people, the importance of having them come to see that who they are and what they do is significant.

Empowering people--providing the context where they can affirm their worth and the worth of their lives--is a central task for any who seek to promote growth. In what does this empowering consist? It does not consist in pep talks or platitudes. It is far removed from sentimentality or naive, childish encouragement. Adults are empowered by finding meaning in the midst of the evil and suffering and injustice of life. Empowering is tied to hope, but a hope in the face of human limits and not apart from them. Empowering seems to occur through emotionally powerful insight into the real. For that, we can only provide reminders. For adults, the reminders must begin with the tasks that are their lot. This mention of tasks appropriate to adult life brings us back to the issue of how our worth relates to what we do. It returns us to this issue, but points to a deeper sense of "doing."

In the West, we set forth ages--childhood, youth, adulthood, and the time of old age itself. In the East, they name tasks--first, the student, then the householder, then the forest dweller, and, finally, the sage. In our culture, it is difficult to know at what age adulthood begins. Freud once remarked that maturity is the ability to work and to love. If this captures a truth, then perhaps we may mark the close of adolescence at the points where one begins a career and chooses a partner to make a life with. Both endeavors seem to be involved in what the East calls the task of the householder.

All this is prologue to make a point. The point is that there is a difference in promoting moral development in youth and in adults. The adolescent is marked by being a student, by the task of exploration. The adolescent is, in David Norton's words, "everything in possibility, nothing in actuality."[12] The adult is one who has chosen a lifepath, foreclosed possibilities (at one level), and embarked on a life project. Perhaps moral development does not take place apart from stage or task. Perhaps moral development in adults calls to mind specifically adult endeavors, tasks marked by adult commitment. If this is so, then part of our development may involve calling to mind and taking to heart the task and its nobility. This seems to be a good way to understand what was happening at the conferences and what gave the conferences an enabling atmosphere, an atmosphere which helped people see the worth of their life work.

Our conferences were set up for adults and focused on the task of teaching as an adult task. As adult teachers and parents, we are committed to that task. We can also grasp with a deeper fund of experience both the nobility and the difficulty of the task. This provides a common experiential base. Given that base and living commitment, there is an empowering when the task and its nobility are called to mind. If called to mind in an authentic way, insight into the nobility of the task can occur and what is perceived as true and good can be taken to heart. This is a true empowering.

The speakers contributed to this atmosphere of empowering. They both spoke of and showed forth the enobling and enabling qualities of a teacher's task. The result of listening to and being in the presence of these speakers was a reawakening of the older notion of teaching as a vocation, a calling, a charge to be faithful to the best of what the tradition has brought to light about the meaning and value of what we do.

I put these remarks under the rubric of setting or atmosphere. What we learned was this: The worth of persons transcends what they do. But what they do is important, and some tasks, like teaching, can become a life project or an important dimension of life projects. Then this commitment can be called to mind. Calling to mind its nobility is a way of empowering people. The atmosphere of the conferences

---

[12]See David L. Norton, *Personal Destinies: A Philosophy of Ethical Individualism* (Princeton: Princeton University Press, 1976), p. 180.

in both physical setting and human interaction was an enabling rather than a limiting atmosphere.

Plot: Exploring a Vocation through Confronting Value
        Pairs

Plot is the element of a narrative which structures time. Plot reflects kinds of human processes. As Wesley Kort notes: "Plots are not so much imposed as they are evoked and the time which they reflect is not so much linear as it is repetitious and, to use Eliade's word, traditional."[13] The time structure of the conferences can be understood in this way. Each conference had, of course, a linear structure--check-in, meals, discussions, films, presentations, departure--a two week interval--then, return, check-in, etc. But since the theme is exploration of value pairs and the resources of the exploration draw upon the tradition of "humane and liberating learning," the conference structure also evokes the time of the tradition itself. We repeat traditional concerns and we recover what the tradition has to tell us. The linear time of a conference is like the tone of musical notes: the cyclic time of the tradition provides the rich overtones.[14]

Recall that each conference took place on two weekends, bridged by a two-week interval which returned the participants to their ordinary setting. Each of these conference weekends took its basic structure from the exploration of two value pairs. The participants discussed the topics (through case study or position papers) before the major speakers addressed them. Thus, the participants already came in touch with the issues in their own living and thinking before hearing the speaker's reflections. If the plot of the conferences can be looked at as a journey, then the value pairs can be seen as presenting obstacles on the way. Participants took the value pairs as reference points--"Today, we confront this topic; tomorrow, that."

---

[13]Kort, op. cit, p. 65.

[14]The metaphor of tone and overtone is found in John S. Dunne, Time and Myth (Garden City: Doubleday and Co., 1973), pp. 21-23.

The topics came in pairs. This was a significant device. Amidst all that changed from the first to second conference, the value pairs were retained. I want to reflect now on how the value pairs influenced the plot.

We worked, in both conferences, with four value pairs:

1. Evaluation and Dignity

2. School as Community and School as Institution

3. Freedom and Responsibility

4. Equality and Excellence

I have suggested that we think of the conference plot under the metaphor of a journey with the topics playing the part of obstacles on the way. But, in true Jungian fashion, those things which first appear as obstacles later become transformed into opportunities for growth. Jung was fond of symbolizing the goal of growth under the image of a mandala; we might regard our topics as the four corners of a mandala. I shall consider these four focal areas, first as topics, and then as value pairs.

As topics, the four areas of discussion first appear as having reference to students. When the exploration deepens, the participants come to see that these four areas pertain to them as well.

The first topic--school as community/school as institution--was always introduced on the first weekend. This may have been fortuitous, for, as I see it, the value of community came to be an important umbrella value. I shall return to this point later; for now, it can only be a hypothesis. But if I am correct in seeing the centrality of community, then this might explain why the topic of freedom/responsibility, so often understood in our time individualistically, became the topic most difficult to deal with.

By far, the topics which proved most inspiring were evaluation/dignity and equality/excellence. No doubt, the speakers treating these pairs made exceptional presentations. But perhaps the secret of

239

their appeal lies deeper. Perhaps teachers find these issues of special concern in their own struggles.

The four areas not only appeared as topics, the topics appeared as value pairs. And this device has a significance of its own.

In the first place, the values are presented in pairs. Immediately, one senses the complexity of value issues.

In the second place, the value pairs are presented in the fashion of both/and, rather than either/or, rather than this versus that. Each partner reveals and conceals something of the reality to which it points. Since each has a truth to tell, we are disposed to embrace, in some fashion or other, both members of the pair. This prevents a one-sided pitting of one value against another. It also encourages dialectical development.

In the third place, the value pairs are connected intrinsically with the vocation of teaching as we experience this task in our time and place. Thus, they are encountered naturally as realities with which a teacher must come to grips in pursuing his or her calling. Pairing the values heightens a sense that the ambiguities are in-built in the task.

When we set up the four value pairs, we gave no further thought to their interconnection. We did not assume that one value or value pair might have priority over others. But during the course of the second conference, I began to see that the value of community seemed more and more central to the exploration, at least as the teaching-learning situation confronts us in our era.

It does, indeed, seem to make a difference whether the approach to the value pairs proceeds out of an individualistic or a communal framework.

Consider for a moment freedom and responsibility. One of the speakers noted, in an aside, that the root word for freedom in the Indo-European language group

240

is "kinship."[15] To be free, in this perspective, would involve being a member of a kinship group whose support and encouragement would enable us to undertake projects, to develop capacities. Not to be free would mean being a stranger, an alien, an outcast. Here the Greek experience provides illumination.

For the Greeks, a man was a zoon politicon--an animal whose proper habitat was the polis (the city-state) and whose highest activity was speaking and listening in the public dialogue concerning the destiny of the polis. The free man was liberated from labor and work, so as to be a part of such action. The worst fate for a Greek was to be isolated (isolato)--placed on an island, alone, without companionship, without the interchange of life in the polis. This was the fate of Philoctetes in Sophocles' play of that name and the play shows strikingly the place of friendship (philia) in the task of becoming human.[16] This is a way of seeing freedom which is quite different from the prevailing view which sees freedom as an individual escape from encumbrances and sees others basically as limits to one's own projects.[17]

The sense of dignity is also seen differently if placed in a communal framework. For Kant, one's dignity resulted from membership in the Kingdom of Ends, and it followed that if human beings are ends in themselves, then it is never right to treat a human solely as a means. To recognize the primal diginity of persons as brothers and sisters in the human family has major implications for how we treat people in evaluating or appraising their work. Charity James' use of Jung's typology with its sensitivity to the dominant and inferior functions of personalities reveals the care-filled way a perceptive teacher comes

---

[15]Charity James made this comment during the discussion following the Keisers' presentation.

[16]William Arrowsmith discussed the Philoctetes in his presentation.

[17]For a provocative, though incomplete, analysis of the modern (and, I take it, individualistic) notion of freedom, cf. Frithjof Bergmann, On Being Free (Notre Dame: University of Notre Dame Press, 1977).

to see the human face. [18]   Nor is this sensitivity
unrelated to a transcendent vision of the person's
radical interconnectedness to all forms of life. A
poem which I remember from long ago used the image of
humanity hanging together as in a mobile and counseled
care "lest a breeze disturb a brother."

Lastly, it makes a great difference in our
awareness of equality and excellence whether we
approach these issues from an individualistic or
communal understanding. From the perspective of the
latter, we are engaged in a common task and recognize
both the diversity of ways to reach the common goal
and the fact that, in the deepest human tasks, the
task itself is valued even apart from the goal
reached. The goal transcends each and all of us. It
is the tradition whose classics express for us the
possibilities of what we can be. Both teacher and
learner stand in the midst of this human tradition
seeking to recover and reanimate the wisdom found
therein. It is from the tradition that we gain those
images, symbols, metaphors, and stories which help us
to understand what we are about. [19]   "He who by
reanimating the old can gain knowledge of the new is
indeed fit to be called a teacher," says Confucius. [20]

The value pairs call to mind, in dialectical
fashion, the dimensions of what we are about in
teaching and learning. If I am correct in giving
priority to a communal approach to these pairs, then
we can say something further about the plot of the
conferences. The conferences become more than just a
journey on which values-in-tension appear as obstacles
to be wrestled with. If community has priority, then
the journey is, in fact, a journey in community-
building through recovery of this traditional theme.
This gives the plot of the conferences a new focus.

_____

[18] See Charity James' article in this volume.

[19] This theme was given voice in the conferences
by Gibson Winter and by the Keisers.

[20] See The Analects of Confucius, tr. by Arthur
Waley (New York: Vintage Books, 1938), Book II, 11.

Character: Exemplars and a Continuum of Colleagueship

"Character in narrative," Wesley Kort tells us, "is an image primarily of the potential of human consciousness to know and manage the world in which it finds itself."[21] Character then reflects human possibilities for good and ill. By presenting characters, the narrator affirms "what the human is or can be."

The characters in our conferences were the participants, the planners, and the presenters. It was from this mix that interactions unfolded. I think I could argue, in turn, that each of the characters has a claim to the title of hero. But I will focus on the speakers, for they stood forth, in a special way, as exemplars.

The speakers were carefully chosen. They were, in the main, well-known in their fields, prominent educators, often of national stature. But the fact of preeminence was not enough. Over and above their expertise, there was the quality of their person and their ability to establish rapport with a non-specialist audience. They were selected as models of excellence, master teachers who love and live their teaching. These presenters spent time with the participants. The participants came to see that the enterprise these teachers exemplify so well is the same enterprise we are all engaged in. Whether teacher by profession, or parent, or administrator who cares for the environment of teaching, we all are teachers and, of course, learners too. Some may have achieved special excellence in their field. Others may work in more hidden gardens. But the calling is the same and there is a sense in which, while distinctions of experts and pupils, gurus and disciples are not to be obliterated, the task makes colleagues of us all. When this insight dawns, we can hear one another more deeply, rejoice in excellence wherever found, and surmount some of the forces of envy and jealousy which made us falsely think that another's excellence diminishes our own. To perceive this continuum of colleagueship demands a breakthrough of sorts, and a willingness to suspend ego-striving to discover the complementarity of excellences which enrich us all. When this occurs, it is a powerful

---

[21]Kort, op.cit., p. 40.

stimulus to growth. In a conference as in a
narrative, character provides images of human
potentiality. When we meet persons who have
actualized in exceptional fashion a human
potentiality, we see new possibilities for ourselves.

Tone: Theory-Praxis: The Ideal as Real

In literature, tone is taken to refer to the
created subjective presence, in the work, of the
author or narrator. It has, as Wesley Kort sees it,
three aspects: selection of material, language
choice, and attitude. As Kort summarizes: "The
writer chooses to tell us something, he uses a kind of
language or uses language in a certain way, and he has
or assumes a certain attitude or set of attitudes
toward what he is telling the reader."[22]

While the conferences do not have a narrator,
they do have an author or set of authors in the
persons of the planners. The selection of setting,
plot structure, and characters expresses the planners'
point of view. Also the language which the planners
use to talk about the task is revealing. The
planners, like any author, do not fully succeed in
having their characters behave as they might wish.
The characters have a life of their own. But the
planners do have an attitude toward what they are
presenting and that attitude arises out of a set of
beliefs, a philosophy of what education is about.

One of my roles in both conferences was that of a
planner. My perspective was that of a philosopher
with a special interest in moral development. The
other planners were distinguished teachers in the
Graduate School of Education at the University of
North Carolina at Greensboro, teachers concerned with
education and curriculum. While I cannot speak for
the other planners, still I shall try to express
something of the tone--or implicit beliefs--which I
saw underlying the conferences. The two beliefs which
I wish to mention were beliefs in the form of
refusals--the refusals to accept those dichotomies
which pit theory against practice and the ideal
against the real.

---

[22]Ibid., p. 91.

The tone of the conferences was anything but condescending. There was no attempt to simplify the complex. But there was a definite attempt to break through the practitioner-theorist split. All of the presenters and participants engage in practice and all engage in critical reflection on practice. Some allot more time to practice; others, to reflecting on practice. But human action would be less than human if both moments did not occur. We seek to be guided by insight in what we do, and theories both result from and lead to insight into praxis.

Likewise, in the conferences we moved against too facile a split between the ideal and the real. Our ideals lie at the basis of who we are and how we encounter the world. Our ideals open our possibilities and provide reminders of what is at the core of our living. Ideals are, then, as real and as powerful as the forces which impede us from realizing them.

The Western approach to ideals follows Plato and tends to perpetuate something of a double-decker view. We are here, and the ideals are there, in a shadowy dreamlike heaven. We are urged to realize our ideals as if they were not real, but only became so as we came to incorporate them in our living. Again, the metaphor of height and mountains to scale.

The East thinks and talks differently. The ideal is what is most real already. We do not strive to put on ideals like a costume or cloak. We instead wake up--brush away the biases and the superficial under-standings--and come to appreciate what we are at our depth, if only we have eyes to see. There are echoes of the East in Pindar's line: "Become what you are."[23] And all the great religious traditions can be analyzed in terms of an ideal, a defect, and a remedy.[24] The ideal is what we are and were meant to be. The defect is what alienates us from what we are and were meant to be. The remedy is a discipline which promises to allow us to see and be again what at our

---

[23]Pythian Ode, II, line 72.

[24]This approach is, by now, a fairly standard one. See, e.g., John E. Smith, Experience and God (Oxford: Oxford University Press, 1968), pp. 165-179. Smith uses the terms "ideal, need, and deliverer."

depth we are all along.

If such is the case, then we can welcome the full
and honest presentation of how things are in their
defective state without losing hope. The quest for
truth and justice marks us even in the midst of our
biases and egocentricity. The contradictions that
elicit change are not simply contradictions between
our saying this and saying that. The deeper
contradictions to be overcome are between what we say
and do, between the web of words we spin to justify
our practice and the urging of our hearts to seek a
better way. We are, of course, both darkness and
light. And as Lao Tzu teaches, when the patient is
sick of sickness, then he is well.[25]

Throughout the conferences, we encouraged
speakers to present the truth of our situation,
however harsh. To oversimplify is no service. Yet we
also wished to speak a human and a healing word. We
were conscious that cynicism induces its own paralysis
which is no less a trap than sentimentality. The
real has a bite. It hurts in different ways. But the
organism also seeks wholeness, and the bite of the
real can be administered as an antidote to the disease
of our drugged slumber.

One reality ought not obscure other realities.
It is here that attention to our language and our
metaphors can lead to insight. How we talk is linked
to how we think. But beyond what we say and think is
what we do and are. As Wittgenstein believed, what is
shown is of equal (if not greater) importance than
what is said.[26] These beliefs--that theory is not
separable from practice and that the ideal is, at
bottom, what is most real--established, in part, the
tone of the conferences.

---

[25]See _Tao Te Ching_, Chapter 71.

[26]The presence of this elusive distinction
between "saying" and "showing" permeates
Wittgenstein's _Tractatus Logico-Philosophicus_ tr. by
D. F. Pears and B. F. McGuinness (London: Routledge
and Kegan Paul, 1961).

Some Closing Words

I started by telling three stories--three approaches to moral development. I went on to tell a fourth story of two conferences held in North Carolina which had, by all accounts, remarkable success. I tried to analyze what caused that success. I did this by looking at the conferences as if they were stories and employing for that purpose the categories of atmosphere, plot, character, and tone. Reflecting on these things, I came to see that what was done could be talked about in terms of calling to mind and taking to heart. I want to conclude with a few words about this theme.

As motto for this exploration, I took two quotes. The first was Andre Gide's remark: "Everything has already been said, but no one was listening, so we have to say it again." Repetition, as Kierkegaard noted, is a form of remembering.[27] The second quote came from a teacher at the conference: "I know these things," she said, "but I forget them".

The conferences can be thought of as strategies to awaken the human by calling to mind and taking to heart. What is called to mind and taken to heart is what lies in the tradition. It is the tradition which is passed from teacher to student, now becoming shallow, now recovered in its depth.

A Polanyi has said, "We can know more than we can tell."[28] As others have emphasized, we are more than we can know.[29] Development for adults seems to demand a recovery of this sense of the inexhaustible richness of Being. But what is common to our being comes to light within the human tradition. This traditio--this passing on of clues to what is going forward--is a dynamic process. We dwell within this

---

[27]See Soren Kierkegard, Repetition: An Essay in Experimental Psychology, tr. Walter Lowrie (New York: Harper and Row, 1941).

[28]Michael Polanyi, The Tacit Dimension (Garden City: Doubleday, 1966), p. 4. (Italics mine)

[29]For example, see the discussion in John S. Dunne, The Way of All the Earth (New York: Macmillan, 1972), chapter VII.

tradition. We bring to light the archetypal richness of our life by appropriating and carrying forward the stories and symbols of the tradition. The tradition reads us as we read it.[30]

Though the tradition is public, the work of recovery is a personal task which no one ultimately can do for us. This is perhaps why Socrates was chary of calling himself a teacher. He only assembled reminders and asked questions. The insights are a matter of grace. In learning and in life, there are two moments--the active seeking and the yielding to what is found.

The work of recovery is our own. But we do not climb the mountain alone, without guides. Nor do we enter the depths without the help of pathfinders. The work of recovery is ours to do, but the insights which come are intrinsically public, able and destined to be shared. The shared insights both constitute the tradition and make us, as we claim these insights for our own, colleagues in spirit with those who have seen most deeply into the human situation. Within the tradition, the heights of genius serve to reveal the depths of common experience and to show what was present all along. To call to mind and take to heart what is our birthright is to awaken the human and change our lives.

---

[30]The phrase was used by William Arrowsmith in his presentation.

Appendices

CONTRIBUTORS

WILLIAM ARROWSMITH is Robert L. Woodruff
Professor of Classics and Comparative Literature at
Emory University. He is General Editor of "Greek
Tragedies in New Translation" (Oxford University
Press) and currently writing on the poetry of T. S.
Eliot and the films of Michaelangelo Antonioni.

KURT BAIER is Distinguished Service Professor of
Philosophy at the University of Pittsburgh and
currently is Chairman of the Board of the A.P.A. He
is interested mainly in ethics, philosophy of law,
social and political philosophy. His best known
publication is The Moral Point of View.

MAXINE GREENE is the Russell Professor of
Educational Foundations and Professor of philosophy
and education at Teachers College, Columbia
University. Her special interests are social and
moral philosophy and aesthetics.

CHARITY JAMES is a free lance writer and lecturer
who has had teaching appointments at Boston University
and Goldsmiths' College (University of London). She
is the author of Young Lives at Stake and Beyond
Customs.

ELIZABETH B. and MELVIN KEISER are Professor of
English Literature and Religious Studies,
respectively, at Guilford College. They have
collaborated before as speakers for religious
conferences and in team-teaching such courses as
Medieval Masterpieces, Modern Poetry and Religion,
Arthurian Myth, and Dante and the 20th Century. Her
special interest is in Medieval English Literature;
she is the author of "The Festive Decorum of
Cleanness" in Chivalric Literature edited by Larry
Benson and John Leyerle, and is currently completing a
book on the Gawain-poet. He is in modern religion and
culture; and has completed two manuscripts:
Recovering the Personal: The Logic of Religious
Discourse in the Theopoetical Quest of H. Richard
Niebuhr" and "Unless Being Itself was Trustworthy":
The Conversion Essays of H. Richard Niebuhr from
Idealistic Liberalism to the Religious Realm of Divine
Sovereignty.

DAVID E. PURPEL is Chairman and Professor, Department of Curriculum and Educational Foundations at the University of North Carolina - Greensboro. His area of interest is in the moral and religious dimensions of education and (with Henry Giroux) is the author of The Hidden Curriculum: Deception or Discovery?

H. SVI SHAPIRO is Associate Professor of Education at the University of North Carolina - Greensboro. His teaching and writing are in the sociology of education. His published work has focused on questions of the state, ideology and culture in advanced capitalist societies.

JOHN G. SULLIVAN is Professor of Philosophy at Elon College. He is interested in the meeting points of psychology, ethics, and the wisdom traditions of both East and West.

GIBSON WINTER is Professor of Christianity and Society at Princeton Theological Seminary. His focus is on symbol and society and the interplay of political, ethical, and religious dimensions in human communities.

KURT H. WOLFF is Professor Emeritus at Brandeis University. He has translated Simmel, Mannheim, and Durkheim and is the author of Surrender and Catch; Experience and Inquiry Today; Beyond the Sociology of Knowledge, and other books, papers, and contributions to symposia and encyclopedias.

PARTICIPANTS

Greensboro Day School

    Marion Bain
    Linda Garrett
    Wynn Harkless
    James Iredell
    Gail LeBauer
    Sue Seagraves

High Point Public Schools

    Ferndale Junior High

        Fannie Atkinson
        Eloise Farlow
        Grecia Sanniota
        Mike Seamon
        Marie Spaulding
        June Stackhouse
        Gail Thacker
        Betty Thomas
        Caroline Whitley

    Griffin Junior High

        Louise Bedford
        Marion Byrd
        Sandra Duez
        Larry Graham
        Harry Leak
        Nanci McDermott
        Ann McNeil
        Robert Rush
        Mary Ellen Townsend
        Dorothy Walker

    Northeast Junior High

        Virginia Carey
        Susan Fagge
        Dick Jones
        Linda Lee
        Billie Lyndon
        Sonja Rhymer

Northeast Junior High (continued)

    Phyllis Sanders
    Ron Singletary
    Teresa Walton

New Garden Friends' School

    Martha Sasser
    Sarah Stohler
    Bob Welsh

Oak Ridge Military Academy

    Phoebe Harman
    Betty Hobbs
    Deedra Mason
    Keith Phillips
    Sally Royster

St. Pius X School

    Sister Ann Adele
    Sister Rose Marie Bryant
    Jane Callaham
    Julie Dameron
    Pattie Hudgins
    Kacy Newton
    Jent Oussaty
    Betty Tarantelli